MY BADGE IS MY INTEGRITY:
The Life of a Harness Bull

by
Edward A. Stein, Sr.

1997

ASHCO PUBLICATIONS
Ashtabula, OH 44004

MY BADGE IS MY INTEGRITY:
The Life of a Harness Bull

© ASHCO PUBLICATIONS, 1997

ISBN 0-9661937-0-9

Library of Congress Catalog Card Number 97-77347

Printed in the United States of America

FIRST EDITION

ASHCO PUBLICATIONS
P.O. Box 3066
Ashtabula, OH 44005-3066

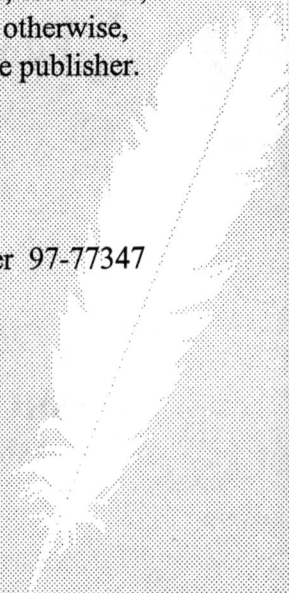

PREFACE

*A*bout ten years before his death in 1986, the author of this book, Edward A. Stein, Sr., was asked independently by both his sons, Martin and Edward, Jr., to write a memoir of his childhood, with some antidotes of his thirty-eight years on the Cleveland Police Force.

His initial response to his sons was negative, believing that no one would be interested and it would be a waste of his time. After much badgering, he agreed to their request--the end result being a three hundred and ninety page record of his life experiences. Little did his two sons realize at the time, that their father would turn what he considered a chore, into a labor of love.

The author's life saw the end of the horse and buggy and the beginning of the age of technology. He, in his eighty-five years as well as others in his generation, lived through more changes technically and culturally than occurred in previous generations.

The beginning of his memoirs reflects a time when life was less complicated, and when most people used "shanks mare" to get where they were going. It was a time when life was harder, and much more disciplined.

The echoes you will hear through the first part of this book are those of a family that lived, played, and died in a German ethnic neighborhood during the first twenty years of this century.

The second part of the book contains experiences of the author's life and events that happened while he served as a Cleveland Policeman. He was appointed patrolman in May of 1925, received his warrant as Sergeant from Elliot Ness in 1938, and retired as Sergeant in the Chief's Office. He relates a bird's eye view of what it meant to walk a neighborhood beat as a rookie patrolman in the twenties and thirties during the era of Prohibition, Elliot Ness, and the Depression.

The title for this book, *MY BADGE IS MY INTEGRITY: The Life of a Harness Bull*, was, in part, from a phrase the author often used to impress upon his sons the importance of having a good name. The word "harness" referred to the police uniform, and the word "bull" was a name given to the police officer.

In order to maintain the flavor and jargon of the time, the grammar and vocabulary of the author was left untouched--some language may be strange to the reader.

These memoirs of a man who lived from January, 1901, to December, 1986, contain a wealth of informative history which will resurge memories of the older readers and stimulate the interest of younger readers.

John R. Radkowski, Ph.D.
ASHCO Publications

ACKNOWLEDGMENTS

Special thanks to the Library Staff of the Western Reserve Historical Society for all their help, and Anne T. Kmieck, Museum Curator, of the Cleveland Police Historical Society, Inc., for her assistance.

Thanks to Don Lemponen, General Manager, Great Lakes Printing, Ashtabula, OH, for all his constructive suggestions and expert advise.

Much gratitude to Deputy Sheriff, Eric Radkowski, and Karen Radkowski, Teacher, for their many hours of proof reading.

And a thank you to Lea Leever Oldham, Teacher, Author, and Publisher, for her guidance, and consultation services.

CONTENTS

v

INTRODUCTION

*L*ong ago it was suggested by my sons, Martin and Edward, that I write down a few memories of my almost 80 years of life which may be of interest to my descendants. While, to my way of thinking they are not of outstanding nature, I can see some value in the suggestion since I have often wished I knew more of my father's past. He was born March 3, 1861, and had he kept notes of his experiences, combined, ours would cover a span of about 118 years at this writing. Surely some things of interest happened during that time.

Edward A. Stein, Sr.

This is not a tale of heroics nor a narrative with a continuous theme culminating in a noble triumph. Rather, it is of experiences which did or could have occurred, to a greater or lesser degree, to anyone in those times. It is impossible to recall every detail of occurrences or every spoken word after these many years. Indeed many of my recollections are inconsequential and would be boring. I will not dwell on the griefs or the sorrows, except where necessary, which I experienced or encountered and; therefore, will give my readers the tip of the iceberg, so to speak, and confine myself to things which I have experienced, observed, were told to me and, in a few instances, what I remember reading at the time.

If the facts and dates do not coincide at times, blame my fading memory but do not doubt my truthful intentions. I will not fictionalize and if the telling offends your delicate senses I make no apologies. I will tell it as it was.

To my sons, Marty and Ed

Edward A. Stein, Sr. (01/18/01 to 12/13/86)

Chapter 1

I, Edward Anthony Stein, was born January 18, 1901, with the aid of midwife Francesca Lex, in a cottage on Louis Street, Cleveland, Ohio, and birth records show the address to have been 50 Louis Street. Francesca Lex is buried opposite my parent's grave in St. Mary's Cemetery, W. 41st Street (formerly Burton Street) and Clark Avenue. My oldest brother, Al, told me that Louis was in a section called Ducktown or Claytown, but don't ask why since it is conceivable that the unpaved streets were of clay or that many people in the area raised ducks. Numbered streets were later adopted for north and southbound streets and Louis Street became W. 32nd. The homesite was south of Clark on the west side of the street which was later acquired by the Cleveland Wollen Mills Company and a brick structure erected thereon. The mill is since out of business.

Let me stray for a moment. Speaking of numbered streets being adopted, it must have been around 1906 that house numbers were changed because I remember when our house number on Buhrer Avenue, where we had lived, was changed to 1925 and still recall seeing two men at our front porch, one on a ladder and one holding it, and the top man tacking the number to the front of the porch under the eaves in line with the front door. You see, I was told, that at that time all streets in Cleveland were named and each had its own house numbers which made it difficult for persons not familiar with street locations to find the street for which they were searching. The city fathers decided it was time to bring things up-to-date since Cleveland had long outgrown its small-town britches.

Although, in a way, you might say neighborhoods were almost small towns in themselves with their own corner groceries, butcher shops, etc. Public square was considered the hub of Cleveland with Ontario Street running north and south thru the Square, dividing the

1

city into east and west sides. Before my time, west of the Cuyahoga River was called Ohio City but the accuracy of this will have to be verified in the Public Library. I do remember it being said that Cleveland was referred to as the Forest City because of its many trees and I also recall the name of Ohio City cropping up once in a while among my elders.

To get back to Ontario, numbers started at Superior and Ontario and streets radiating either east, south, or west increased in numbers. Numbers also increased for those streets north of Superior, downtown, but not for long since Lake Avenue, overlooking Lake Erie, was two blocks north of Superior and about the northern boundary of the city. Wherever possible streets running north and south were numbered and those running east and west were named. Example: W. 3rd, one block west of the Square, was formerly Seneca Street; W. 6th was Bank Street and W. 9th was Water Street east of the Square, East 6th was named Bond Street and E. 9th was Erie Street. My brother, Al, occasionally let these street names slip into his conversation since he was accustomed to using them. In numbering or naming some thoroughfares, there are exceptions, the reasons perhaps being buried in the city archives. Thoroughfares, called roads, were generally those with a curve or angling across or into thoroughfares, a good example being Scranton Road on which we lived and Ansel Road on the east side.

I have faint recollection of our move to 45 Arthurdale Avenue, but this may be imagination since I must have been about one year old at the time. Arthurdale is now Woburn Avenue, but the house number is unknown to me. I read somewhere that Cleveland's southern boundary was Willowdale Avenue. South of Willowdale to Big Creek was Brooklyn, and from Big Creek south (boundary unknown to me) was Brighton. Ergo, 45 Arthurdale Avenue, Brighton, Ohio. All have long since been incorporated into Cleveland, and, indeed,

Arthurdale may have been so incorporated at the time of which I am writing.

I have clear recollections of our family living on Arthurdale from about 1902 to about 1905--our family consisting of Dad and Mother, brothers Al, Joe, and Ben, sister Lucy and me. In between were Frederick and Alfred who died in infancy and are buried with Dad and Mom in St. Mary's Cemetery. German and English were spoken at home since Dad and Mom were from Prussia, Germany.

We had a cistern in the back of the home to which all rain water from the roof was directed and it was used to wash clothes and pumped with a long iron pump handle into an iron sink in a small room attached to the kitchen. However, I cannot remember what disposition was made of the wash water since there were no sanitary or storm sewers; they came later. Wash water had to be boiled in a copper wash tub when washing day came around and since there were no gas lines the fuel was wood and coal.

Copper Wash Tub
Courtesy of the late Veronica Jaworski

Drinking water was pumped from a well situated on the outside of the house near the kitchen door and, I remember, at times Mother attached an empty cotton salt bag to the spout to strain out the silt and occasional crawly things which fell into the well. We lived!

3

Antibiotics, of course, were unknown then. There being no piped-in water, a pail of well water with a dipper was always in the kitchen for drinking purposes. We had no bathroom, no plumbing, and no sanitary sewers so a privy in the backyard, called a backhouse, was a necessary structure. In more up-to-date circles they were called outhouses.

A Saturday bath was a must and the tin bath tub, green painted sides, was taken from the wall of the small room attached to the kitchen. It took a lot of water heated on the kitchen stove and bath water was sometimes used twice. Also, a bath during the week was looked on as unnecessary. Our morning ablutions were usually made from a metal basin in the kitchen, although bedrooms normally were equipped with a large crock pitcher set in a large crock basin into which the water was poured. This crockery was usually set on the dresser or on a separate

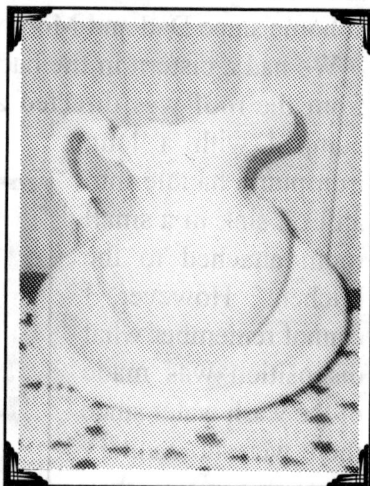

Pitcher and Bowl

stand equipped with a mirror. To dispose of the used water, it was poured into a large crock jar, setting on the floor, called a slop jar.

As for bathroom facilities, we had a two-holer privy in the backyard across from the chicken coop. I don't remember what ventilation design was carved in the door, but it usually was a half moon and star, or either one. Privy ventilation designs could, I was told, usually be selected by the owner. I do remember some designs were in grape cluster shape and I can readily see where designs would become a major subject of family discussion and ideas could run rampant.

4

Anyway, it was a good place for the bees and flies to enter in the summer. We had a saying "busy as a bee in a privy" and I guess that's where it originated.

This two-holer privy was constructed to afford a comfortable sitting position. The carpenter knew his business. The holes had beveled edges and some privys had two or more sizes so, as you grew older, you graduated from one size to another and when you reached the largest size it was an achievement. Use of this facility in the middle of a dead cold winter night was an experience and soon made you realize you were a member of the human race.

The thought will naturally occur to a thinking person as to what the hell happened when the privy reached its holding capacity. That problem was solved by, what were known as, the honey dumpers. Some called them honey dippers. No matter! Years later I learned they were employees of the Cleveland Night Soil Division. An apropos name, don't you think? The duty of the honey dumpers is self-evident and, I was told, the fee was $2 a privy. These good men drove a team of mules hitched to a wagon with a coal oil lantern hanging from the rear axle.

Coal oil, my dear readers, when we became more educated, graduated to the name of kerosene. The wagon contained about eight wooden barrels with covers and on the appointed night (they worked only at night) they came to your home. They needed no trumpets to announce their coming since the aroma preceded them for a block or two if the wind was right. At the scene of their endeavor, they removed the privy from the hole and proceeded to their appointed task. What happened after that I don't know. Mom was no dummy, she took me in the house. I heard her say, "Wass ein gestank!" What a stink!

We had a happy home life. Brother Al was working as a bundle boy (wrapping bundles) in a downtown department store. Joe, Ben and

Lucy attended St. Mary's School on Broadview Road west of Pearl Street. St. Mary's Church has long since burned down but the frame school building is still standing. One spring day, Lucy took me to school, presumably to show me off. I was a redhead about three or four years old and the sister teaching the class took me to the front of the room and asked me how old I was. I couldn't understand at the time why everyone laughed when I said I was 14.

We had milk delivery every day by a man with a closed wagon who drove down the street ringing a bell and the housewives would come out with their pitchers. With a long-handled dipper he'd dip out the desired measure of milk from the five-gallon can and in summer the flies were free. Milk and meat had to be bought almost daily since ice boxes were unknown and milk would sour; however, winter was no problem since food was kept in a cold room or in the cellar.

About that time sewer pipes were installed in our street. They were large red clay pipes in which we played hide and seek before they were installed. There was no trench-digging machinery so storm sewer ditches were dug by hand. A number of men were employed at this work and Bonner's Saloon at the corner of our street and State Road (now W. 35th Street) must have done quite a business. Let us digress for a moment and explain more about the men whom we called "Ditch Diggers."

They were good, hard-working men, referred to as Guineas or Honkies and from my observation of ditch digging during my childhood, the work gang consisted of about eight or more men plus a boy, called water boy, whose job it was to see that the men got drinking water when one of them called, "Water boy." The water was pumped into a metal pail from someone's well along the street or a faucet if they had piped water. In the pail was a metal dipper to drink from. If they were near a saloon, every once in a while the water boy would be given five or ten cents by one of the men for a can of beer.

6

The "can" was a metal pail holding about a quart and apparently, it came with the job. Sometimes the bottom of a lunch bucket was used which often came in two sections, the upper section usually was for the sandwiches and the lower for coffee.

The water boy would go to the nearest saloon and have the required measure of beer poured into the pail. You can be sure it didn't go far among thirsty men in summer. The man furnishing the money got the first drink, usually a long one, and the pail was then passed down the line until empty. It was suspected that the water boy often got the first drink. The next time the money was paid by another man.

To get back to Bonner's Saloon, it had an open-sided shed in the back used by teamsters and persons with wagons or other rigs to shelter their horses in inclement weather while they went into the saloon for refreshments. Of course, inclement weather wasn't always necessary. Horses have brains! I've seen drivers come out of the saloon feeling no pain, crawl on the driver's seat and head the horses home and go to sleep. The horses would get him home every time. Also, the horse knew the driver's favorite saloon and would stop in front every time they passed it by.

I still remember quite a few of the saloons and the open-sided shed in the rear. They were equipped with mangers for hay or feed which the wagon driver brought along. Each wagon or buggy was usually equipped with a nose bag, mostly called feed bags, but there is no necessity to describe them here since they are still around and found wherever horses are kept. A necessary equipment was the hitching iron and whip held upright in the whip socket attached to the dashboard. Dad had a hitching iron which was round and weighed about 10 pounds to which a strap was attached. When we left the wagon we put out the hitching iron and hooked the strap to the bridle. If the horse took a notion to walk away he was held by the hitching iron and its weight soon changed its mind. I've seen horses run away with the hitching iron dragging, but with the horse's head held to the side because of the weight it didn't get very far. Many wagons and buggies had a pet dog on the seat beside the driver, or it would run under the tailgate and I'm sure this is where the saying originated for a conceited person, "he thinks he's the whole team and the dog under the wagon." Fire stations usually had a Dalmatian breed dog as pet which rode along on fire calls and the standing joke was that the dog was taken along to find the fireplugs.

On Arthurdale Avenue one summer day Mom took me along to visit a Mrs. Wenger living in a cottage two or three doors down the street. Mom knocked at the back door, which was partially open, but no answer. She pushed the door open a little wider and we saw Mrs. Wenger lying on the kitchen floor beside the stove. She had apparently suffered a heart attack--my first dead person.

Our next door neighbors were Mr. and Mrs. Richland who had a daughter, Charlot and a son, Carl. They were fine people and Lucy and I always enjoyed her custard pie. Poor Mr. Richland was a consumptive and Mom, Dad, and I visited him in the Consumpton Ward at City Hospital where he later passed away. Consumption is now called tuberculosis and kids were allowed to visit in the ward then and it's a wonder I didn't "ketch consumption." Mr. Richland was interred in Calvary Cemetery, Newburgh, Ohio, now part of Cleveland.

At the end of our street was the car barns, a place where streetcars came to the end of the line. The name was a holdover from the days when they had horse-drawn streetcars and horses were stabled in a barn at the end of the line.

When the funeral day came Mr. Richland's casket was carried down the street to the black funeral car waiting at the car barns on State Road (now W. 35th). At that time if one traveled with horse and buggy on State Road, one eventually arrived in Columbus. To me the

8

shiny black funeral car, the size of an interurban car, was an impressive sight, especially the black upholstery and curtains on the inside. The casket was pushed into a compartment with a door on the outside toward the front of the car. Pallbearers and mourners were dressed in black with the ladies wearing a heavy black veil attached to a black hat and black dresses down to the heels. We attended service at St. Mary's Church on Broadview Road and afterward the casket was carried by the pallbearers down the street to the waiting funeral car at the corner of Pearl Road. It was a long solemn ride, particularly since I was getting hungry and Mom had brought no lunch, expecting we would be home by noon. She had a dollar but it being a no-stop ride there was no opportunity to get off at a grocery to buy a snack for the three of us. Some of the people must have been on a similar ride before since they had brought along food. However, Mr. Wilhelm, the conductor and neighbor, saved the day for us. He had brought along a bag of sugar biscuits and told Lucy and I to "dive in."

To get back to our home, heating it in winter was something else again. The kitchen was the warmest room, wood-burning stove, you see. The dining room had a wood and coal-burning base burner, as it was called, resting on a square sheet metal mat. Some of the mats had quite colorful designs, but they all served a useful purpose in preventing the spilled hot coals or ashes from burning the floor. The base burner was a large pot-bellied stove with a nickel-plated flat rail around the front and sides on which we'd warm our feet. The door had Eisenglass windows and when there was fire in the pot they shone with a warm mellow glow. To me it was a high iron monster. It was fed by swinging back the cover on top or by opening the door in front. A coal pail with appropriate size pieces of coal and a small coal shovel were handy. With it came an iron poker to poke up the fire and an iron shaker to shake down the ashes into the ash pit on the

9

bottom of the stove. To start a fire a little coal oil was first poured over the fuel after making sure there were not hot ashes or coals still left. Mingled with the coal would be some crumpled paper and a match would do the rest.

The stove was kept polished with regular stove polish. I tried polishing my shoes with stove polish but it left them with a silver sheen. The base burners really heated up a room and my first memory of toasted bread was Mother putting a slice of homemade bread on a long knife and holding it over the hot coals until it turned brown. We had no door or window weatherstripping and I don't believe they were known then. In the ceiling over the base burner was a square hole with a metal grate. This opening let the hot air into the upstairs bedroom and it helped some, but not much. Standing over the grate on a cold winter morning was a good place to dress.

None of these arrangements or sanitary conditions bothered us. We came of healthy stock and beside the usual colds or sore throat, I only remember brother Al having diphtheria. Mom did say he had a severe case of scarlet fever in his childhood. As for myself, I am told I had the three-day measles and nothing else. I seemed to be immune somehow since during my years in the police department it was necessary to go into homes with all sorts of contagious diseases but I never "caught" anything. In my thirties I had a ruptured appendix, in my seventies a heart attack and sight deterioration but these things come with age. A gall bladder operation can also be included in this. Outside of the usual colds and odds and ends we did alright. I do recall Lucy having the flu during the epidemic of 1918. Mom and Dad lived to be 73, brother Al 80, brother Joe 84, brother Ben 18, Lucy and I are still around. (Lucy died in 1982 and the author in 1986.)

For lighting, we had a coal-oil lamp, one on the kitchen table and one on a small shelf on the wall with a reflector. The job of cleaning

10

the glass chimney usually fell to brother Joe. A coal-oil odor in homes was usual. Coal oil was also used by some persons to kill lice, head lice in particular. We never used it--no lice. The beautiful parlor coal-oil lamps were something to see. They had various flower designs painted on the globes and reservoirs. Some lamps were of plain-colored glass. When lit, lamps cast a mellow glow and when walking down the street in the evening they were a pleasure to see. Today these lamps are collectors' items and, like everyone else then, when gas lamps and electricity came into use, the lamps were stored in the attic and finally thrown out. Attics in those days were called garrets. We, too, had a garret on Arthurdale Avenue, which was entered by a door leading from the upstairs bedroom.

Our next move, about 1905 or 1906 was to 1925 Buhrer Avenue. The house still stands albeit changed somewhat. In August, 1977, I was treated to a ride by my sons Edward and Martin, accompanied by my sister Lucy, and we parked in front of or near our old homes. Marty took pictures and they turned out well. 1925 Buhrer Avenue seemed to be an old house at the time we moved in. I do not know the reason for moving, but St. Michael's School and Church, being only two or three blocks away, depending on which side of Scranton Road you counted the streets, may have been a factor. Certainly, piped-in water and a water closet with sanitary sewer must have been.

I recall these years as being happy ones and I particularly remember Mother humming and singing while doing her household chores. Dad worked at Bushman's Furniture Store downtown as a furniture finisher, brother Al was learning the upholstery trade, brother Joe was apprenticed at the Jones Optical Company. He was with them for many years and foreman with the American Optical Company when they purchased Jones Optical and moved to Youngstown. Ben and Lucy attended St. Michael's School, but I was too young to go. In those days if you completed the 6th or 7th grade you were thought to have had enough schooling and then went to work. Brother Al left after the 5th grade while both brothers Joe and Ben after the 6th or 7th grade. Lucy, I believe, finished 7th grade and became apprenticed to Mrs. Grau, Milliner.

Lucy, Ben, Edward Stein
1925 Burher Avenue

The house consisted of kitchen, middle room, and front room. The middle room had a small room on the side with a bay window. Middle rooms are now called dining rooms and front rooms are called living rooms. A center hall led from the dining room to the front door. Across the hall from the living room was another room which was used as a spare bedroom. From the hallway to the right of the dining room was a stair leading to three upstairs bedrooms. These rooms were colder than the end tails of hell in winter and Mom would wrap hot flat irons in dish towels and put them at the foot of the bed to keep our feet warm.

As on Arthurdale, this house also had a cellar which was entered by lifting a trap door in a small room behind the kitchen. A short stair led to the cellar where the winter supply of potatoes, apples and canned fruits were stored. It was small and had a hard-packed earth floor. I do not recall what material the walls were made of, but it could have been stone or brick. The cellar extended only under the kitchen with the rest of the house on a foundation of sandstone block with a crawl space of about two feet between the ground and the floor of the house. The foundation had square holes in each side for ventilating the crawl space--nice for drafts in winter and kept the floors cold. The squares had grates which prevented cats and other crawly things from using it for shelter.

Our plumbing system was much improved, we now had sanitary sewers and piped-in water with one cold water faucet in the kitchen. You can see that Ma and Pa improved themselves--no well at the back door and one faucet in the house. A hot-water tank we had not. Also, instead of a privy in the backyard with the chickens, we now had something more modern--a water closet. It was attached to the small room in back of the kitchen. This small room was the one which had the trap door leading to the cellar. The side opposite the trap door had a clothes hamper for soiled clothing and two wood wash tubs with a washboard. The tin bathtub, sides still painted green, hung on the wall over the trap door.

To explain the water closet in more clinical detail, it was a two-holer with a brass handle in an upright position to control the water. It was turned on by turning the handle clockwise then flushing the water into the sanitary sewer when one completed one's assignment. All privys, and our water closet, were equipped with torn paper, usually newspaper, of the appropriate size strung on a string and hanging from a nail in the wall. Farm folk used Sears-Roebuck catalogues and by the time spring came around they were up to the harness section.

Ours was a two-entrance water closet, a door from the inside room two steps down and a door from the outside at ground level. Good planning there! It was a cold place in winter and not conducive to lingering long since it had no central heating. However it was an improvement over the old backhouse since we didn't have to run through the backyard and dodge the chicken manure around the hen house. I will not offend your delicate senses by speaking of the thunder mugs which were part of all bedroom furnishings. The fancy ones had covers and cupids painted on the sides.

Across from our home lived the Koch family who were teamsters for the Osborn Manufacturing Company. Osborn's had their building on the east end of the old Superior Viaduct, later replaced by the new Superior High Level Bridge. I do not know what they manufactured, but Koch had the contract for deliveries. As I remember, Mr. Koch had four or six teams driven by his sons and hired teamsters. Anna Koch, the youngest daughter and my age, was my childhood playmate and we spent many happy hours in the barn climbing around the horse stalls and the fringed top surrey. Sometimes we played in the hayloft, but were soon called down by her mother because of the danger of falling through the openings in the floor through which hay was forked into the mangers below.

Saturday was particularly interesting when, from in front of our house across the street, I watched the teamsters wash their wagons and groom their horses. A few healthy swear words were par for the course. Teamsters were noted for the variety of descriptive swear words they used, especially with a balky horse. It seems that some horses respond better to a few salty words. Mules especially. It could be this is the first place I heard the great American expression "sonovabitch." I heard it from a teamster, that's for sure, either at Koch's or at Duffy's Saloon. We never heard swear words at home with the exception of a donner wetter (thunder weather) from Dad.

A team of horses with the brass and brass-studded harness shined up was a pleasure to see. A good teamster took pride in the appearance of his team and wagon much as some persons take pride in a clean and polished automobile.

Vegetable hucksters, fish peddlers, farmers with their produce, ice wagons, banana peddlers with two-wheel pushcarts loaded with bananas, two-wheel ice cream pushcart peddlers and buggies were in abundance. While these peddlers didn't come around every day they did make their appearance in neighborhoods in summer at least once a week, especially the ice cream peddlers and banana pushcarts.

During the hot summer weather many teamsters and drivers tied a straw hat, made for that purpose, on the horse's head to keep the sun off. It's a wonder the horses didn't get sunstroke. Some had holes in the hat for the ears and some tied a wet sponge between the ears and wet it when hot. The last time I saw a horse with a hat was when Leona and I were in New Orleans in the 60's. (Note to the reader: Leona was the author's wife.) Sprinkling wagons were a lot of fun on a hot summer day. The purpose of the sprinkling wagon was to flush the manure and mud from the pavement. The wagon consisted of a very large wooden cask mounted lengthwise on a wagon chassis built for that purpose. It was usually pulled by a team of horses. The driver sat in front and operated the opening and closing valve with a push-and-pull handle. The cask had an opening on top and when the contents ran low, a canvas hose was attached to a fire hydrant and the cask refilled. The sprinkler would be driven down the middle of the street and we kids, being barefooted in summer, waited for the driver to open the water valve. When it gushed out, we'd run in the stream of water until the driver shut the valve. The gutters would be awash with water and we'd jump around in it too, not withstanding the

15

Ice Wagon
Courtesy of Western Reserve Historical Society--Cleveland, OH

manure and mud floating toward the sewer opening. I guess that's where we were immunized from disease--those of us who did "ketch" something. Yelling and screaming was part of the fun.

Hopping ice wagons was an amusement in hot weather. We stood on the back step of the wagon and enjoyed the cool air flowing from the blocks of ice while the wagon rolled down the street. We were happy when we found small pieces of ice to put in our mouths.

The fish peddler was especially busy on Friday. He blew his horn as the horse walked down the street and whoever wanted fish for the evening meal came out with a plate. The fish were kept in a large box of ice behind the driver's seat. Besides selling fish, the peddler's job would be to gut them and remove the scales for the customer. Mom usually bought Lake Erie blue pike which were in abundance then.

All horses were bothered with biting flies in warm weather and a fly net helped to keep them off. There were large flies called horseflies and there was a continuous switching of tails and stamping of feet when the flies bit deep. The more affluent people owned a horse and buggy, consequently a barn with a manure box was necessary. Of course, horses could be boarded at a livery stable but this would be too inconvenient and expensive. When the box was filled, a farmer came periodically and emptied the box into his manure wagon. This was used as fertilizer by him. I have no idea if the farmer paid the owner or the owner paid the farmer for this service.

The manure boxes were breeding grounds for flies and every home in the vicinity had its share. I remember Mom using flypaper, Tangle Foot brand. It was in demand then. The paper was put on a table or a strategic place, glue side up, and once the fly lit on the paper that was the end of Mr. Fly. He never got off again. Once in a while clothing was inadvertently laid on the paper but we soon learned. Mother also used to take advantage of a thick poison-saturated black paper sold in stores. This was placed in a dish or shallow pan, wet down and sugar added. The flies went for the sugar and consequently were finished. This was a slower process and I enjoyed the Tangle Foot more. Another home invention used by people was paper cut in about one-inch wide strips, about six or eight inches long and tacked to the upper door frame in such a way that the paper did not get stuck between the screen door and frame. I am not quite clear on the mechanics of it, but I have seen it and it worked to some extent. When the screen door was opened it chased the flies away.

Another method I saw Mom use was to darken the rooms, open the kitchen screen door and flap a towel at the flies in the direction of the open screen door. They would take off for the light and it was quite effective. Fantastic? I was there. It was during these years that the city fathers instituted a "Swat the Fly" campaign. Fly swatters were free in most stores and, I think, the price set by the city per 100 flies was 1¢. I don't remember where the flies were delivered to or who counted them.

During the hot weather, hand fans were in vogue and most ladies carried one, especially at social events or picnics. They were all types and sizes. Some were of palm, some of cardboard with a picture on the front and advertisement on the back, and some folding fans. The fancy folding fans were things of beauty with gold or silver sprinkles or sequins sparkling in the light.

We had gas streetlights mounted on iron posts and every evening at dusk the lamplighter with his short ladder over his shoulder walked down the street, leaned the ladder against the lamppost and lit the lamp. The disadvantage of gas lamps was that they spread the light only a short distance from the lamp and the street between lamps was dark. Later we had arc lights suspended from electric light poles.

Summer evenings were peaceful with crickets fiddling in the grass and an occasional horse and buggy with laterns hanging from the rear axle rolling down the street. Some buggies had large fancy coal-oil lamps attached to the sides near the driver and some had a coal-oil lamp with red glass attached to the rear. The sound of a horse clip-clopping down the street is something I've always carried with me.

18

Chapter 2

*T*wo blocks from our home was the 9th Precinct Police Station, Althen Avenue and Pearl Street (now W. 25th). It was always exciting to watch the patrol wagon, pulled by a fast-moving team of horses, race down the street on a call. Police then still wore helmets and I can still see the driver on his high seat and the other officer on the back step hanging onto the hand rails. The patrol wagon, called paddy wagon, was equipped with two benches facing each other. Often times I saw the wagon return with men, either drunk or sober, who perhaps had been causing a disturbance in a saloon. Sometimes their song would rise in the evening air. Little did I know that one day I would be assigned to this police station while in the police department. Later on I may touch on a few occurrences in the department.

Mom taught me to make the sign of the cross and say the Our Father while standing at her knee. I didn't understand at the time and resented it but it was something I had to do. When I went to school I realized I was prepared in this direction when some of the other children were not. We were taught to say our prayers before each meal and at bedtime. A large picture of the Sacred Heart in a heavy gold frame was part of our lives and hung in the living room. I kept this picture for many years. Dad had a statue of the Blessed Virgin and the Infant Jesus which was his favorite. Underneath the statue was scratched the year 1886 and the initials M St. I believe this to have been a wedding gift to him. I recall Mom saying to me that God is all seeing, He knows the past, the present and what is going to be. Mom used to sing little German songs while she worked. When she sang and hummed I was content.

One of the songs I still remember was this:
Kam ei n vogel geflogen,

Sezts sich nieder auf mein fus,
Liebe vogel fliege weiter,
Bring den Grossmutter einen gruss.
(The spelling may be somewhat incorrect)
The translation would be:
"A bird flew in and sat on my foot.
Dear little bird fly away and take my greetings
To grandmother."
Sorry I can't make it rhyme as in German.

Christmas was always a good time and looked forward to well in advance. We'd pop corn and with needle and thread, Mom, Lucy, and I would make long strings of popcorn for Christmas tree decorations. Santa always brought the tree and presents. The tree was put in the coldest room of the house, usually the front room, to keep the needles from drying and falling off. We had no problem choosing a cold room on Buhrer Avenue. Electric lights for trees were unknown and Christmas candles were attached to the limbs by small holders. The candles were of various colors and lighting them was a job for grown-ups. The lit tree was a beauty to behold and usually gathered around and sang Stille Knocked, Heilige Knocked. Dad had a good voice, more on the tenor side.

Santa Claus and his reindeers was the topic of conversation between Lucy and me. We imagined many wonderful things and did not doubt his ability to come down the chimney or through the keyhole. Once, a few days before Christmas, there was a stamping of feet on the back porch and a knocking at the door and in came Santa Claus with a bag on his shoulder. Santa had a red face and white whiskers. The bag was stuffed with toys. Later I figured the outline of the toys must have been pieces of wood. Santa spoke to me in German and asked if I could say The Our Father. I started it but was unable to finish because of being frightened and I hid behind Mom's long skirt. I heard Mom say something to him in a low voice and he said he would leave the toys for Christmas and left. I never forgot it. Some years later I found out it had been Dad. I should have suspected him, a German-speaking Santa Claus.

Christmas morning was the most exciting day of the year and Mom had no trouble waking us since we were long awake just waiting to see what presents Santa had left us. I wasn't particularly happy with clothing or Mom's hand-knitted black gloves which he had left us. A big treat for each of us was a large bowl filled with hard-colored candies in the shape of animals, a variety of nuts in the shell, a few cookies, and an orange at the side. Christmas was the only time we had an orange because, I suppose, they were too expensive. Perhaps 15¢ a dozen. We ate our share of fruit in season during the year such as apples, pears, grapes, and strawberries, especially at canning time. The blue Concord grapes were my favorite.

The week between Christmas and New Year was particularly happy since Lucy and Ben didn't go to school and playing with our toys was in order. We nibbled at the candy and made it stretch as long as we could because we knew after it was gone there would be no more. Mom had baked a variety of cookies for the holidays and we were particularly fond of pfeffernuss during Christmas week. They were great for munching. If a large batch had been baked, they sometimes lasted till February and by that time they were hard as stones and made good dunking. Another cookie Mom would make was the springerlies. They had raised pictures on each one, mostly of flowers. The way the pictures were formed on the cookie was by pressing a wood block, into which the picture had been carved, onto the cookie dough. The dough was of a special mixture and taste.

For New Year's Mom would always make radekuchen. They are a little difficult to describe. To begin, "rade" means wheel and everyone knows what kuchen is. Actually, it is not a kuchen but a cookie. Rade is not pronounced like raid, but as rod-en-kuchen. (Stick around my friends, I'll make German readers of you yet.)

21

Mom mixed the radekuchen dough and rolled it flat. Then came the "rade" part! It was a small brass wheel with a zig-zag edge attached to a small wood handle. With the wheel the dough was cut in strips about one inch wide and about five inches long. In the center of the strip Mom cut a line about three inches long. She then took both ends of the dough and folded them through the center slit and straightened it out. This resulted in a twisted center. Do I make myself clear--you cooks? While all this was going on Mom had the iron kettle going with hot lard and when the lard started to blue smoke a little the radekuchen were put in until they were a rich brown. No trouble seeing the color, they floated on top. After removal and the fat had drained off and the cookie cooled, powdered sugar was sprinkled over them. Good eating! Especially when still warm. Nobody knew what cholesterol was then--thank heaven! I am astonished at all the details I remember but I guess it is because I was part of it all and I did help Mom in the kitchen many times. Of course, Lucy was Mom's big kitchen helper while I was the gopher--go for this and go for that.

Since we didn't have storm windows or weatherstripping, on a cold snowy winter day the wind would heap tiny mounds of snow on the inside sill at the corner of the windows. The windows were so thick with frost we had to melt it with our breath to see out.

I did not care for Monday washday in winter on Buhrer Avenue. Water had to be heated in a copper wash boiler on a wood and coal-burning stove. The boiler was filled with water, a brown bar of soap, German model brand, (later we had Fels-Naptha) was cut up or shaved into the water and all clothes boiled. Mom had a stick about a yard long with which she stirred or tamped down the clothes. Wooden wash tubs were set side by side on a bench, one tub having warm water with a washboard in it and the other, rinse water to which liquid bluing had been added. Washboards were made of wood with a corrugated metal sheet covering the rubbing side on which the clothes were rubbed to remove the soil. It was a backbreaking chore

22

for some women. After a thorough rinsing, the clothes were run through a hand-operated wringer to remove excess water. The kitchen was filled with steam and moisture and the window panes ran with water.

Drying clothes in winter was something else again. Mom used lines strung in the kitchen and also hung the clothes on a wooden rack which she unfolded and stood in the dining room. To dry clothes the house needed to be warm and humidity must have reached 100 degrees. When Mom hung clothes to dry in the yard during the fall of the year sometimes one or two pieces would be forgotten because they had not dried well, especially the long-johns. When left out overnight they'd be frozen stiff as sheet metal and had to be handled carefully or the frozen cloth would break with the ice. In summer there was no problem, washing clothes was done on the back porch and clothes hung on a line to dry in the sun.

Mom always looked neat and somehow managed to look neat even on wash days. About 4:00 p.m. she'd change to other clothes before Dad and my brothers came home from work. Mom had pierced ears and wore small gold and black inlaid earrings. In her later years she wore none. Women wore high-collar waists to which, usually, an ornamental pin was attached at the collar. Mom had one shaped like a butterfly, white stones for the wings and red stones for the eyes, which glittered when the light struck it right. She always wore a broad gold wedding ring, as did Dad, with the wedding date engraved on the inside. I have given these to my son, Martin as a keepsake.

Long sleeves were the style and for dressing up long white gloves in the summer and dark gloves in winter. Also in style were the long elbow-length leather kid gloves. Two or three petticoats under the long skirts were the norm--with lace trimming, mind you. A far cry from the cut-off fringed jeans worn at this writing. It has been argued in some quarters the petticoats aided in the protection and preservation of virtue, too.

To keep hands from freezing in winter, fur muffs were a must--also stylish. It was a good depository for handkerchief, house keys, purse, and other personal items--long hatpins, too, in case one was attacked. Muffs were a status symbol, the bigger and more expensive the fur, the more statue. However, muffs faded out in about the 20's and, in later years came back in style for a short time.

There was no shortage of decoration on ladies' hats. Mom, like most ladies, had several hats, one for every day and one for Sunday. Decorations seemed to be seasonal, too. In summer there were ostrich feathers, flowers, or imitation fruit and in winter hats were of velvet or other material covering a wire frame and decorated with odds and ends. Let us not forget the long six to eight inch, hat pins to hold hats in place on a windy day. A more accurate description could be given by my sister Lucy, a first class milliner who learned her trade from experts.

The ostrich plumes on a hat could be an annoyance on a crowded streetcar. Dad brought home two ends of ostrich plumes one time. He said he had been on a crowded streetcar and the woman beside him kept turning her head in conversation. The ostrich feathers kept brushing his face so he took out his pocket knife and cut them off. To this day I do not know whether Dad was joking. I know this, he was capable of it.

As for men, I recall the peg-top pants. These were wide at the hips and narrowed down to the ankles with cuffs barely reaching the button shoe top. They looked best on men who were spare in the short ribs. Yellow or bright orange button shoes was something to write to your relatives about. A buttonhook was part of the shoe purchase. They were given away free by the shoe stores. I had my own buttonhook when I was growing up.

For the record I will describe Dad as best I can. He was not tall--about 5 foot 8 inches and of stocky build. He had hazel eyes, fair complexion, and a brown moustache. He had a full head of hair which remained black until his later years. There are no bald heads on the Stein side of the fence. He wore gold-frame glasses and, as was the custom in his youth, snuffed Copenhagen. Many men snuffed tobacco then and I still remember some of his friends asking him for a "prees"--snuff. While "prees" is not the word for snuff it has the same connotation, for example, as "Give me a cigarette." Pop was a good man and thoroughly honest. He was a man who kept his promises. As the saying is, "His word is as good as his bond." It was! I've tried to follow his example and don't recall ever intentionally breaking a promise. There are times, due to unforseen circumstances, when promises cannot be kept, in which case I would explain the circumstance and get released from my promise.

Edward Stein, Age 12 & Martin Stein, Father
1913

Pop was a devout Catholic, drank a glass of beer occasionally, smoked perhaps two cigars a month. He was strictly a meat and potato man and very seldom ate dessert, sweets, or green vegetables. The first joint of the ring finger of his left hand was permanently bent. He said it had been broken many years before but did not say how. He got along well with people and appreciated a joke. He always had a humorous comeback for the ladies and they enjoyed it. I remember one time when I was helping him deliver a davenport to a home, the hallway to the living room was small and it was a tight squeeze and took some maneuvering. The wife was looking on and, in German, said to him "That's a hard job." Dad replied, in German, "It's about as hard as a 65 year old woman giving birth to a baby." She enjoyed the joke. Pop wasn't a meek man by any means and had a temper too. He had a saying, which translated to "It's a sad home where the rooster is silent and the hen crows."

Pop always wore a black derby and across his vest he wore a gold link chain with a gold C.M.B.A. emblem dangling from it. The letters stood for Catholic Men's Benevolent Association. Attached to the chain was a large silver watch. I have given it to my son Martin as a keepsake from his grandfather. He wore a culluloid collar to which was hooked a ready-made knotted tie. Keep the collar away from a burning match or you've had it. Later the white rubber collar was introduced which was not as flammable. You see, shirts with attached collars were unknown then. The celluloid and rubber collars had an advantage, you know. When they became soiled they were washed with soap and water but if they became too old they turned yellow at the neck line. Collars were attached to the shirt with a brass collar button in front and one in back and detachable cuffs were held to the shirt sleeve with a metal clasp.

Collars and cuffs were usually sent to a commercial laundry or taken to a Chinese laundry to be laundered. The Chinese were expert launderers and during my teens I paid either 2-1/2 ¢ or 5 ¢ a piece to have my collars laundered at the Chinese laundry at W. 25th and Althea Avenue. I became well acquainted with Charlie, in fact, he tried to teach me Chinese, but I didn't have the patience. I do recall he did his calculating on an abacus. Charlie lived upstairs with his helper, another Chinaman. One evening I saw Charlᵥ in a back room on a stool. He was sucking on, what ɪᴄ large banana stalk. The end of it was in a kettle of water aᴵ sucked and blew out smoke it would gurgle. It must have been ѕ ᴢ sort of water pipe. In retrospect I believe it was a hollow bamboo stalk. I've seen Greeks on Bolivar smoke water pipes but not that kind.

While discussing Chinese laundrymen, in the basement of the Pearl Street Bank, W. 25th and Clark Avenue--now a chain grocery--was a Chinese laundry reached by an outside stair. The Chinaman wore his hair in a long queue down his back and black skull cap. When I went to school the boys going home that way would yell down the stairway "Chink, Chink, Chinaman" and run. Sometimes he'd come up the stairs after them but never were they caught and I imagine he didn't try very hard. My way home was in a different direction so I missed the fun. Chinese then were looked on as a sort of mysterious race, usually associated with smoking opium in an opium den somewhere and kidnapping young girls. They were supposed to eat rats, too.

One of the big events on Buhrer Avenue was having gas piped into the house. This was an improvement since Mom didn't have to cook meals or iron clothes with flat irons heated over a wood-burning stove anymore. A gas-heated stove, referred to as a gas range, also took the place of the base burner in the dining room. The gas company must have just laid gas pipes then because many of our neighbors also turned to gas heating.

Fourth of July morning was something. No one slept long because at the break of day the firecracker racket started. There was a continuous banging and booming throughout the day and far into the night. Firecrackers, sparklers, rockets, and other explosives were sold in all stores. Large caps were placed in a row on streetcar tracks and when they were run over it you could hear it for blocks. Kids had cap pistols which were harmless and made a banging noise. Lucy and I had a stick with an iron knob on the end with a slot in which was inserted a cap. The bottom was movable so that when it was struck on the sidewalk the cap fired.

It was on a day before the 4th of July when Mother took me downtown. We were waiting for a streetcar on the Square about where the Terminal Tower is now when we heard much screaming. On Ontario street a few doors from the Square, was a 5 and 10 cent store from which the screaming came. We saw smoke pouring from the upper stories and soon the horse-drawn fire engines arrived. The smoke became thicker and the screaming worse. The firemen were busy and everything was in an uproar. Mom and I watched it for a time from the opposite side of the street, but when the streetcar came along we boarded it. Good thing we did or we might have been there a long time with the streetcar tied up by fire hoses criss crossing the roadway. The next day the newspapers had the story. It seems they had counters of fireworks on display on an upper floor and someone ignited a sparkler. The sparks set off the firecrackers. As a result of the fire and panic the floor collapsed and many persons lost their lives. Within a few years the city fathers passed an ordinance banning the sale of fireworks within the city limits. The ordinance is still in effect. This, tho didn't prevent anyone from setting up stands with fireworks across the boundary line of the city.

On the southeast corner of Clark and Scranton was a candy store--long since replaced by a dry cleaning establishment. This store sold Hoky-Poky's. For a penny we could buy a Hoky-Poky and for another penny we could by an all-day sucker. Once in a great while, on a Sunday, Dad would take Lucy and me there to each buy a Hoky-Poky. They were extra special and delicious. A Hoky-Poky, my dear readers, was nothing more than a piece of ice cream, about two inches square, wrapped in a piece of wax paper, much like an ice cream slice is now. We never had ice cream. Indeed, I think the

Hoky-Poky is the first taste of ice cream we had, so you can see how good it was.

Then comes the all-day sucker. I liked the all-day sucker but it was a disappointment for the reason that I expected it to last all day--like they "sez." It didn't! You could suck on it only as long as it lasted, like any other sucker, which wasn't long enough.

Then there were "Likrish Straps." The "Likrish Straps"--Licorice Straps to the educated--were favorites among the kids. They were long and thin with a hole through the length. Six for a penny. Lots of chewing and spitting of "tobacco juice"--fun and tasty.

Jaw breakers--they were the thing. I guess everyone knows what a jaw breaker is, even today. It's a round hard candy, black in color with a seed in the center. I don't know if the jaw breakers today have a seed but they did then--and six for a penny. Good sucking! Six would last longer than an all day sucker. One time brother Ben had a nickel--he was working and could afford it. He asked me to buy him a nickel's worth of candy, expecting a variety, I think. I got a nickel's worth of candy, alright--jaw breakers--30 of them. Ben was so damn mad he threw them at me, one at a time. You can be sure they didn't go to waste. I had my share of jaw breakers that day.

The only thing I recall about election time on Buhrer Avenue is Dad talking about William Howard Taft, Theodore Roosevelt (we called him Teddy Bear Roosevelt), the Bull Moose Party and William Jennings Bryan. We had a picture of Taft hung in our front window which was the thing to do to show our political choice for the election. I also remember Dad talking about our Mayor Tom L. Johnson, proponent of the 3¢ car fare. His statue is still on the Public Square. Pop pronounced his name as Tom Ale Younson.

As I mentioned earlier, Dad and Mom were born in Prussia, Germany. Dad in Marienburg and Mom in Braunsberg. Whether it was East Prussia or West Prussia I do not know but one, and perhaps both, are now in the Russian Zone since World War II.

From Mom's conversation, I believe her family to have been fairly well to do--at least comfortably provided for. I believe Grandfather's (Rogasch) first name was Bernard. He was in the roofing business and, also, had a farm. They lived in Braunsberg where mother was born. They had two or three boys of whom, I believe, Uncle Bernard Rogasch, Rochester, was the oldest. Mom was the oldest of three girls. Mom and Dad never spoke of their earlier years and I wish they had but I suppose they were too busy raising a family of five children to give it much thought.

Then, too, coming to America and settling among strangers was a new life, although Dad did have a few acquaintances from Germany in the area. I learned many German songs from Mom and Dad and to this day I can still sing them. A few years ago, in the condominium where we are now living in Tucson, we had a German couple living in our area with whom we became acquainted. They had both been born in Germany and the husband had served in the German Army during World War I. Occasionally I'd surprise them with a German song and the husband would say, "You know more German songs than I do." Brother Al took a trip to Germany with Mom when he was six years old. One of the relatives he visited over there was Grandfather Rogasch who had a farm and hired hands. One time, according to what Al told me years later, Grandmother, who was looking for the hired girl, asked him if he'd seen her and Al told her that the hired hand called to her from the hay loft, asked her to come up and she did--understand? Mom went back to Germany about 1913 with sister Lucy to visit her relatives in Berlin, Koleburg, and Braunsburg while I stayed home and guarded the portals.

It was a lonesome time for me. I became an expert fried potato and scrambled egg cook that summer.

I have a great respect and admiration for Dad and Mom. They were wise and had seen the elephant and heard the owl. When one is young; parents are just someone who'll be there when needed and be there for all time. It is only in more mature years that one gains a different viewpoint. I read a definition some time ago of a teenager-- "A person who believes he won't be as dumb as his father is when he becomes his age." Also, there comes a time when a teenager attempts to analyze the parents and is surprised to find they are human and have feet of clay.

Dad was a rather quiet sort and not one to speak of himself. I do know that he learned the trade of male nurse, served his time in a hospital and received his papers, or what amounted to a diploma then. He carried his skill and knowledge of herbs and medicine with him when he came to America. He had a stepmother, a sister and one or two half-brothers. I recall one or two Stein's from Canton, Ohio, visiting us on Scranton Road who, apparently, were children of his half-brothers. I asked Dad one time about his early life and all he told me was that he had a poor childhood and it was best forgotten. He wasn't one you could press for information either.

One time I asked Mom how she had met Dad and there, too, I ran into a wall. She said, "Oh, you know how young people meet." What an exercise in futility. That's about the same sort of answer kids got those days to the question of whether a stork brought them or if they were found in a cabbage patch. It was kept a deep, dark secret but we learned, usually from a more-enlightened school companion. This brings to mind when I was a child of the times Mom had one of her friends over for a visit and I would hear them talking in low tones. When I entered the room conversation ceased. It must have been a subject not fit for my tender ears. I wonder if the subject was sex.

Dad was the adventurous one it seems. Considering he left Germany to come to America to start a new life among strangers, it took a lot of drive and determination. Then, too, he must have read about exciting things happening in America. You see, he was born at the beginning of our Civil War and his teens were about the time

31

of Custer's Last Stand, our Indian troubles, and Buffalo Bill, so he must have had a wish to see what it was all about, particularly the streets paved with gold as they were told. I know he was an avid reader of western stories written in German by author Karl May--the spelling may be Mai. I doubt whether good old Karl was ever in America but he wrote a good story. In fact, I've read since that Karl wrote these westerns while in the klink in Germany and never had been to America. Once in a while one of my errands on a Sunday was to go to St. Michael's library after the 3:00 o'clock devotion and pick out a book of May's for Dad. I never did find one he hadn't read before. There were quite a few books on various subjects but many of them were in German and there was nothing which interested me.

While on the subject of library books, I cut my eye teeth on fairy tales, graduating to Altsheller's frontier stories. The Long Knives, Kentucky Riflemen and many others of adventurous nature. I usually managed to devour 5¢ worth of salted peanuts (1/2 lb.) at these Saturday afternoon sessions at the library. At home I read the Rover Boys, Claud Lightfoot, practically all of the Alger stories. *"Sink or Swim,"* and *"From Rags to Riches."* Alger books could be bought for 10¢, hardback, in the dime store then. I know, brother Joe used to buy them. They were good, clean reading for youngsters coming up and always pointed up a moral--work hard, be honest and save your money. The stories usually followed along the line of a boy working hard shining shoes on the street and saving his money. Besides keeping his poor widowed mother in doughnuts, he is able to save enough to buy a whole shoeshine stand on a corner for himself. Then he saves more money and opens a small haberdashery, then graduates to a clothing store and becomes wealthy. All this time he is being kind to old people and shoeshine boys. As a climax he uses his wealth to help poor children.

I wish it were so but it did point a child's mind in the right direction. I was so immersed in Alger's *"Rags to Riches"* idea, helping old

32

people who would leave you a lot of money, that one rainy day I was about to enter the grocery at Meyer Avenue and Scranton when I saw an old lady with an umbrella crossing Scranton. In my mind's eye she was about 35 or 40 years old. As she reached the sidewalk, she slipped and fell. I rushed over and helped her up. I retrieved the umbrella and gave it to her. She thanked me kindly and walked into the grocery. No money! I wish I had saved the Alger books they are collectors' items now. A treat for me at Christmas was to receive a book, not that I was studious, but I did like to read and I soaked up a lot of information one way or another which helped me later in life.

Mom and Dad were both good-hearted and generous according to their means. However, Mom was the conservative one. Dad never had much spending money in his pocket, not that he bought anything for himself but just bought things to bring home for Mom, for us children, or for the home. Sister Lucy is a great deal like him in this respect--generous to a fault. I don't know what wages Dad earned but it was sufficient to raise a family and keep food on the table. When brothers Al, Joe, and Ben worked, it helped. Then, as I did too, all earned money was brought home until one was 21 years old. From this you received weekly spending money and Dad and Mom furnished everything else, shelter, food, and clothing.

Mom is the one who sewed our clothing when they needed repair and she also made Lucy's dresses and my blouses. Mom made her own dresses, quilts, and feather beds. Home was where Mom was and family life revolved around her. She always saw to it that we were neat and shined up when we went to school or church. Family clothes were handed down then, when one outgrew his clothes they were handed down to the next in line. I was the last and usually they were worn out by the time my turn came so I got new clothes. I do remember wearing altered pants and a coat handed down through the family ranks. I didn't like it at first but soon became used to it. Almost everyone in our class was in the same boat--large families, you see. I don't remember ever wearing my brother's shoes since, by the time I caught up in growth, they were worn out. Dad had a shoemaker's last and bought large squares of leather with which he resoled our shoes. Most fathers did this and some became quite good at it.

One time Mom took me to Greenfeld's Clothing Store, Clark and Pearl Street, to buy a suit. The store sold men's and boy's clothing and all the other fixings which a well-dressed man should wear. At the front of the store, on the inside, were glass display cases which had celluloid collars, ties, cuff links, and other items. Greenfeld's, Spany and Reich, corner of Walton and Pearl, and Epstein's at Vega and Pearl were known to everyone in the area and that's where men's and boys' clothes were bought. The owners of these stores were good, solid citizens of Jewish extraction. Many a poor child was clothed by them when the parents were too poor to pay. I particularly remember Mr. Epstein who always spoke German to Mom and called her by name. He had a nose that met you at the door but he was a "Mensch" (a Yiddish term for a man of honor). His son worked there also and wasn't cheated in the nose department either. Epstein's is the place I received a free watch. I'll come to that after I get through with Greenfeld's.

Clothing stores had gimmicks too. At the time Mom took me to Greenfeld's I was about in the 1st grade. The salesman gave Mom a suit for me to try on and walked away. When I put my hand in the coat pocket I felt a small soft package. I pulled it out and it was a coin purse stuffed with something which, I was sure, was paper money. I became very interested and showed it to Mom. She opened it and found it to be stuffed with paper. Mom knew about store shenanigans too! She'd been around! She put the purse back in the pocket, said nothing, and didn't buy the suit. I remember the salesman hanging around in the background. Was the purse put into the pocket on purpose to lure the customer into a sale? My thoughts lean in that direction.

Came my Solemn Communion when I was about 12 years old. I had had my First Communion several years before. For Solemn Communion we were expected to wear blue serge suits with bloomers, white shirt and tie, and patent leather shoes. The girls had to be dressed all in white--everything. No question whether one could afford it or not--it was done! We headed for Epstein's who, with each suit, gave a solid nickel-plated pocket watch. Boy, how proud I was. I carried it a long time. It was made of good material and kept good time but if it conked out that was it. There was no repairing, it was thrown away.

Around the turn of the century, Dad learned the barber trade and opened a barber shop. I don't know where it was but I still have two hobnail glass bottles, one blue and one light amber in color, used by him for water, toilet water, hair tonic, or such like. The bottles should be antiques now. Haircut and shave was 15¢ or 25¢. Dad's shaving mug with his name "Martin" lettered in gold on it I have given to my dear son Dr. Martin Stein as a keepsake. Barber shops then, and I still remember seeing them in shops when I was growing up, had a rack on the wall with cubby holes. Each customer had his own shaving mug in a cubby hole with his personal saving brush and soap in it. Each mug usually had the owner's name on it--or a recognizable picture of some kind. No mixing of germs, you see. There was such a thing as barber's itch which was conveyed by unclean instruments, brush, razor or towel. My friend Larry Mellert had it and his face broke out in a rash. He let his beard grow until the treatment cured it. As for myself, I never had it, perhaps because I used my own straight razor.

To get back to Pa--we called him Pa and mother Ma--he always tried to make a few extra dollars to help out the family budget but I don't think he was cut out for the business world since he always worked hard for a living and never seemed to overflow with cash. Some people measure success by position held, amount of money or property accumulated. I think differently. I believe a person is a success if he had lived honestly, paid his debts, and raised his children to be honest and law abiding citizens. That, to me, is success and something to be proud of in the evening of life. According to my thinking, Ma and Pa were a great success since none of us ever landed in the slammer and kept a jump ahead of the sheriff. Bill collectors we knew not.

Everything was paid in cash then--by us anyway. Credit cards were unknown and if we didn't have cash it wasn't bought. Some corner grocery stores and butcher shops had book accounts. Everything a family bought was put "on the book" and when payday rolled around they were expected to settle up. Now we have credit cards and they are quite convenient. In fact, I have one or two myself. The trouble with the book accounts was that some people ran up a large bill and never paid. I well remember one time in my teens we dealt with a corner grocer. I went in to buy some item and had to wait a long time while the owner took down a phoned book order. I joked about the long wait I had and he said "Yeah, but look at the big order I got."" That grocer went out of business and I heard it was because of the many unpaid book accounts he had. People had checking accounts but I don't recall them ever having been used to pay a grocery bill at the counter. Checking accounts were $1 a year for handling and checkbooks were free.

36

Chapter 3

As said previously Dad learned his trade in Germany and must have been good at it. There were some friends who remembered him when they had certain ailments and came to him for medicine. Coughs, chest colds, pneumonia, blocked bowels were some of the things he was called on to treat. He was also called on for Schrepfen in the Spring. He was good at extracting teeth too. I watched him. Mom held the victim's head while he pulled the tooth--no novocain. The cuspidor was put in use (they were called spittoons) into which the patient spit his blood. We had one of blue granite baked on iron. I'm sure Dad boiled his instruments, or at least washed them, somewhere along the line, either before or after. At least none of his patients died that I heard of. No molly coddling, they were made of sterner stuff. A survival of the fittest, one could say. The price was 25¢ a tooth. You pay your money and you takes your chance. I will say that Dad knew his limits and was careful not to step beyond them. Later on, laws were passed and the Health Department tightened their rules and rightly so.

People then cured many of their own ailments with home remedies. I heard that some people put an axe under the patient's bed to cut the pain. Also, warts came from toad pee and hair from a horse's tail put in vinegar for two weeks will turn into a snake. I tried it, it didn't work. I never handled a warty toad so I can't vouch for the effectiveness of that treatment. Horse tail tea was another remedy for cold in the bladder--or thereabouts. Mom called it zinkraut tea. I used to pick it in the cinders along railroad tracks where it flourished. A remedy which Mom used to effect, and which Leona and I can vouch for, is elderberry blossom tea to break a cold or grippe. I've used it myself. In the spring of the year I'd go to the valley below our home and pick the blossoms by the half-bushel basket. We'd dry them in the attic and then put them in containers for future use. If the need arose, we'd steep them in hot boiled water, meanwhile take a hot bath. After the bath we'd drink the tea and jump in bed. Cover up good and be prepared for a change or two of night clothes during the night, perspiration to no end. In the morning we'd feel a definite change for the better, albeit a little weak. You future Stein medicos, don't smile, try it! Quinine, I presume, will do the same. Yes? No?

Hospitals were usually looked on as the last resort and relatives weren't surprised if you died there. You see, hospitals hadn't reached the fancy equipment stage--no $200 a day, or more hospital beds either. Home remedies were looked on with a jaundice eye by the medical profession but there were no laws prohibiting them. Doctor calls to your home were three bucks a throw. I know, Dr. Schultz, who spoke German, made sick calls to our home on Scranton Road. One time Dad dislocated his right arm at the shoulder while lifting a piece of furniture from the wagon. Dr. Schultz put it in place at home. I saw him do it.

One Saturday, after lunch, Mom told me to take a bath and stay around the yard. This was unusual since bath time was after supper. Dad came home about 3:00 o'clock, which was unusual too. I suspected something was up when Dad told me, quietly, that Dr. Schultz was coming over to examine my throat. When he came, Mom took me up to her bedroom and had me lie on her bed while Dad and the Doctor conversed downstairs. I still didn't know what the hell was going on. After some small conversation with me, Doc Schultz placed a white cloth, shaped like a cup, over my face. He started to pour a sickly sweet liquid on it and that's when the fox walked into the flock of geese. I let out a yell, cried, and squirmed while dad held me down. In the distance I heard Dad ask Doc if I was alright and he answered--in German--"they all do it."

38

That's the last I remembered. Faintly I heard Mom call my name, I wanted to sleep but she wouldn't let me, she kept calling. Finally I awoke but Mom stayed around to see that I didn't slip off to sleep again. I was a sick boy for a few days. My adenoids had been removed. I had been chloroformed.

To keep on the subject of Dad and his doin's, in the spring of the year many people wanted to be bled. I don't know what the heck for but I imagine it was because of high blood pressure and the loss of blood made them feel better for a time or, perhaps, the idea was a holdover from the dark ages. Anyway, many barbers "bled" people. I read somewhere that's

Barber Pole--Courtesy of John and Anna Kinnenun

how the red and white barber pole originated--white stripe for bandages and red stripe for blood. What a gory subject! Do I offend you?

Many years ago I had my hair cut by an old-time German barber. We'd converse in German and he'd compliment me on my high German. Once our conversation turned to the subject of barbers bleeding people and he said he had engaged in the practice at one time and told me why he quit. He and another barber attended a barber's picnic at a beer garden and both became pretty well oiled on the lager beer. One of the men wanted to be bled, so feeling no pain the three of them went to the friend's barber shop. The operation was performed by his friend who used a more direct approach. He cut a vein, or artery in the man's arm and bled him. The difficulty was that they couldn't stop the bleeding and the patient became white. They ran around the shop in their anxiety trying to find something to stop the bleeding and were afraid he might die in the chair but finally it stopped. This sobered them and after a rest they took the man home. He lived. My barber ceased the practice.

Dad brought his expertise with him from Germany and, apparently, knew his business because many times his friends would call him to their homes to be bled or for other treatment. I was seven or eight when he'd take me along on one of his Sunday calls. I remember one time going with him to a couple's home. The husband must have had a high temperature which he couldn't break with conventional medicine of the time. I don't know what ailment he had but I later heard Dad's treatment was effective. I was with Pa in the man's bedroom and his wife was also there. Dad had the wife bring a long flannel nightgown--pajamas were not in vogue then--and soaked it in hot water. I don't know what ingredients Dad put in the water, possibly hay seed, and had the man put it on and covered him up in bed. The hot nightgowns were alternated with cold ones--on and off. The man grumbled and shivered every time the cold wet gown was put on. After leaving instructions with the wife to keep alternating we left.

Dad used an effective remedy on me one time when I was a child. I couldn't shake a chest cold so he heated up a flaxseed poultice which he made and put it on my chest. It worked. Some of the home remedies are not to be sneezed at. Now, of course, medical science has a better method--x-rays, pills, blood tests, operations and the rest. There's more money in it. Pop was no quack in the sense that he would be looked on today. He had acquired his knowledge by study and under the teaching and direction of doctors in Germany. I recall leafing through the German medical and herb books he brought to this country. He could whip up a good cough medicine from various herbs and his liniment was something to make a horse run away. Still, it was sought after by a certain clientele.

One time Dad took me along on one of his schrepfen deals. The English word is "Cupping." The tools used for this schrepfen consisted of a bottle of alcohol, a short candle, a wire with wick attached to the end, and anywhere from six to a dozen small bulbous-shaped glasses about the size of a whiskey glass. Then, the main item, the brass block with the cutters which were operated by pressing a trigger. I have since given this instrument to my good son Martin and suggest my descendants see him for a demonstration. I do not recall the exact mechanics of this operation but it was on a summer Sunday morning and the scene of the operation was on the back porch of a man's house. He was sitting on a stool, stripped to the waist, bent forward and next to him was a bucket of water. Dad placed the cutting instrument against his back, pressed the trigger and put the glass against the cut. From the distance between the blades there may have been more than one cut under the glass. I have a faint recollection that the glasses had been pre-heated or boiled in hot water. There was some maneuvering with a lighted candle or lighted wick around the glass. It must have been to heat the glass to create a suction. When Dad was finished he had four or six glasses attached to the man's back--looked funny. As the glasses filled Dad would take them off and pour the contents into the bucket of water. What a subject! But that's the way it was. I don't know if there were any cures but I never heard Dad to lose a patient. A survival of the fittest again?

While we're on the subject of medicines and treatments it brings to mind the drug store at the corner of W. 25th and Althen. It was owned by a Mr. Krebs who had learned his pharmaceutical trade in Germany. He was a short, thin man and wore a black skull cap in his store. To me he seemed ancient. I was first in his pharmacy when Mom took me there to make a purchase. It had a distinct, pleasant, medicinal odor. Mr. Krebs knew his herbs and medicines, alright. When we lived on Scranton I'd see him, about twice a week, go down to the valley. The place was called the valley because it was on a lower level and where the river flowed. It was about a quarter mile from home and I spent many happy hours there. We speak of it later.

Mr. Kreps took along a paper bag and I'd watch him browse around, picking plant blossoms, plant leaves, and digging in the ground. When returned the bag was full. These were herbs with which he concocted medicines and ointments. Of course he handled prescription drugs too.

Drugstores were not the department stores they are now where anything from a fishing rod to an electric appliance can be bought. Every drugstore window had one or two large glass globes of colored water in it. At night, with a light behind them, they could be seen for quite a distance. They served the same purpose for drugstores as barber poles do for barber shops. The stores usually had a few comfortable chairs arranged on the side for people to rest while waiting for the prescription to be filled. Sloan's liniment was a standard item as was tar soap and catarrh medicine. Lydia Pinkham's Vegetable Compound, too. (A baby in every bottle as the joke was).

42

Brother Ben worked for Mr. Krebs after school and all day Saturday. His job was to sweep up the place, dust the furniture, wash windows and run errands. A dollar a week, silver, and glad to get it. Ben had a brilliant idea of what he should do with one of his dollars. He wanted to buy a goat.

The ultimate for a kid was to own one or two goats, harness them to a small wagon and drive them down the street to the edification of small onlookers--if you could wangle the idea across to your parents. At the corner of our street was Bislich's grocery store and Mr. Bislich bought a goat for his son which they housed in a shed behind the store. The son had the goat harnessed to a small wagon and drove him down our street to the envy of all of us kids. The only thing I didn't like about his driving habits was that he had a long stick with which he would "goose" the goat to make him run faster. I didn't think "goosing" a goat was nice but I can see that Bislich's son had an inventive mind.

Ben pestered Mom to buy a goat. I don't know what Dad thought of the idea but I know he liked pets and, perhaps, he secretly approved. Finally Mom consented with the provision that he pay no more than a dollar. There were no flies on Tom. Came a Saturday morning and Ben went to the stockyard with a silver dollar to buy a goat. We impatiently awaited his return. He returned alright--no goat. Goats were more than a buck a piece. In retrospect, who would have had the trouble with the goat? A shelter would have had to be built and kept clean, a harness purchased or made and no small item would be the food. Besides, goats had a positive personal aroma.

It's amazing what impressions and memories a child stores away. I still recall the kids yelling to each other, "To hell with Spain, remember the Maine." I didn't know where Spain was and certainly knew nothing about hell, so it must have been the sound of Spain or

43

hell rolling out of the voice box which intrigued me. A snatch of song we sang, which may have dated from the Civil War, was-- "Rally round the flag boys, We'll rally once again, Shouting the battle cry of freedom." Then there was another one "Pull for the shore boys, pull for the shore." I believe it had something to do with the Spanish American War.

This brings to mind the Memorial Day parades I watched with the surviving Civil War Veterans from around Cleveland taking part. They were at least 65 to 70, some with moustaches and some with long beards. I particularly recall one with a beard down to his waist walking with a cane. The Spanish-American War veterans were more numerous, younger, and more spry. Some of the Civil War veterans wore old uniforms worn during the war and the Spanish-American war boys wore their old Army uniforms. I'd watch the Memorial Day parades with Mom when she'd take me downtown. A few veterans were still around when I was in my teens.

It interested me to go into the Soldier's and Sailors Monument on Public Square where they had a Civil War attendant for sightseers. I'd ask him questions and he'd talk. Occasionally he had another war veteran visit him and they'd talk about some action. One time I heard them mention Bull Run.

Dad was a kind-hearted man and usually brought something home for Lucy, Ben and me like sweets or peanuts in the shell. One time he brought home a cigar box with shelled peanuts. They had been in a large box which had fallen off a wagon into the street. The box had broken and Dad had gathered up some of the peanuts for us. I was healthy and hungry then and didn't mind the horse manure I found with them.

At W. 25th and Clark next to No. 5 Fire House, was a moving picture show named Wonderland. This Wonderland show was something out of this world to me. Dad loved shows and once in a while would take me or Lucy along. I recall the fast moving flicker films for which the admission price was 5¢ on weekdays and 10¢ on Sunday. Part of the show were slides with ads from surrounding merchants. Also in vogue at the time were colored slides usually depicting a sad scene or story. With the slides they usually had a young lady singing a sad song in connection with them, accompanied by a pianist below. Sad, nostalgic songs were the thing then. I still remember part of one melancholy song which went something like this:

> "Please Mister take me in your car
> I want to see Mama
> They say she lives in heaven
> and tis very, very far.
> My new Mama is very cross
> and scolds me every day."

> The refrain was something like so:
> "Always in the way
> I can never play"

By the time the song was finished there were wet eyes in the audience. Gad! Tender hearts.

When I went to school I loved to go there on Sunday afternoon after Devotion. The show was just a block from the church. I loved the 101 Bison westerns the best. They were about Indians, cowboys and the U.S. Cavalry. The cavalry always came to the rescue and defeated the Indians. The pictures were accompanied by a pianist hammering out fast music, especially when the cavalry was coming to the rescue. The show was filled with noisy kids who whistled, stomped, and cheered the cavalry on.

Across from the show was Bromerneier & Preisels Popcorn Stand and Ice Cream Parlor. For 5¢ I'd get six large popcorn balls in a bag and munch on them during the show. They also had roasted peanuts in the shell, home made taffy, and other goodies. In summer, the show was very hot. It had no windows, no ventilation or refrigeration, just two electric fans on shelves opposite each other to keep the air moving. It was a small show by today's standards and had one aisle down the center dividing the audience. It was the only show there was until the Amphion and the Marvel opened a few blocks down the street. With all the kids eating popcorn and peanuts, or munching on candy, the air became quite stagnant. To overcome the stagnation the manager walked up and down the aisle spraying cheap perfume with an atomizer. It didn't help much.

About Mom, she was a slender person slightly taller than Dad. She had brown eyes and fair complexion and wore rimless eye glasses. She always dressed neat and had an erect carriage. I am told I resemble her. When I was a boy, Mom and Dad would take Lucy and me on a Sunday afternoon to visit Mr. and Mrs. Stephen on their farm. Years later Mrs. Stephen died and I visited the mortuary where she was. It was in my territory and as I walked in the door to pay my respects there were two ladies standing at the casket. As they saw me one of them said "Eddie Stein." She was the oldest daughter of Mrs. Stephen and remembered our visits when I was a child. I asked her how she recognized me in my uniform. She said I looked just like my mother. It's an odd coincidence but Mother must have been about

46

the same age at the time we visited the Stephen's as I was when I visited the mortuary. I like to think my two sons have inherited Mom's erect carriage.

Mom was kindhearted and many times I saw her feed beggars and tramps at our kitchen door or hand them a bag with sandwiches. Her policy was never to turn anyone away asking for food or drink. Word gets around these travelers and at times customers were frequent. It was generally thought that a secret sign was marked on the sidewalk in front of the house where food could be had. Perhaps there was, else why would we get all the trade?

With Dad working six days a week, leaving early and coming home about six in the evening, Mom necessarily had to be the disciplinarian. She was wise, she didn't wait for Dad to do the job but, after a few warnings, took care of it herself. As the very last resort Mom used a strap. I don't remember Lucy ever being disciplined except for a scolding, perhaps because she didn't need it. Being a lively youngster, I guess I was the worst offender and having a feisty temper didn't help. My theory is that a little temper and stubborness is okay as long as it's controlled. It keeps one from being pushed around during life.

The strap was a symbol of authority and hung from a nail in the kitchen. Mother used psychology there. It was a piece of thick harness leather about 1-1/4 inches wide and about 15 inches long cut into about 6 thin strips approximately 8 inches long, leaving a handle of about 7 inches. Just seeing it there was a reminder. It was rarely used but when Mom lowered the boom it was effective. She didn't hit very hard but a swipe or two stung, you can be sure. I know. I can see now, but didn't understand then, Mom was in her forties and did not feel well during that time so our shenanigans must have gotten on her nerves many times. One weekday Mom took me to church and

47

we left before mass was over. We sat on the front steps of the church for a while and Mom told me she wasn't feeling well. After a rest we started across the street towards a shoemaker shop and on the way she said that if anything should happen I was to go to the shoemaker. I was apprehensive but didn't know what it was all about, you see I must have been all of five at the time. When we entered the shop Mom spoke a few words to the shoemaker and he brought a chair. Mom sat down and fainted. The shoemaker, whom Mom and Dad knew from being his customers, brought a glass of water but Mom was still in a faint. In a few minutes she opened her eyes, took a few swallows, and after resting until she felt better we walked home. Mom laid on the couch and told me to go to Mrs. Koch across the street, tell her she was sick and ask her to come over. When I returned with Mrs. Koch they had some conversation and Mom told me to go to Mrs. Koch's home for the day until Dad came home in the evening.

During the day Mrs. Koch checked on Mom several times and brought her soup. Dad could not be notified because we had no phone and I doubt if Koch's had one either, although being in the teamster business they may have. Very few families had phones so all notifications had to be made by someone in person. I didn't find out what Mom had, but thinking back it was probably the 24 hour flu.

Chapter 4

St. Michael's, being a German parish, all sermons, prayers and songs were in German. Men and women were separated--the men on the right side of the aisle and the women on the left. Talk about women's lib. This silly arrangement was corrected later on but I remember it being there for some years. In the vestibule of the church, on Sunday was a kirchenforsteher (church councilman) who sat behind a table and collected money. Everyone entering was expected to lay down 5¢, the going rate, before going into the church proper. It was not insisted on but was expected. Some kirchenforsteher were more expectant than others and would let you know. This nickel, or whatever, was sort of an offering and went into the church fund to pay expenses. Of course, the regular collection wasn't forgotten either. Rumor had it that one time one of the kirchenforsteher who took up collections was suspected of dipping into the till. He was watched by other kirchenforsteher secretly in the vestibule and caught red-handed lifting the coin from the collection basket. They beat him up right there and that took care of his sticky fingers. Swift justice there by these kirchenforsteher--and no appeal to the U.S. Supreme Court either.

The first St. Michael's school I remember was a two-story square frame building, painted yellow, on the corner of Scranton and Clark. A library stands on the location now. Herby Wentz lived across from our home and attended the first grade. He was about a year older than I was and since I would be six in January, 1907, I suppose Mom thought she would give me an early start and arranged to have Herby Wentz take me to school September of 1906. It didn't work out, I was too young and missed my Mom too much. I believe the good sister noticed this and must have talked to Mom or, perhaps,

I pawed up too much dust when she readied me for school in the morning because three or four days later she kept me home. How happy I was! When September 1907 rolled around I was more mature and going to school was no problem. Public schools had kindergartens to ease the way into the first grade but St. Michael's did not.

I have fond memories of the first grade sister. She was an understanding person and helped us put on our rubbers in rainy weather and bundled us up in cold weather. We had to learn our A,B,C's in the German and English languages. The blackboard had the alphabet in both, 26 letters for each. This sister had an interesting way of teaching us the German alphabet. She'd tell us a story with the climax being the letter we were being taught. I distinctly remember the small German letter "n." A little fib was in order to impress it on us. She said she had a bird in the cloakroom and closed all the windows so it couldn't fly away. Then she went into the cloakroom while our eyes remained glued to the door. When she came out her hands were under her black apron and at her desk she pulled out the bird--it was a card with the German letter "n." It was a bit of a letdown but we didn't mind. To this day I remember the letter "n."

The big deal of the year was the school play for the parents. Each grade had their own little play or act. I don't know the right of it but most grades were represented in one way or another. Girls had their own acts and the boys had theirs. Never the twain mingled. Anyway, the plays were practiced on the school auditorium stage long in advance of the play night. The sisters had to drum parts and verses into the heads of the unwilling children. This was all after regular school hours and on the children's own time. Regular school must go on--yeah! I can now see why we weren't exactly sold on the idea since it cut in on our valuable time. Most of the plays centered around the American flag with singing of patriotic songs, such as "Hail Columbia the Jam of the Ocean" or "My Country This of Thee, Sweet land of SLIBBERDEE."--each one holding a small American flag and waving it in time to the piano being played in the orchestra pit. Great stuff! It must have been a pain in the neck to the good sisters of Notre Dame. The boys were full of shabernack too.

I well remember the first grade play I was in. There were 50 in our class and the theme was about George Washington chopping down the cherry tree and "I did it with my little hatchet. I cannot tell a lie." About that time Dad brought home to me a hatchet carved out of wood by a friend at work. Dad knew I had to have a hatchet for the play and this was his way of helping out little Eddie. I wish he were here so I could thank him properly. It was a good imitation, the hatchet part was painted aluminum color and the handle yellow. I took it to the practice session one day and it was a mistake. Sister jumped on it like a chicken jumping on a hot June bug. She recognized a big opportunity. She told me to ask Dad if he could have 50 hatchets made like it. Dad told me right away that the hatchet took a lot of work and to make 50 was an impossibility. Good old Pop went to the sister's house and talked with her with the result that he agreed to make the 50 hatchets himself--but not out of wood. For several weeks Dad worked in our shed making hatchets. It was after coming home from work, so it was quite a sacrifice. He collected quite a number of yard sticks; then, out of cardboard, he cut the hatchet part and nailed it to the end of a cut-down yard stick. The yard stick was painted yellow and the hatchet aluminum. It wasn't a bad job and filled the need nicely. I was permitted to keep my wooden hatchet for the play and was the envy of all the kids. I was a big shot for a time, particularly since Pop had donated the hatchets.

The script was that we were to be all dressed in white blouses, blue pants, and black shoes. Each one received a hatchet and held it over the right shoulder--shoulder--arms position. There were about 10 of us in the front row and each one had a piece to say about George Washington cutting down the cherry tree and not being able to tell a lie and the "Marl" of the whole damn thing. Good old George must have turned over in his grave. I was the "Marl" quoter and was situated about the third from the end in the front row. After the ones ahead of me had spoken their little pieces, accompanied by a swipe of the hatchet at an imaginary cherry tree, Eddie Stein spoke his piece, like so, "And we boys know the Marl, we'll live it out if we can." I didn't know what a "Marl" was and what we should live out, but there it was. Years later when I was ruminating about this "Marl" work and its meaning it dawned on me the word was "moral." This made a little sense but not much.

The girls had their plays too on the same night, a waving of small flags and the "Hail Columbia" bit. Lucy was in one, front row I think, and the body action of the actors represented picking flowers from a hillside--or on a hillside--accompanied by the song "Bring flowers from the hillside. Bring flowers from the de-e-e-ell." I can still sing it and I think Lucy can too. We've laughed about it many times since. Price for attending these Sunday night plays was announced from the pulpit as "Finf and zwanzig zent und reservierte zits. Zen cents extra." (Admission 25¢ and reserved seats 10¢ extra). The good padre of the parish and the assistant padre were expected to watch these plays from the front row--and they did. I wonder what thoughts crossed their minds. Maybe figured it was good penance.

One of the more exciting acts I remember was put on by the eighth grade boys. Eighth graders were big guys to us, you know something like supermen. They looked down their collective noses at us small fries, if they noticed us at all. Their act followed a patriotic theme again. The Civil War! One half of the boys

52

represented the Southern Army and the other half the Northern Army. Each side was equipped with BB guns. How they all finagled them I don't know. The Northern half held the American flag and the Southern half the Stars and Bars. The Battle of Bull Run was on. The BB guns must have been well, and intentionally, loaded with oil for when the battle began the North and the South started to shoot. No BB's of course, just oil.

With all the shooting the stage became a cloud and miasma of oil. Every time the gun was fired it spit oil and soon the auditorium was filled with the odor. First the South chased the North across the stage, then the North rallied and chased the South across to the other side and a good time was had by all. This must have been the second Battle of Bull Run since the North was victorious--it was expected. The next scene showed the wounded returning home. This was right up their alley. Some had their heads in bandages daubed with red paint, some with crutches, some with an arm in a sling and most limped. It was a dramatic way to learn the lesson of the Battle of Bull Run. I'll bet the sisters were glad when all the plays were over so they could relax for another year.

In all my years at St. Michael's School I recall only about four nuns who didn't have a German accent. We were taught reading and writing in both languages and with my background it was not difficult for me. For a few children whose parents were born in America and only spoke English at home it was rough going. These were no-nonsense Notre Dame nuns and ruled with the rod. They had to in order to keep a class of 50 lively boys in line.

For the first grade and, perhaps, the second also, we wrote on slates with slate pencils. The slates were of two sizes, one about 10 by 12 inches and the other about 12 by 15 inches. I had the small size with the plain wood frame. The larger ones had a red felt cover

over the frame. Slate pencils were six for 5¢ and came in a small red and white striped cardboard box. To this sweet day I don't know how the sisters stood all the screeching of pencils on slate. To wash off the things we had written each child had to be equipped with a small sponge which could be wet in a bucket of water sitting in back of the room. I remember some kids thought this was unnecessary and used a quicker way--they spit on the slate and wiped it off with their sleeve. I tried it once and that was enough, it was too sloppy for me. Mom's cleanliness apparently had rubbed off on me.

Bible history and cathecism, prayers too, were taught in the German language for the first three or four years. It was memorized word for word and we took turns standing and reciting our lessons--in German yet! What a hodge-podge my chum Clarence Fastnacht made of German. His parents were American born. When he recited the Hail, Mary full of Grace and reached the part "und in der stunde unseres todes. Ahmen" (and in the hour of our death. Amen). It became tangled in the area of his larynx and came out "Stinsey Stodes. Ah-men." It seemed he was determined to strangle each word before it struggled out to freedom. In the fifth and sixth grade we had prayers and catechism in German and English and from the seventh grade on it was only in English. We had "learnt" German.

During the various grades; columns of multiplication tables and "spelling words" had to be memorized every day and to this day I think a thorough groundwork in this branch of learning is best. I was a little weak on the rules of grammar but I skinned by. Now they pronounce Arkansas ARKANSAW, then the accent was on the "kan." Words and pronunciations change with usage. One of our German sisters taught us how to pronounce the word schedule--her pronunciation was shedooley, strike out the "c" and accent on the "doc." I never had the occasion to use the word much until I began

54

work when I heard the correct pronunciation and adopted it in a hurry.

We had penmanship lessons every day also--the Palmer Method. I believe it is still used today. The method may be different now but then it was taught through muscular movement. With this movement you grasped the pen, poised it over the paper and for the ovals you rotated your arm on the muscle of your forearm. With the slant marks you upped and downed on the same muscle. This was supposed to teach one muscular control and writing was supposed to be with the muscle only while the pen was held steady. It never worked for me and I did better when I used my own style.

We had segregation then but didn't know it. The boys were in classrooms on one side of the school building and the girls on the other. It wasn't until the ninth grade that they permitted us to be in the same room together. I guess they figured it was time the boys found out about girls and visa versa.

Till about the seventh or eighth grade, we had a unique monthly report card to take home to our parents. It was in two columns, one indicating our general absorption ability and the other behavior. Of course it was in German and the highest accolade was Sehr Gut--Very Good. I give you an example from the highest to the lowest rating:

Sehr Gut (Goot)	-Very Good
Gut (Goot)	-Good
Ziemlich Gut	-Pretty Good
Geniegent	-Satisfactory
Ungeniegent	-Unsatisfactory
Schlecht	-Bad
Sehr Schlecht	-Very Bad

If one received Ungeniegent you could expect Ma or Pa to visit the teacher. If you received either of the last two you might as well leave home, for when Ma or Pa came home from the teacher you'd wish you had. As for me, I was about average, hovering around good and sometimes Ziemlich Gut. Occasionally I'd wander into the upper category of Sehr Gut in one column and one time I received Sehr Gut in both columns. I don't know why, I must have been sick that month.

The priest of the parish came once a month to each class room to distribute the report cards. We didn't know what rating we had until he called your name and announced the score. He was not at all hesitant in dishing out a whipping in front of the class to anyone with an ungeniegent, schlecht or sehr schlecht. Nowadays he'd have a lawsuit on his hands. I could relate a story or two about this chastisement which, to this day, leaves a bitter taste.

The good sisters each had their own little article for punishment. One we had, had a length of rubber hose about 2 ft. long and when you were struck with it there sounded a "zonk." Many years later I met a classmate of mine and we discussed St. Michael's. He asked me, "Red, do you remember the pounding with the rubber hoses?" I never received a pounding and I don't think he did either. He was a nice fellow and later became one of our city officials. One of the class secrets we had and passed along to each other was that if you held your breather when sister slapped your open hand with the hose and stood on one leg at the same time, it wouldn't hurt. I heard that was for the birds. All in all I think our class was no better or worse than the average at the time. I only recall one of my class ever serving time in the penitentiary--Joe Braun. It happens! All the rest whom I ever heard about turned out to be good solid citizens. Give some credit to the rubber hose.

Chapter 5

I liked Joe Braun and came up with him through the eight grades. He was a quiet and unassuming boy and knew his lessons and caused no trouble. Whatever caused him to go off the track I don't know. Perhaps the wrong company, who knows? The last time I saw Joe I was in my early twenties in a restaurant. Like many restaurants it was owned by a Greek. It had two entrances and a u-shaped counter. I was eating a sandwich when Joe entered the door on the opposite side of where I sat. He didn't see me and if he had I wonder if it would have made any difference. He must have been a bit oiled with bootleg booze although he appeared sober. He walked along the counter opposite me and announced "I'm Joe Braun. I just got out of the penitentiary." He repeated this to the customers sitting at the counter. I don't know what reaction he expected but by this time the Greek was alerted, he walked around the counter, took Joe by his collar and his arm and pushed him out of the front door. That's the last I saw of Joe Braun.

Children can be cruel. Not intentionally but because they don't understand. We had a boy in class whose nickname was Stinky and I always felt sorry for him. His mother was widowed and apparently had a hard row to hoe. His clothes were hand-me-downs and he had a downtrodden manner. I can now see it perhaps was because he was ridiculed by other classmates. I don't know why he was called Stinky except that he looked stinky. I never called him Stinky, I used his name Paul. We were about to celebrate our Solemn Communion and all had to wear blue serge suits, white shirts and white ties. One day, the week before Solemn Communion, Stinky did not appear in class. Sister told us, in a very nice way without mentioning a name, that one of the class would not be dressed in a blue serge suit or in a white shirt and wanted us to understand that nothing was to be said. We all knew it was Stinky so, to the credit of the whole class, when Stinky appeared in an old, but clean, suit and a blue work shirt, the class never peeped and never did anyone say anything to him to my knowledge. I can see now that Stinky must have been kept home from school on purpose by his mother that day so sister could instruct us. It still gives me a good feeling when I think the whole class did have a kind spot. For all his hang-dog manner he was smart. He was a good student and knew his lessons better than most. I would say he ranked at the top of the class and if the term were used at the eighth grade level, would have graduated cum-laude. I don't know where he went from the eighth grade but the last time I saw him he was a councilman in his church, had a nice family, and was a respected businessman in the electrical line. So much for nicknames.

We had a magic lantern with colored pictures. The slides were about 1-1/2 inches wide and about 5 inches long. A room was darkened and a bed sheet hung on the wall. In order to light the lantern, a candle or coal-oil wick, situated in back of the slide, was lit. The front had a magnifying glass and behind it, between the glass and light, was a channel through which the slides were pushed, thus magnifying the pictures projected on the bed sheet. We all enjoyed it and I was very much impressed since we didn't use it very often. We had boxes of slides and the set would be an antique now for sure. It could be considered the forerunner of home movies.

We had many other ways to spend our time too, like picnics. One Sunday the St. Michael's Church Choir had a picnic at Hobo Park. Dad loved to sing and must have belonged to it. I was about six or seven and have the picture of the picnic group somewhere in the family archives. Dad, Mom, Lucy, and I went. We used the streetcar for transportation since we didn't own a horse and buggy and certainly not an automobile, such as they were. Hobo Park was on the lower end of about 54th, south of Denison. Years later I went to the picnic location and there were small factories on the site. The reason I remember this picnic so well on that Sunday afternoon is because of all the free pop we had. We called it soda pop-- "different flavers." Pop bottles had a round top with a heavy wire ring attached to a rubber plunger in the neck of the bottle. If one wanted to imbibe, the rubber plunger was pushed down, releasing the rubber seal and the fizz water was ready to drink. The health department put an end to that method of bottling some years later, too unsanitary. I don't recall paper cups being in vogue then.

Hobo Park was in a shady grove of trees and perhaps belonged to a farmer. I recall walking through the grass when I kicked a lady's handkerchief with something knotted in one end. I thought nothing of it but when I arrived where the soft drinks were on ice I heard one of the young ladies of the choir say she had lost her handkerchief with all her money and that she wouldn't have car fare to get home. I told her what I had seen and took her to where the handkerchief was. She was very grateful--with a thank you. There was a lot of money tied up in the corner of the handkerchief, you see--30¢. If the Boy Scouts of America had been in existence than I would have "done did" my Boy Scout deed for the day. I think Boy Scout organizations came into existence about 1910, championed by Teddy Roosevelt. It's a wonderful organization but the Catholic Church frowned on it and I don't know why. The same with the Y.M.C.A., perhaps because these organizations were not well known then. However, this changed many years ago.

About two or three times a year a Back Peddler came to our door. He was a Jewish man with a beard and at the time I thought him to be old. In retrospect I suppose he was in the prime. At the age of six or seven who can judge age? Mom would let him into the kitchen with his black oil cloth-covered pack where he'd proceed to open it, making somewhat of a ceremony of laying out a variety of colored items such as straight combs, curved combs for the ladies' hair, small hand mirrors, ribbons, pins, needles, spools of thread, yarn and many other items. These he arranged in a fashion to attract the eye. It was good salesmanship. Lucy and I were fascinated. Mom always bought some small item, more out of the kindness of her heart. After all, she could buy what she needed right in the neighborhood--and cheaper.

The Back Peddlers were small businessmen you might say. Each had a route or territory and, I'm sure, marked their customers in a book. Mom must have been so inscribed. I read somewhere that Jews immigrating to this country were set up in the business by other Jewish businessmen to give them a start in this country. It was a commendable thing to do. Quite a few ended up owning clothing and department stores. One time the peddler gave Lucy some small trinket, perhaps because Mom bought something more than needles and pins that day. She never failed to offer him a cup of coffee, especially when the weather was cold. I believe he liked to come to our house if only to rest his tired feet. One time he sold Mom a large black comb with the word unbreakable printed on it. I recall this because he pronounced it "unbreakawbull", with the accent on the "kaw." The comb lasted us many years. Plastic was unknown then so it must have been made of hard rubber. The teeth never broke off.

One of the things which pleased children in the neighborhood was to hear the Grind Organ Man. He was usually of Italian extraction and carried the grind organ by a strap over his shoulder. Fastened to the back of the organ and extending downward was a heavy pole or stick on which it rested when the organ grinder removed it. It was about chest high and had a handle on the side which he turned causing the most wonderful melody, so we thought, to roll out of the organ. The organ was about 2 by 2-1/2 feet in size and about 10 inches thick. Some organs had fancy pictures and scenes on them. However, this was not the main attraction. On the Organ Man's shoulder perched a small monkey dressed in a red jacket and a small red hat. Mr. Monkey was controlled by a chain fastened to his collar.

The object was to go into neighborhoods with children--and play the organ while the children begged pennies from their mothers to watch the monkey do tricks. At a signal, the monkey would get on the sidewalk and turn a few somersaults and hold out his small red hat for the penny. Sometimes he'd take the penny from your hand. He'd jump back on the Organ Man's shoulder and chatter while the Organ Man took the penny from him. After working about all the change he could from a particular stretch of street he'd walk to another spot and do the same thing. It was a hard way to make a living I think. I never did see a Grind Organ Man with a horse and buggy so all his traveling must have been by streetcar or shanks mare.

Another man seen in the neighborhood was the Scissor Grinder and Knife Sharpener Man. This man carried a stand about 3 foot high on his back. The stand held a grinding wheel. He'd walk down the street ringing a bell. Everyone knew what the bell meant and those who had a job for him called and he'd set up his grind stone in the yard and go to work. I don't know what he charged since it was something Mom didn't have to have done as we had our own sharpening stone.

We had umbrella menders too. They carried an assortment of umbrella ribs in a case with assorted umbrella handles. We never had an umbrella mended so I don't know much about the technique. There were more umbrellas around then and a well-equipped home had an umbrella stand in the hallway at the front door. The stands were of various shapes, some long, upright made of crookery with a 10 inch opening into which you put the wet umbrella to drain and others with a simple metal hoop attached to a cloak stand. There were more umbrellas then because people didn't have autos and walked to the streetcar for transportation and to the stores for shopping and needed protection against the rain.

Banana peddlers were common. Pushing a long two-wheeled cart loaded with bananas was a hard job. He bought them at a

61

commission house on the east side and pushed his cart over the bridge to the west side of town. I think bananas were 25¢ a dozen, however I may be off on this. We never ate many of them at home so we never bought from a peddler.

In the fall, farmers with their home-grown produce, especially potatoes, made their appearance. We always bought a sack or two of potatoes for our bin in the basement and a bushel of apples for our apple bin. Toward the spring, it was necessary to knock off the sprouts from the potatoes. Mom canned all sorts of fruit in the fall, especially peaches and pears. A small stick of cinnamon in each jar of pears gave it flavor. Good desserts. We never bought fruit in cans.

About 1908 Mom and Dad built a home. It was built with plans of my Uncle Bernard Rogasch, in Rochester, albeit the rooms were larger. You see, Pa and Ma had five kids as opposed to Uncle Bernard's two. Dad took Lucy and me one summer evening to see how the house was coming along. The basement had just been dug and the kids in the neighborhood were having a high old time jumping into the hole and climbing out. We moved on a cold day just before Thanksgiving and with all the moving, the doors were open and the house cold but this was soon corrected. We now enjoyed a basement, first, and second floor and a large attic.

It was a big improvement over the house on Arthurdale with its outhouse, and the house on Buhrer with its water closet and one inside water faucet. It can be seen Dad and Mom were industrious and frugal to be able to build a house of this size in the length of time they had been in this country. They were good solid citizens and made a good addition to this country. We now had central heating, electric and gas lights combined in the same fixture (in case the electric lights didn't work), a bathroom with all the newest fixtures, hot and cold running water throughout and a large basement with fruit cellar. A clothes chute too, from the second floor to the basement.

The woodwork was walnut and in the dining room, approximately six feet from the floor we had a shelf on which to put fancy colorful dishes for display. Between the dining room and living room and between the living room and front hallway we had walnut sliding doors which separated the dining room and kitchen. The pantry door to the dining room was walnut and a two-way swinging affair. The pantry door to the kitchen was standard. In the pantry was a counter on which to roll bread or pie dough. Beneath the counter was a large flour bin and drawers to hold towels and kitchen utensils. Ranging the wall on the kitchen side of the pantry were cupboards with glass doors and cupboards underneath. At the end of the pantry was the first floor opening to the clothes chute. Clothes chutes were something new to us and our friends.

The kitchen was at least 12 by 12 foot, perhaps larger, it contained the cook stove at one end, the kitchen table at which seven had meals, the sink at the porch side, and a couch on the pantry side. The ice box (not refrigerator) was on the landing leading from the first floor cloak room to the basement. In later years I thought the kitchen arrangement was poor since Mom had to step fast between the stove and sink preparing meals, especially when she had a late start. Modern kitchen floor plans now are much more convenient for the homemaker with the stove, sink, and refrigerator usually arranged along one wall with ample and convenient cupboard space.

Then the noon meal was referred to as dinner and the evening meal supper. I don't know about the higher echelon of society but among us butter folks that's the way it was. The heavy meal of the day was at supper with the exception of Sunday when it was at dinner. Now the dinner is lunch and supper is called dinner. Confusing? I was never too excited about Sunday night supper since it usually consisted of cooked wieners, cold cuts, and potato salad. Dessert was a must at all meals except breakfast. Mom always had homemade bread with real butter.

63

Margarine was called factory butter and was the white color of lard. With each pound of factory butter we received a coloring bean. The bean was crushed into the margarine and mixed, resulting in a yellow butter color. Margarine had a peculiar taste then which has been eliminated to a degree. To this day I don't care for the taste of margarine.

To get back on track, the second floor had four bedrooms leading from a large, square center hall. At the south end of the hall was the bathroom and at the north end were the stairs leading down and a door to the attic steps. The east and west sides of the upstairs each had two bedrooms. My bedroom was on the east side overlooking the backyard and the street and had an airing porch.

In the basement we had a large washing machine operated by turning a wheel with a handle. This was my job many times. Later Dad bought a washing machine operated by water power. A short hose was connected to the faucet and the water pressure turned a four-pegged wooden disk, which had the appearance of a small milk stool, on the inside of the machine thus agitating the soap water and clothes in a half circular back-and-forth motion. A second hose ejected the water back into the sink. The faucet and wash water never mixed. Water was cheap then. I seem to recall the rate was $1 per year.

I was told the price for the house and lot was $3,500. About 1920 it sold for about $10,000 when we moved to Bernard Avenue. Quite a few years later I stopped in the neighborhood on a call and was informed it had been turned into a rooming house.

The next ten or twelve years are packed with memories and it is difficult to know what to include. I will skim the top and make no guarantee memories or occurrences will be sequential but I will try. I was observant as all young people are and up to this time have no complaint on the contents of my memory box. Perhaps observing was good preliminary training for police work which, with quick judgement, I found was so necessary.

Chapter 6

*I*spent a happy boyhood and my teens. I have recollection of Halley's comet about 1910. It is supposed to appear every 75 years. We could see it in the sky towards the northwest. It was bright with a long tail, the head pointing towards the west. It was the topic of conversation that summer, I can tell you. I was sitting at the bedroom window looking at it and I thought it would be nice if I could see it from the same room 75 years later. I don't think I'll make it. Since I recall Halley's comet so vividly, I long ago took the time to find out what records have to say about it:

The comet was discovered by Edmund Halley who was born in England in 1656 and died in 1742. He was a captain in the Royal Navy, accepted a professorship at Oxford and appointed Royal Astronomer. On June 29, 1456 Pope Calixtus III issued a Papal Bull against Halley's comet. Since Halley's birth was still about 200 years in the future, the comet must have been unnamed at that time. However, it was the same comet. Mankind then feared it would bring a plague, famine, or other disaster so, therefore, the Papal Decree was issued asking that "Christendom pray that the comet--or symbol of the "anger of God," be fended off or that it be entirely diverted against the Turks, the foe of the Christian name."

In 1910 horses and wagons were still in abundance but the auto was rapidly taking its place. Statistics show that by 1920 there were about 8 million autos in the nation. The makes were varied, all in competition with each other. Some companies went out of business and others were absorbed by larger corporations. Ford and his Model T (Tin Lizzie) was in the forefront and the company is still there. About 1917 Ford changed the shiny brass radiator shell to black enamel. The headlights were changed about that time too. There were not many structural changes until about 1929 when Ford manufactured the Model A.

Church picnic bus rides were on a Sunday or holiday and I always longed to go on them. It may have been because I'd watch the horses curried and brushed until the hides were glossy and the large wagons washed and shined for this event, especially Decoration Day or the fourth of July. The brass studs on the harness were polished and the harness decorated with small American flags at the harness and collar. Some teamsters tied a red ribbon to the whip which was held upright in the whip socket, some decorated the harness with small white bone or celluloid rings, depending on the taste of the teamster. The wagon was equipped with two benches facing each other, each seating eight to ten, with the picnic baskets usually at one end. The outside was draped with red, white, and blue bunting. At a church picnic, tickets were bought for a nominal sum, perhaps just to pay for the teamster's time. The wagons lined up in front of the school or along the street and about 10 a.m., they drove off. The last wagon usually had a keg of beer, ice, and bottles of soda pop. When the wagons rolled past our house, the youngsters usually sang and waved small American flags. Old fashioned patriotism was in evidence.

I went to one or two church bus rides but the one I remember best is the time we went to Herbst Grove on Broadview Road. Herbst Grove was only a few miles out of the city, not far by today's standards. Maybe the reason I remember that one best is because it was a cold, rainy Sunday and the teamster had imbibed too much beer at the saloon and was well loaded by the time it came to go home. Mom had been undecided whether to go to the picnic because of the weather. Actually, I believe she just wanted to show Lucy and me a good time. To get there we had to take a streetcar to Pearl and Broadview and meet Koch's wagon at the Old Johnson House on the

66

corner. It was a two-story yellow painted brick building on the northeast corner with a porch across the front facing Pearl. In years gone by, the Johnson House was a stage coach stop where travelers stayed overnight and had their meals. In the rear was a long open shed for horses and rigs.

Although it was rainy and cold, Lucy and I had fun but couldn't run around much because of the wet grounds. Beside the picnic grounds Herbst Grove had an open-sided dance floor. The saloon was in a separate building facing Broadview which was traveled by farmers or others going to Strongsville or Medina who'd stop to wet their whistle.

I don't recall much about the picnic except eating our lunch and playing ball on the dance floor with other children. About 4 p.m. it was time to go home so we headed for the wagon which was stopped in front of the saloon. Other picnickers were already in the wagon. We waited and waited and could hear arguments going on inside the Brau Haus. The teamster, Koch's son, finally drifted out and it was evident he was in no pain and had been fairly well anesthetized with Leisy's Lager. He climbed onto the driver seat and when a second man staggered out, they engaged in language which would back a sailor into a corner. It seems the second teamster had made some disparaging remarks about working for Mr. Koch or, perhaps, about Koch himself. Our teamster threatened to have the other one fired. I don't believe it happened because I saw him around Koch's barn after that. Finally our man drove off with us and while we were apprehensive about reaching the Johnson House safely, the team made it back without trouble.

About 1909 Dad and brother Al started a small furniture and upholstery repair business above Gut's Wagon Works, Prame Avenue and W. 25th. The place was a starter but not suitable for furniture finishing which was Dad's line. It was too dusty because of the blacksmith's forge, the open doors, and the heavy, dusty work in constructing wagons on the ground floor. When Dad varnished a piece of furniture the dust settled on it giving it a dull finish and no amount of hand rubbing would eliminate it entirely. Shortly afterwards they rented a more suitable place.

Mr. Gut was a short, stocky, and very strong man. He was a blacksmith by trade and now employed six or eight men in the wagon shop. One time Dad had some work to be done on the wagon and sent me to Gut's shop. The horse Dad had at that time was a little frisky but a good worker. It was big and more powerful than old Dick. As I parked the wagon in Gut's wagon yard one of the workers started to burn rubbish in a metal container. While the flames were nowhere near the horse, nevertheless he became excited and started to prance around. I was on the ground and held him by the headstall but it didn't make much difference, he was too strong for me. Mr. Gut happened to come out and saw I was having trouble. By this time the horse was standing on his two back legs and pawing the air with his front legs. I grabbed his reins and attempted to pull him down but my strength was not sufficient. Mr. Gut grabbed the reins out of my hands, pulled the horse down, cussed him out, up and down and the horse stood still. Mr. Gut said "you gotta show the sonovabitch who ISS de boss." Guess the horse knew I was scared.

The place they had moved to was actually two separate stores with connecting doorways in the rear leaving free access to each store. Dad and Al did not intend to have showrooms, but workshops only. The upstairs was occupied by the building owner, a woman and her daughter, and roomers.

Dad and Al needed a horse and wagon for deliveries so Old Dick was bought and Mr. Gut made the wagon. The wagon is clear in my memory. Actually, it is part of my life with Dad since we delivered furniture together, sang songs while Old Dick trotted along and made many a stop while Dad hoisted a glass of lager at a saloon and brought out a sandwich to me from the free lunch counter. The lettering on the side, near the front, was A & M Stein Upholstery Co., Phone--South 445-J. I remember the phone number because it was the first phone the family ever had, albeit a business phone.

A good part of my education in the handling of a horse was obtained during those years. Many times Dad left the chore of currying and brushing the horse to me, besides cleaning out his stall and, at night, feeding him his oats, hay, and a measure of bran. Bedding down the horse with clean shavings for the night was part of it too. Hitching the horse to the wagon was something I liked and I believe I can still do. The first horse Dad bought was black and his name was Dick. I had read the story of Black Beauty and liked to imagine Dick was it. He was a gentle horse of undetermined age and putting on his bridle was as easy as counting a mare's teeth. Some horses fought the bridle because they disliked the bit between the teeth but with Dick there was no problem. I'd first put on the collar, then take off the halter and slip on the headstall and fasten it with the bit between the teeth, then throw the rest of the harness on him, buckle the cinch and back him between the wagon shafts. A horse will expand its belly so the cinch is not too tight so it's necessary to thump it. I'd put my knee against Dick's bread basket and pull on the strap until the buckle was in the position I wanted it to be. After this, the harness is fastened to the shafts and the traces to the whiffle-tree. Then I'd put the lines over the dashboard, see the whip was in the socket, climb aboard, back the wagon out of the barn and drive in front of the shop. The last thing I did was put the hitching iron out and snap the strap to the bridle. Dick didn't like to be hitched to the

iron and pulled his head away as much as to say we didn't need the
iron with him. We were now ready to load the furniture for customer
delivery.

Delivery wagons for small packages were common. All large
department stores had them. An experienced delivery man jumped

Delivery Wagon
Courtesy of Western Reserve Historical Society--Cleveland, OH

off the wagon with the package as soon as the horse stopped, ran to the house, made the delivery and ran back. When the horse saw him coming it would start off. Then came the tricky part--while the wagon was in motion, he'd grab the seat handle with the right hand, face the rear of the wagon, swing his left foot up to the hub of the turning wheel so the hub rotated between the heel and sole of the shoe, stand and lift his right leg over the moving wheel and onto the wagon, make a half turn and sit down on the seat facing forward. This was done in one fluid movement and faster than it takes to tell. I practiced on Dad's wagon. It was a matter of timing and I became adept at it.

I don't know where Dad bought Old Dick but I do know Dick used to pull a laundry wagon. Every time we'd pass the Cleveland Laundry loading yard on the east side of town, Dick tried to pull in and we'd have to jerk his head around to keep him going. It is a habit of horses, and perhaps other animals, to go where they were used to having been. It brings to mind when I was with Dad in the wagon-- we'd see a horse automatically pull in front of a saloon and stop without urging by the driver. This was because of it being a regular stopping place by the driver. Not far from Al and Dad's shop was Schaeffer's Saloon. There was a wagon ahead of us and the horse pulled up in front and stopped. Dad knew the driver and joked with him about it. The driver said in German "Ehr weiss Bescheidt," (He knows what to do). The story goes that one day a driver didn't show up for work so the boss made the deliveries. After a couple of days the driver reported for work and the boss told him every saloon he stopped at while on the job.

Dick was a reliable horse but shied at paper blowing in the street and was frightened of puffing locomotive engines. We knew this but Dad could control him. At West 64th, north of Clark next to the

Nickel Plate Railroad tracks, there was a slaughterhouse and meat packing plant. In it was a butcher shop where fresh cuts of meat could be purchased cheaper than in a butcher shop. One day Dad pulled up the wagon to go shopping and left me with Dick. We faced the railroad crossing and everything was quiet, no train coming. I hoped with all my might no train would show up because I figured I'd have a time with Dick. Sure enough, in the distance I heard an engine puffing. It came closer and closer. Dick started to get nervous. His ears were twitching and pointing toward the tracks. I knew the signs. I looked towards the slaughterhouse hoping Dad would come out but he didn't show. Apparently he had not thought of a locomotive so there I was, about 12 years old, with a jittery horse likely to run away and no Pop, no Mom to help. I was on my own and knew I had to make out by myself. The engine puffed closer and closer pulling a small string of freight cars and making plenty of noise about it. By Dick's actions I knew I was in for something so I hung onto the reins calling "Whoa, Whoa Dick, Whoa boy," etc.

A man's voice with a few healthy sonsabitches might have settled him down a bit but he kept prancing back and forth and sideways with his rear end and stomping with his front feet paying no attention to me. I suppose my nervousness contributed to Dick's insecurity. I knew what a run a way horse, gone nuts, could do. I had seen one or two performing, one on Carnegie and one on the Brooklyn Bridge. The vision of a smashed wagon and injured horse was before me. I did some emergency thinking--whether to ride it out or jump, was the question. Not being completely addled, I opted for the jump. I made up my mind that when I calculated Dick's snorting, prancing and shaking of head and reached his take off point, I'd jump. I did. I timed it just right. Dick took off like a shot, pulled the wagon across the tracks, just missing the end of the last freight car, and continued on. It was a good imitation of a quarter horse race take off.

White as a sheet, I ran into the slaughterhouse and told Dad the horse had run away. He came out and we followed him to the end of the street where he had come to a halt in the swamp in Walworth Run, wagon and all and that is the only thing which stopped him. Dick was still very nervous, but unhurt, while the wagon had a cracked shaft and whiffle tree which Dad patched up with bailing wire. We had a little difficulty getting out of the swamp but with some backing and maneuvering it was accomplished. Dad and I drove back to the shop, the slaughterhouse forgotten.

Scranton was a nice street, paved with asphalt and substantial, well-kept homes. Mother complained that about 4 a.m. every market day she was awakened by horses clip-clopping down the street on the way to the West Side Market with farm produce. In the late afternoon they'd all clip-clop back.

Our house was next to a vacant lot and, since we had our usual complement of chickens, it was my job after school to let them in the field and watch them while they foraged for bugs or for whatever chickens forage for. I didn't like this chore since it took away from my valuable time. The point in watching the chickens was that they were brainless and had no sense of self preservation when it came to food. They'd run into the street and peck at manure for the oats and seemed to be totally oblivious to the approach of a car or horse's hoof. I'd chase them back into the lot and as stupid as they were, they soon learned the boundary line of their freedom.

Chicken feed attracts rats and we had a few of them holed up under the chicken house. I'd hide under the oilcloth hanging over the ladder hooked onto the fence in the chicken yard and wait for them to come out and forge for feed. The King BB gun I had was accurate at the distance and I'd ping them when they showed. They'd jump a foot in the air and run back under the chicken house. They were tough critters and I never did know if I killed one. Perhaps they died somewhere else.

73

The chicken coop was actually a shed, one half for the chickens and one half for garden tools, and other things. In summer, when we mowed the lawn, the grass clippings were taken to the hot attic under the slate roof and strewn on the floor to dry. After it was dry it was swept into a pile and stuffed in a burlap bag for winter chicken feed. It was a good idea because this drying-out process kept the nutrition intact. The mowing and stuffing was my job. The chicken shed was colder than a refrigerator in winter and Mom would heat up the feed and mix cut up grass clippings with it. We always had 10 to 15 chickens and, somehow, they survived the cold days. About 5:00 p.m. in winter when it became dark, the chickens would huddle close together on the roost for the night. The nests were under cover beneath the roost and during laying time I've seen Mom bring out an apron full of fresh eggs. They were in demand by the neighbors and, I suppose, that's the way Mom made her pin money. The chickens were a good source of food after they quit laying and a treat for us on Sunday was to have a chicken for dinner. Mom knew how to make soup from a chicken and her fried chicken, to me, was out of this world. Leona is also an expert at fried chicken having been taught by Mom.

Chapter 7

Summer evenings were tranquil. We had a wooden platform lawn swing in the backyard which seated four comfortably. Mom, Lucy, and I would rock back and forth listening to the crickets in the garden. It was especially nice on a moonlit night. The annoying thing was the mosquitos pining around our ears. The darn things hid in the grass and shrubs and way laid any human in the vicinity. We had a fairly effective repellant--punks or citronella. The punks were bought for a penny a package, six packages for a nickel. We'd light punks and the smoke helped drive off the mosquitos but it wasn't entirely successful since they'd zing in on you in unexpected areas. Swatting was the only sure cure. The citronella was of vaseline-like consistency with a not too unpleasant of an odor, and when rubbed on exposed areas served to keep off the little critters quite effectively.

Our front porch was a favorite place. People then did a lot of porch-sitting in the evening. It was a good place to rest after a day's work and a good vantage point to see what was going on in the street, while enjoying a newspaper and a pipe. The greatest majority had no transportation such as a horse and buggy and, not many owned automobiles. Radio and television were unknown. Therefore, porch-sitting was the thing. The few who did have autos were looked on by us common people as being more in the bucks and, possibly, rich. Just owning a horse and buggy was considered a cut above the ordinary. It was on a warm summer night that we waited for the newspaper, Extra, to come out on the result of the world's championship fight. About 9 or 10 p.m. the newsboys came bellowing down the street. Some had reached the long pants stage and made use of their new found voice power. "Wuxtree, Westree, Wuxtree. Jack Johnson K.O.'s Jeffries."

Besides keeping tabs on the street, we were able to talk to neighbors or acquaintances strolling by. A walk on a nice summer night was a pleasure and there was no fear of assault or holdup. Such a thing never entered anyone's mind. Lucy and I took a walk with Mom many times. Compared to now, the street was quiet. An occasional horse and buggy lit by a lantern or an auto with carbide-burning headlights would go by. After 10 or 11 o'clock the street became silent with little traffic.

The streets were lit by arc lights which attracted insects in summer. In spring, the May bugs, also called June bugs, were plentiful. We called them May bugs because they'd come out about the end of May. They are a destructive beetle and feed on flowers and foliage and the larvae feed on roots in the ground. Ben and I would have a pail with cover, pick them off of the pavement and feed them to the chickens in the morning, which were nuts about them. They had good nutritional value and saved on feed.

Our house was one lot away from Valentine Avenue near City Hospital. When we moved to Scranton it was known as the Poor House, where poor people stayed because they had nothing and no means of support. Everyone was sorry for them--and rightly so. In back of the Poor House, overlooking the valley (now steel mills), was the Pest House. This was a place to give wide birth to because if you walked to close, you'd catch some sort of pest. Actually, it was used for people with contagious diseases such as small pox. In line with the Pest House was the Consumption Ward building which I wrote about previously, where our neighbor Mr. Richland passed away. I still remember the people from the Poor House sunning themselves on the extensive front lawn and resting in the shade of the large elms. About 1910 or 1911 the county built a Poor Farm and Correctional

76

Farm, called the Workhouse, in Warrensville, a suburb on the east side of Cleveland. Then all the poor people were moved to the new location and the Poor House became the Cleveland City Hospital. Mom liked to walk, particularly in fields and woods. One day she walked with me down Valentine Hill, across Jennings Road and to a wagon road leading to the prairie below. This area was all new to me since we had just moved to Scranton and I was too young to start browsing around by myself. Halfway down the wagon road, on the hillside, we came upon an old cemetery. It must have been there for many years since there were only three or four fallen headstones left. It was there long before the turn of the century I'm sure. Mom surmised it was a place the city buried indigent people who had died in the Pest House years before. It was evident that it had long since been abandoned. I'm sure Mom was correct. Many years later in the office of the Detective Bureau I received a call from an officer who said that a road crew working on Jennings Road, in the rear of City Hospital, had unearthed an old skull and there was no sign of other remains. I asked in whose possession the skull was at that time and he said he had it but that the road crew had been playing catch with it. Geeze! My memory went back to the time I was with Mom. I told him where the old skull came from and instructed him to take it to the morgue. I'm sure I was the only person in the whole city who had the answer to the mystery of the skull. That would be a good title for a paper book. That was the last I heard of that old cemetery.

At that time, the hospital grounds fronting on Scranton was like a park with elm trees, green lawns, and flow beds. The student nurses in their long, ankle-length, blue dresses with white starched aprons, collars and nurses' caps, strolled on the grounds and young student doctors in their white outfits were not far behind. I don't recall the two fraternizing except for a greeting or so. Usually each sex was seen separately. Perhaps it was a rule. At the south end of the hospital was a two-story brick building with iron bars on the

City Hospital
Courtesy of Western Reserve Historical Society--Cleveland, OH

windows. This was said to be the Crazy House, where they kept crazy people. The word insane or disturbed was not used in my childhood circle of acquaintances. A crazy person to us was someone who was violent, frothed at the mouth and spit at you, and if the spit struck you or you were bitten, you'd be poisoned and go crazy. I always steered clear of this building perhaps because of the iron bars and the supposed crazy inhabitants. Actually, I believe, it was used

78

in prior years to temporarily house persons with disturbed minds who were either released or admitted to the insane asylum on Turney Road. At that time I believe the building was empty because I never saw anyone around it. The insane asylum was in the town of Newburgh before it was annexed to Cleveland. Around town the expression "You belong in Newburgh" was often used in a joking way. To me City Hospital is almost a story in itself and we'll finish with it a little later.

Sometimes on a summer evening the neighbors gathered on the hospital lawn to sit and discuss weighty topics of the day. It was sort of a Town Meeting, you know. We kids ran around and had a good time and let the world go hang. It was there I had my first brush with the law. One evening one of the neighbors put up a bed sheet and showed colored slides. I forget what they were about but we all sat in a row looking. The action wasn't interesting enough so a few of us boys began horsing around, "wrassling" and such. Suddenly I was tapped on my skinny rear end and when I turned to defend myself there was the majesty of the law, wallrun moustache, blue helmet, white gloves and a billy in hand. He was from the Auld Sod because, in a thick brogue he said "You bye's behave yourselfs." Gad! We offenders straightened out then and there and sat in a row like bunnies with our ears straight up. We "learnt" quick. Lots of respect. This officer was the policeman on the beat and just doing his "dooty."

Getting back to City Hospital, we could see the emergency entrance from our backyard plus all of the north and most of the front side of the hospital. Here the horse-drawn ambulances and police patrol wagons brought injured victims of fights or accidents. The city ambulance was black with a white cross on each side. The horse was sturdy and usually ran at a trot--in first gear so to speak. Apparently its main function was to haul indigent persons to the hospital for treatment. Once in a great while, the horse would gallop in with the

City Hospital Ambulance
Western Reserve Historical Society--Cleveland, OH

ambulance bell clanging. This would be an emergency. There were private ambulance companies which made a business of it. Usually their ambulances were fancier, more shined up than the drab city ambulance. The horses were also better and had their harnesses shined. One privately owned ambulance was the Express Ambulance used in emergency cases. It was a two-wheeler pulled by a fast horse and a sight to see it tearing down the street, the bell clanging, and the driver leaning forward lashing the horse. When I heard an ambulance bell I was usually waiting at the emergency entrance. All I had to do was jump the back fence, cross the alley and I was there.

Police patrol wagons always came at a fast trot. Horses were well-groomed and, after standing a short time, would paw the pavement impatiently. Besides hauling prisoners, the patrol wagon was

80

equipped with stretchers and served as an ambulance when necessary. The driver sat high up in front and the other officer rode standing on the back steps holding to the vertical brass bars.

There were many things I saw which I've never forgotten. One is a boy being carried in on a stretcher, white of face, with his right foot, shoe still on, beside him. It was cut off at the ankle and the driver said it had happened at a railroad track. Oddly enough, these sights never bothered me and, perhaps, were good training for worse things seen while in the Police Department.

Across from our home was Sackett Alley. It led from Scranton to W. 25th, where the streetcar line was. Opposite the alley was Warnecke's candy store and young Johnny Warnecke had the paper route from end to end through the hospital. Papers were 1¢ and Johnny would ask me to go along for company. I wasn't keen on going because I didn't want to "ketch" anything. In fact, I was a little fearful of all the sick men lying in the large wards. There were about six or eight men in long dark gray nightgowns in beds on each side of the room. Johnny and I walked down the aisle between the beds selling newspapers. Each man had a small brass box about three inches square with a spring cover into which he'd spit when the urge came. Usually there were several men hawking and spitting at the same time. The hawking and spitting wasn't properly orchestrated in the high and low key section, therefore, an innocent, clean-out, fresh-air minded new assistant newspaper peddler wasn't exactly enamored with the whole damn paper route, especially handling pennies from these sick men. All in all, brass boxes were, perhaps more sanitary than a spittoon alongside each bed. Less work, too.

The nurses all liked Johnny. He was friendly and had a smile for all of them. I went along out of friendship and was glad to leave when his peddling was over. I didn't know that Johnny had an ulterior motive in taking me along. First, he was anticipating a vacation and needed someone to fill in for him. Secondly, it kept him tied down every evening with no relief paper boy. Lastly, I was handy to the hospital. Came the day he asked me to fill in for him while he was on a two-week summer vacation. I'd have no part of it and turned him down. He said to me "What do you think I've been taking you along for?" It was news to me. I believe that had he explained this to me in the beginning with the idea that I would learn the hospital route and, in his absence, make a few pennies for myself, my interest would have overcome my dislike and I would have paid more attention to the paper route with all its hallways, twists and turns, upstairs and downstairs. Not that I wanted or expected anything but all I ever received from Johnny for helping him carry and peddle his papers was a piece of candy which he said he had swiped from the candy store when his dad wasn't looking. Johnny's older brother reluctantly filled in for him.

Dad bought me a pair of roller skates one day and it was one of the good things which happened to me. I learned to roller skate on the sidewalk in front of the hospital. It was a good place because there were few pedestrians. One day I had a good idea for roller skating where the sidewalk was smoother and shaded by large elms. It was on the cement walk alongside the driveway leading to the front entrance of the hospital. I liked this sidewalk and driveway and used to watch the carriages of visitors drive down and stop at the front entrance. Occasionally there'd be an auto. Whoever constructed the sidewalk couldn't have made it the proper thickness of cement since it gave a hollow sound when skated over. The noise made it more interesting so I used it frequently until one day I was stopped by a man from the front office whom I had often seen around there. I figured he was the front office manager--or higher still. He wore a dark suit, and a white shirt with high starched collar. He told me to stop since the patients had been complaining about the noise. I had never given this a thought. Perhaps he was the one who was annoyed, not the patients. However, I stopped the practice and that's the last time I skated on hospital grounds. Again--respect for authority.

The side of the hospital on Valentine and the side facing Scranton had mysterious goings on. Frequently the air in the neighborhood was permeated with a strong carbolic or disinfectant odor. We kids let our imaginations run rampant. In our discussions, we laid it to poison used on patients in the hospital, or to doctors cutting up live people during operations or, even, dead ones. Yeah!

Adding to the mysterious doin's were the moans and screams emanating from the second floor. The second floor windows had heavy iron screens on the outside and often a man with a long dark nightgown would stand in front of the window cursing and calling to be let out. Sometimes it became so bad the neighborhood people would be attracted to the noise and line the hospital fence to see and hear what was going on. Many times on a summer night I heard the calling, wailing, and moaning continue all night. Mom complained of it many times. In the dead of the night it gave me a creepy, scared feeling, accompanied by goose bumps. The only explanation I can think of is that it was a mental ward. They had a particularly violent case one night. It was in the evening and the light was on in a room occupied by a man who must have gone berserk since he smashed the window, broke out the window frame with a chair and hammered at the heavy window screen until it loosened. All the time he was shouting and cursing. We all wondered what he'd do if he broke out since it was on the second floor. Suddenly two or three men in white jackets appeared and wrestled him out of sight. That was the last we heard of him. The men didn't have a corner on the moaning market, the ladies did their share too. I particularly remember one with long hair at the window calling to be let out.

One day I was walking past the hospital when I heard banging at one of the windows on the second floor. A man in a long dark nightgown stood on the outside window ledge and jumped down. I can still see him in the air with the nightgown around his thighs. When he landed on the grass below he stayed there, moaning. Two men in white jackets rushed out of the front entrance, took one look at him and returned to the hospital. They came out with a heavy wooden stretcher. I heard one say he may have a broken back.

Occasionally I'd find a note written in pencil asking that someone be notified of the rats in the hospital eating their food, and making other complaints. Apparently they were thrown out in hopes someone would pick them up. I'd show them to Mom and it was decided to mail them to the city health department.

One day I was in the back yard, Mom and Lucy were in the house, when I saw a man in a long nightgown crossing the lot next door towards the gate in our fence. I ran into the house and told Mom. She locked the back door, called to Lucy to lock the front door and when we looked out of the window one of the white-coated men from the hospital had him by both wrists and asked him where he was going. He said he was coming to our house to ask for a drink. Mr. White Jacket escorted him back to the hospital.

It was in the early morning hours of a night in the latter part of June when I was awakened by exploding firecrackers. I recall thinking that they were starting the fourth of July celebration early. Usually they did start the firecrackers a day or two before the fourth as a preliminary testing. This night the noise was accompanied by a woman's screams. It was a warm night and I got out of bed and went out onto the airing porch to hear better. It was then I learned the firecracker noises were shots. There were more shots and more screams. A light came on in a house two doors behind us and a breaking of crockery and banging around started. The neighbors were aroused and came crowding around the back in their nightgowns--men and women. Shortly after, the police arrived and after several more shots and a scrambling and thumping a man was brought out and taken away. He had been shot three times.

The next day we found out that a man had been brought into the emergency room, for what reason I never found out, had run away from the hospital help, crossed the street, banged on the door of a house and asked for a glass of water. He was refused so then he went to the house where all the action took place. He banged on the door and when it was opened, he barged in and locked himself in the bathroom. Then the homeowner fired several shots at him through the bathroom door. The next morning I hung around the neighbors who gathered on the lawn discussing the occurrence. There was plenty of angry grumbling and a decision was made to go to City Hall and see someone. The homeowner, or tenant, said his wife would not stay in the house and had gone to her mother's until they moved away. A few weeks later they did.

I was about fifteen or sixteen when I observed a commotion at a large touring car parked at the emergency entrance. With the car were two white men, one behind the wheel and the other alongside. In the back seat was a heavy set, muscular, colored man--handcuffed. In telling how things were then, colored folks were usually referred to as niggers, coons, or jiggs. In the Police Department they had other, more descriptive, monickers. In the Detective Bureau I worked with a man who was raised in the Dakotas, there they were called jaspers.

Digressing for a moment, it's an oddity that almost all nationalities or races have their nicknames although all are human:

English are referred to as Johnny Bulls
Germans--Krauts
French--Frogs
Italians--Wops or Guineas
Hungarians--Hunkies
Americans--Yanks or Gringos
Jews--Heebs, Kikes, or Yidds
Chinese--Chinks
Japanese--Japs

The black man must have been a mental case. He was violent. It seems they had tried to walk him into the emergency entrance but he wouldn't go so a tussle took place leaving one of the white men with a bleeding face. In retrospect, I believe them to have been county deputy sheriffs who had been ordered to take him to the mental ward at the hospital for temporary confinement and observation. He kept repeating "Jesus Christ, the Lamb of God" meanwhile twisting and turning the handcuffs. I was watching him when suddenly they parted--one cuff on each wrist. He jumped out of the car, ran down Valentine Avenue, down the hill, and across Jennings Road. We chased him, the deputies, spectators, and I, along the way. He had picked up a thick limb of a tree and ran down another incline to a small clearing and faced us with the club swinging. It was an effective club, alright. No one could get near him. The deputies tried and jumped back every time he swung. By this time, people lined Jennings Road above us. The police had arrived and some circled behind him in the prairie to get him from the rear. The other young fellows and I were facing him about fifteen or twenty feet away when one of the deputies, a short, thin man, walked up and attempted to take him by the arm. The black man swung at him and just missed whereupon the deputy drew a revolver and fired about four shots at him. None of them seemed to take effect. The black man walked backwards to another small clearing and stood swinging the club. It was evident something had to be done in a hurry, and it was a situation which had to be resolved before this demented man broke through and attacked someone else. The shooting started by the deputies and the police, and each time one of the shots struck him I saw him wince. He was shot in the head because he leaned over, leaking blood, and pulled out teeth which he dropped on the ground. He was tough. Apparently the shots had not hit him in a vital place. He still stood, swinging the club. We kept sneaking up on him, the circle getting smaller and smaller. Finally we rushed him, I dove for his legs and knocked him over and the rest piled on. The club was kicked away and he was done. He died at the hospital several days later. I don't recall any mention of the action in the newspaper.

Chapter 8

Every year, St. Michael's School had a May Walk. Each class, accompanied by its sister, would walk from the school to Brookside Park, a good two-mile walk. The children brought their own lunches. This was a time we all enjoyed. When we arrived at the park we were more or less on our own and the sisters usually paired off and walked about the park by themselves. The lunch was a big thing since Mom had packed a shoe box full of sandwiches and goodies.

The zoo didn't amount to much then as zoos go, and the biggest attraction was Minnie the elephant. Minnie had been purchased through collections of pennies from the school children. Actually, I believe the whole scheme was thought up by one of the newspapers. Brookside Park was a great place. It had a large pavilion on a hill overlooking a large pond. At one end of the pond was a candy and popcorn stand and a place for hiring rowboats. Some Sundays, a band played in the pavilion. It was a place of shelter in case of rain and, also, a place to have your picnic lunch. Sometimes Mom, Lucy, and I took the streetcar there on a Sunday and just walked around, sat on the grass, or just strolled around the pond. Circling the pond was a roadway which was traveled by horse and buggy or automobile. It was quiet and tranquil. Park police were referred to as Sparrow Cops and rode bicycles. They didn't belong to the Cleveland Police Department, but to the parks Department and only had arresting powers in the park. The police department had their own policemen on bicycles too--no motorcycles for them then. I've seen many of them race down the street to answer a call.

One time I was on a May walk and a few of us boys climbed the hill and walked into the woods surrounding the park. There are no woods left now, it has long since made way for homes. On this particular day two friends and I were picking flowers to take home to our mothers. It was a nice sunny day and as I walked among the trees I spied a man sitting on the ground with his back against a tree. He was bleeding from the head and in his right hand, in his lap, was a revolver. I backed away in a hurry and told my two friends, who also looked, to do the same. A short distance away we heard elder boys, possibly eighth graders, to whom we ran and told what we had seen. They came and looked too and said it looked like suicide and took off to notify someone in the park. We scrammed the hell away from there--fast. I heard later the police brought the man down and whether he was alive or dead I never found out. It was a grisly thing for my young eyes.

In the woods surrounding the park was an old log cabin. How long it had been there or for what purpose I do not know. On our walk with Lucy and me, Mom would sometimes rest on a bench in the shade in front of the cabin and tell us stories in German. One I remember was Hansel and Gretchen. With the trees, the sun shining through the leaves and the bees buzzing around the flowers it was the proper setting for fairy tales.

On one of these walks I was alone with Mom and we had walked quite a ways through the woods and fields, climbing over farmers' split-rail fences, when I saw a snake coiled up on the ground in a sunny spot. I was going to show my bravery, protect Mom perhaps, and picked up a stick to beat it with. Mom stopped me and said the snake wasn't hurting anything and to leave it alone, it was there for a good purpose. I was glad to follow her instructions that time since I actually didn't want to tackle it. Mom decided to return and about that time we saw a horse and wagon being driven down a one-wagon track dirt road through the fields headed in a westerly direction.

There wasn't a house in sight, just fields and patches of woods. Some years later when I became familiar with the area I'm quite sure it became Memphis Avenue which runs westerly and, after turning north turns into 117th Street ending at Lake Erie.

The sisters of St. Michael's School had a rule that when a pupil passed a sister in the hall, or outside, he was to say "Gelobt sei Jesus Christus" (Praised be Jesus Christ). The boys had to tip their caps and girls to bow their heads. Remember--the boys were on one side of the school and the girls on the other. No women's lib in those days. This rule was alright, it taught us respect, but it also "learnt" the sisters about the uncertainty of rules. When a whole class of boys came marching through the hall on the way to 10:00 a.m. recess, noon hour, or evening let-out time, it was our pleasure to roar it in unison. One tried to out-holler the other. St Michael's School hadn't been built with top quality acoustics in mind, so when two or more classes passed a sister in the same hall it was a nine-day wonder we didn't shatter the windows with reverberations or cause the doors to fall off the hinges. This was especially so when there were two or more sisters walking behind each other and each one was accorded the same salute. When the sisters were walking on the girls' side of the hallway they received the greeting from the girls in unison too. However, their greetings were more dignified and delivered more sweetly--in an up-and-down lilt, like a swallow in flight--very respectfully. So, you see, sometimes the greetings by both masculine and feminine gender would create quite a cacophony of sound. It got to the ridiculous stage so the word was passed to lay off the noisy greetings and say it quietly.

In the third grade we had double wooden desks with a board separating the pupils. The desk covers were solidly fixed so the books were slid under it on a shelf. In each desk was a hole with a bottle of ink and a groove to hold the pen and pencils. I suppose they still have them. All of us had pencil boxes of our own with an assortment of pencils, pen, and penholder. The better equipped student owned a pen wiper. It was a small chamois used to wipe the ink from the Esterbrook steel pen point. If it wasn't wiped off, it would rust.

Occasionally a boy complained that something had been swiped from his desk. And there was. Every class, everywhere, usually had a pupil or two with sticky fingers, either at school or away from it. It's part of growing up. A boy don't get to be a man with clean britches on.

Our third grade sister, like most of the nuns, was born in Germany and spoke with a German accent. She loved to tell stories about her sainted father. Each story differed from the other. Once he'd be a big shot businessman, next he owned a store, the third time something else, ad infinitum. She'd take off on her narratives, in German, about twice a week. It was a joke among us kids but we knew we had to listen anyway since it was during class and no way out. We were a captive audience, you see. The best one she told was about the bravery of her father during the Franco-Prussia War about 1870. In one of the battles he was in, the man holding the flag was shot down. Her father jumped forward to rescue the flag--"UND DANN HAT MEINEN FATER DIE FAHNE GEGRIFFEN. ACH GOTT!" (and then my father grabbed the flag. Oh God!)

Like all kids I had my fist fights in the school yard and on the way home. It was usually of small account and the result of someone, perhaps unintentionally, pushing or punching me. My feisty temper was at fault too. I never could stand being pushed around, it sticks in my craw. It was a good way to learn how to get along and taught one how to hold one's temper. Also, it taught others not to push you around.

One afternoon in the fourth grade Charlie Kowalski and John Holler had it out in front of the class. They were paired in a double desk in the front of the room. Charlie and John didn't see eye to eye--a personality clash perhaps. I do not know what brought it on but suddenly they both jumped up and proceeded to do battle. Fists were flying, as were tempers. Sister pulled them apart and put one in a seat in back of the room. We knew what this meant--an after-school fight. After class was out we trooped down the alley behind the school--our fighting ground. It was out of sight and hearing of the sisters' house. We formed a circle, Kowalski and Holler squared off and the fight was on with all of us yelling and egging them on. It was a good one with the opponents evenly matched, although Kowalski was the taller, Holler was quicker. He could turn around in a hen's nest and never break an egg. They both gave a good account of themselves with Holler having his nose bloodied which he wiped on Kowalski's shirt during the clinches. By the time the fight was stopped, Holler's shirt was in tatters. At least one had a black eye. In my judgement, although looking a mess in the bloodied shirt, Kowalski came out a little ahead in the deal. The fight was stopped by a woman who came into the alley from her backyard. As a peace offering she told the boys to come into the house and have some kuchen. She even tried to get them to shake hands and make up but she didn't know Charlie and John. Both were too exhausted to accept so they went home. I imagine sister heard about it but wisely asked no questions. I guess she knew everyone has to turn over his own rocks. They were separated in class after that.

Some of the fights started in the school yard and ended up after school hours in an alley. One was between my chum Carl Becker and Ben Jagelski. Individually they were good kids and easy to get along with. Again, the cause was boyish temper. We'll get back to them shortly.

In the spring, and usually lasting until school let out for the summer, we had pugging in the school yard at recess and at the noon hour break. Pugging was a form of playing marbles. The boy with the agate or flint sat on the ground with his legs spread wide, placed the agate or flint in front of him and the boys would line up in front of him at a certain distance, depending on the type it was, and pug at it with brinnies. Pugging was the act of aiming and throwing the brinnie. A brinnie was a round marble made of a particular type of clay, baked hard and colored. I don't see brinnies any more nor do I see marbles being played. Agates were usually 2¢ a piece, graduating upward in price according to coloration and size. Flints were tops. They were small, hard to hit and 10¢ a piece-- big price. Since the flint was the most expensive and had to be hit from a greater distance, they were highly prized. Brinnies were about 10 for 1¢. The owner of the agate or flint would keep all the brinnies and relinquish his ownership of the agate or flint to the one who hit it. The new owner then set up the agate. When a line of five or six boys were pugging at an agate they did not take turns but pugged as they pleased resulting, many times, in two claiming to have made the hit. A scuffle usually started with all the puggers jumping in and grabbing all the brinnies they could lay their hand on--for free.

To get back to Becker and Jagelski, one of these scuffles took place when they both claimed to have made the hit. I was there. During the scuffling and pushing someone hit Jagelski or Becker on the backsides with a board. It stung. I saw the board in someone's hand but don't recall who. They didn't investigate and one blamed the other, although neither had proof. Just as the fight was getting into shape, recess was over and the fight was postponed until after school let out at noon. This time the fight location was in an alley across from the school. It was rolling along when Jagelski's sisters came by on the way home. Of course, they told Mom Jagelski and Grandma Jagelski when they reached home. Ma and Grandma came storming up the street with sticks waiving to protect their offspring. Grandma Jagelski was a hefty gal of belligerent Low-Dutch stock (Platt Deutsch). I don't say Low-Dutch in disparagement, it was an area in Germany so called. With Grandma, Ma, and the sisters, Jagelski was well covered although he hadn't asked for it. Ma was yelling in English and Grandma in Low-Dutch as they waded into the spectators with their sticks. The fight broke up. I would say the fight was a draw at that point.

The smartest two belligerents I saw were Leo Hildebrandt and Carl Thoemas. Leo was the son of the Hildebrandt Provision Company owner, and Carl was later the organist for Our Lady of Good Council Church and taught music for a living. The fight was actually promoted by classmates over some imaginary insult. "He said this about you." "You said that about him." "He'll meet you in the alley after school." All pure fabrication. I watched it happen, I was in school when they were baiting them. After school we all trooped to the alley off of Kinkel Avenue. Lots of alleys around, paved and unpaved. In school they had been making threatening motions with their fists so we expected it to be a good fight although I had never known either one to be feisty. We formed a circle and they squared off. We were all doing the usual yelling and egging on when each turned around to us, stuck their tongues out, thumbed their noses at us, picked up their books and ran down the alley. They were one up on us, we couldn't sucker them into a fight. They had connived on the side.

About four blocks from our school was the Lutheran Church and School. In those years there was religious prejudice, something we encounter very seldom now. My own philosophy is each to his own religion, they all lead to the same place if you believe and keep to your faith. Catholics were called "Cat-lick Mackerel Snappers" because we ate fish on Friday. Of the Lutherans it was said "When Martin Luther rings the bell, all the Lutherans go to hell." There was ill-feeling between the Lutheran school children and those from our school. How it started I'll never know. Certainly, it was not condoned by the minister or priest. One time I saw five or six eighth graders from St. Michael's School, carrying clubs and ropes, start an argument with the Lutheran group. I'm sure neither group actually wanted to fight. There were some threats made and it was decided the best boy from each group should fight it out in the street to decide which school was the winner without the involvement of both groups. It was a decision worthy of Chief Justice Oliver Wendell Holmes. One of the Lutheran boys stepped forward and then a big Catholic boy stepped out and said "Sonovabitch hold my coat" and while in the act of removing his coat the Lutheran boy stepped in and knocked him to the pavement. Our "Sonofabitch" boy said "I quit" and that was the end of the fight. It was a silly, pointless business and didn't prove a thing. I heard later that our priest visited the minister of the Lutheran church and the monkeyshines stopped. Leona's Grandmother Engel was Lutheran and it was the minister from that church who visited and prayed with her during her critical days.

There were still vacant lots on Scranton Road. Two, side by side, were between Valentine and Clover Avenues. One was owned by

Mr. Stroemple and the other by Mr. Henkle. Henkle and Stroemple were very good friends and decided to each build a home on his lot and as Stroemple was a building contractor, he was to do the constructing. Stroemple, at the time, was living on Clover Avenue on the corner of the alley behind Mr. Ball's manure box. Mr. Ball had five or six teams of horses which he hired out to the Pittsburgh Plate Glass Company. In summer the manure box became quite noticeable in Mr. Stroemple's house. Then, too, with the manure came the usual flies which wasn't a thing to be happy about. I was a friend of Mr. Ball's son, Charlie, and got the story from the horse's mouth, as it were. There had been previous manure discussions between Mr. Ball and Mr. Stroemple and one fine day an argument developed between them. Perhaps Mr. Ball had not had the manure hauled away often enough. Some threats were voiced and Stroemple went into the house and came out with a pistol. When Ball saw the pistol he figured he was about to be gunned down so he turned around to get his own gun from the house when Stroemple shot him in the back. He carried the bullet in his back for the rest of his life. Stroemple had a trial and served time in the Workhouse. Stroemple was No.1 enemy.

I remember Stroemple and Henkle's houses being built and, to all appearance, they were exactly alike. The agreement had been that both were to be built from the same plan, look alike and be of the same measurement. The building cost was to be shared equally. One day Henkle had occasion to go to Stroemple's house and found out Stroemple had built his house on a larger scale than the plan called for. Simply put, Henkle was paying for at least part of Stroemple's house since the measurements were larger. Now Stroemple was No. 2 enemy. The feathers hit the fan. The feud was on between them.

Henkle, his wife, his daughter and son-in-law, would stand in the driveway between the two houses and berate Stroemple. Stroemple would stand on his front porch and aim a toy cannon at them and holler "Boom, Boom." I witnessed it. The neighbors were familiar with the story and no one would talk to Stroemple. Pop didn't either for a time, but then forgot about it.

At the south end of the hospital was a city playground equipped with sandboxes, swings, chutes and other playground equipment. I had a lot of fun there during summer vacation and spent many of my Saturday mornings on the grounds. I could see our upstairs airing porch from the playground and Mom and I had an understanding that when she wanted me she'd hang a white towel on the porch. This worked well, unless I forgot to look.

One day Mom and I were scheduled to go somewhere so I was dressed in my Sunday best. Since time was a little heavy on my hands waiting to go to wherever we were scheduled to go, Mom gave me permission to go to the playground providing I didn't get my clothes dirty. That was one day I forgot to look for the towel and when I got home Mom asked me where I had been since she had been waiting for me. I told her I had forgotten to look for the towel. Quietly she asked me what I had done there and I told her that I had been playing in the sand box.

> "Mm-hum! Yah! Wass noch?" (Yes, what else?)
> "Oh, I climbed on the bars."
> "M-hmm. Und?" (Yes. And?)
> "I swung on the swings."
> "Yah! Und wass noch?" (Yes. And what else?)
> " I slid down the chute."

That's when the cows walked into the pasture. Mom lowered the boom right there. She swatted me a few times and said she had warned me not to get my clothes dirty, and on and on. Yah! Again I "learnt" to do what I was told.

In front of the playground on Scranton the city had a concrete water trough for horses, one of many scattered around town at strategic locations. Many saloons boasted water troughs but they were made of wood, and I noticed horses preferred the concrete through. You see, the water circulated in the city troughs and remained fresh while in the wooden troughs it sometimes became stagnant. Duffy's saloon across from our home had a wood trough in which he kept minnows but they didn't last long since the boys fished them out.

The city trough at the playground was a favorite place for me to make a few pennies on a Saturday morning or in the evening, checking horses. That's what we called it--checking horses! It was simply waiting for a horse and wagon, or team of horses, to come along and stop for a drink. Many horses had check reins. A check rein is a strap attached to the head stall and hooked onto the top side of the cinch. The purpose of the check rein was to keep its head up so, when a horse came to drink at the trough the check rein had to be unhooked so it could drink. Some horses had no check rein and didn't require our service. However, most of the buggy horses had them. Each time a horse pulled up we'd see if it was check reined and, if it was, we'd reach up and take it off the hook and let it drink. Some horses enjoyed the cool water and put their head in halfway to their eyes, blew bubbles, pulled up their head, snorted and slobbered around. Most would take one drink, raise their head with the water draining from their mouth and then go for a second one.

After the horse had drunk its fill I'd slip the check rein back on. Occasionally a horse didn't want it hooked up again so it was quite a job. We usually received a thank you but, many times, and this is what we counted on, the driver gave us a penny or two. One time I received a whole nickel which was quite a sum for me and made my day. I didn't tell Mom about it since I had plans for it--a picture show. Farmers were apt to give a pear, apple, or whatever they were taking to market. Once in a while the horse was too strong for us and the driver had to climb down and check rein it himself. During vacation time I was usually at the trough after breakfast to get the morning traffic. Sometimes there were two or three of us and we'd take turns. This is one way I made pennies to go to the moving picture show which cost 5¢. Occasionally I'd check horses later when the buggies and fancy rigs came out for an evening drive. Horses and buggies weren't the only ones on the street, automobiles were very prominent too.

I will recall one lady driving down Scranton in her buggy several times a week, usually in the evening. She was fair complexioned and had red hair, pompadour style, earrings, wore a large straw hat with ostrich plumes, long white dress, and long white gloves. She had a Lillian Russell figure and knew it. In other words, she was well stacked, especially in the bodice area. She drove a high-stepping blood red bay hitched to a single seat shiny black buggy with shiny red spoke wheels. They sparkled! I don't know where she lived or if she owned the horse but they cut a good figure--woman, bodice, and horse. I noticed the eyes of the local yokels would follow her. She'd sit straight as a ramrod in the center of the seat, one rein in each hand, while rolling down the street. Occasionally she'd pull up at the trough and with a gracious nod give me permission to check her horse. Never did I get a penny, just a sweet thank you as though conferring a favor. One time the horse would not let me hook him up so Lillian Russell drove away with its head lower than usual.

The only reason I can think of for a check rein is to make a better appearance, but in my opinion a check rein should not always be used since it prevents the horse from putting its weight into the collar for pulling. However, there may be other reasons for its use. I've seen carriage horses with their tails bobbed, but can readily see where this could be a cruelty since it deprived the horse of its defense against biting flies.

We kids would sit on the curb on a summer day and watch the horses. When we saw a white horse we'd wet our finger, press it into the palm of our other hand and then thump the palm with our fist. This was good luck. The idea was to determine who spotted the white horse first, therefore having the most luck. We could always spot a pacer by his peculiar side-to-side gait. If I recall, a pacer was a horse used in harness racing and to see one hitched to a delivery wagon looked out of place, but it happened.

The Valley Race Track was located where the Clark Avenue Bridge now is. When Mom took Lucy and me up to visit Mrs. Adler, who lived in the second story of a house overlooking the track, she'd set me at the kitchen window and I'd watch the horses being exercised on the track.

On a summer Sunday afternoon Dad hitched up old Dick to our fringe-top surrey and drove him around to the front of our house. We'd drive all the way to about Snow and Pearl Roads, a distance of four or five miles. There we'd stop and get out, walk around in the fields, perhaps picking flowers. It was out in the country then. Now it's all stores, shopping centers, and other developments. By the time we returned home it was time for supper.   Brother Al was courting his future wife, Elizabeth Raps, about then and would take her for a ride in the surrey.   Al would drive while Elizabeth sat beside him in the front seat.   We still have a picture somewhere in the family archives with Al and Elizabeth in the front seat, and Mom and Lucy in the back.   Al later said he'd be embarrassed at times since Old Dick, just as old people sometime are, was afflicted with flatulence. People in the caviar circuit will know what the word means. To us bread and butter people the dictionary defines it as "the presence of excessive gas in the digestive tract."   I will say no more except that Al and Elizabeth must have had some pooping good rides. By this time, buggies were getting to be somewhat of a rarity since the auto had taken over most of the show.   About 1918   Dad bought a 1917 Model T touring car and, along in there some-

Model T Touring Car
Courtesy of John and Anna Kinnenun

where, Al and Dad bought a Ford delivery tuck.

Chapter 9

*I*ran a lot in my youth, especially on the way home from school. Never to school--only away from school. Actually, I liked to run. I was Mom's errand boy and, whether necessary or not I usually ran at a jog. Perhaps it was to get it over with and return to my play at home. Much of my running was between our house, the butcher, the grocery, the baker shop, milk depot, and Dad's shop. At the milk depot we paid 8¢ for a quart of milk and 4¢ for a pint--in glass bottles. Then we had Thiel's grocery store on Valentine which required a jump over the back fence and down the street. From being errand boy I remember prices of many items since we paid cash for everything. Walter's Bakery and Helm's Drug Store were two more stops. When I think of the price of food then and now it's unbelievable. Unbelievable, also, is the difference in wages. Bread was 5¢ for a one pound loaf, fried cakes or sugar doughnuts were six for 5¢, sugar biscuits were the same price. Ginger squares, about 2" by 4" by 1" heavily coated with maple sugar, were the same price. We expected a free cookie at the bakery and a piece of bologna at the butcher shop with each purchase and got it. Schwab's butcher shop received most of our trade for meat except when Dad came home from the West Side Market on a Saturday night with a half bushel basket loaded with meats, cold cuts, sausages, and wieners. My favorite on a Sunday morning was fried ring bologna or fresh liver sausage. The butcher at Schwab's was a heavy-set fellow and liked to tease Lucy, so she didn't like him. Years later a friend from work, who lived in Independence with her sister and brother-in-law, asked her to come over for a visit. As Lucy walked in the door she recognized the man as the butcher from Schwab's. He didn't know her after all those years and Lucy didn't say anything. He had been the mayor of Independence and was well liked in the community.

Schwab's had sawdust on the floor, as most butcher shops did in those days. On the wall was a row of meat hooks with carcasses of beef hanging from them, and on the open counter displaying various cuts of meat and roasts kept free to the flies. I saw it. I heard later the butcher complained about the women customers pushing their fingers into the meat to test for tenderness. About twice a week I'd be sent to Schwab's for a "pound and a half of ground meat mixed," the mixed part being a little pork mixed with the beef. Mom made a lot of meat loaf, stuffed cabbage, and the like. Roasts were for Sunday, you see. I noticed the butcher put his thumb on the edge of the scale when weighing the ground meat. Having led a sheltered life and being innocent in the ways of the grown-up world I thought it necessary to do this to balance the scale so it would hit the right figure. One day I told Mom about it and the next time she went there herself to get her ground meat but there was no thumb weighed that time. I wasn't there, but Mom told me. She said she had talked with him about it and I noticed after that his thumb didn't get weighed in with the ground meat. Knowing Mom, she didn't take a backseat and must have given him a piece of her mind.

One time there was a change of butchers at Schwab's. The meat was still on the open counter and this day I had to buy meat other then ground meat. When I got it home and Mom unwrapped it the meat had maggots. The flies had done their duty. Whether Mom sent me back with it or threw it out I don't recall. All I do remember is the big hot-haw I caused in the butcher shop the next day when I told him, in front of two or three customers--out loud, yet!

"Your meat had worms in it," I said.

"It did not," he said.

"It did to."

"It did not," he said.

"It did too," I stood fast.

102

I wasn't about to be called a liar. Sweet Moses on the mountain! I forget whether I got my money back or fresh meat instead. I "learnt" a little something from this, though. Don't accuse someone in front of other people.

We used to hitch wagons home from school, or anywhere else for that matter. This was a common practice, especially when the tailgate wasn't too high and the horse was going slow enough. In back of us on Valentine Avenue lived the Karps. Young Roy Karp was a good kid and a year younger than I was. We enjoyed playing in the field next to our home but I noticed that his Mom didn't let him play with me too long at a time and kept an eye on him from the house when he was with me. I didn't know why and still don't. In thinking back about this it could have been either because I was Catholic and they were Lutheran (there was prejudice those days, you know) or because about this time I was using a few salty swear words. These words may have been of above average variety and heard, no doubt, from a teamster or at a saloon door. If this was so, Roy may have brought some of the words home to an appalled mother. Anyway, it seems I was an evil influence.

One day, after school Roy asked me to go with him to Schwab's butcher shop. I did and he bought about a half pound of baloney. As we started back down Sachet Alley, a horse and wagon drove by with the tailgate just right. I asked Roy if he wanted to hitch a ride with me--evil influence again. He agreed and after stuffing the paper wrapped bologna under his blouse we hung onto the tailgate swinging our legs. Too much action for the bologna, it slid out of the paper from under Roy's blouse and fell into a fresh pile of horse manure. We looked at the meat, a la manure, and Roy was a very worried boy because he knew what awaited him at home. His Mom was no-nonsense and ruled the roost. There we were looking at the manure-covered baloney wondering what to do when I spied my brother Ben in the front yard sprinkling the lawn. I had a brilliant idea. I asked Ben to sprinkle off the baloney and he did. Roy wiped it reasonably dry on his blouse and rewrapped it in the paper and took it home. I didn't hear any yelling or crying so I was sure he had got by with it. The next day I asked Roy about it and he said his mother had wondered why the baloney was so wet and that was all. I asked him what they did with it and he said, "we ate it." Must have been manure from a healthy horse.

In winter I enjoyed hitching a ride to or from school on a farmer's sled. The need for salting down the roads to melt the ice had not been thought of since horse traffic could manage and most autos were not used in winter. They were stored away in a shed or barn, the radiator and oil drained and the auto put up on wooden blocks to avoid tire damage. We'd stand on the sled runners and enjoy a smooth and quiet ride. It was less noisy than a wagon wheel on pavement. Most horses had bells on the harness and on the wagon shafts so there was a continuous tinkling of bells as the horse and sled moved along. A cutter with bells and a fast horse between the shafts made a musical and exciting ride. We could tell it was a bitter cold morning before we left the house for school when we heard the wagon wheels squeal. The iron tires on the wagon wheel running over the cold snow made a continuous wee-ooo, wee-ooo, wee-ooo squeal.

Christmas vacation was our time to hitch our sled to wagons. We'd have a long rope fastened to the front of the sled which we'd pull through the bottom bar of the tailgate and then slam ourselves on the sled while it was pulled along. Sometimes we'd miss the sled and land in the road and if you didn't let the rope go, the sled ended up hanging under the tailgate and the rope would be jerked out of your hand.

Some drivers objected to the hitching of rides, I suppose because of possible accident or rule by the employer. I remember a big freight wagon, in particular. The teamster saw us after we had hitched on. He yelled, "Get off there, you sonsabitches" and lashed at us with the whip which wasn't long enough to reach us. We left in a hurry but soon hitched another ride.

Valentine Avenue had a hill which ended at Jennings Road. It has all been changed now by freeways. It was a good coasting place in winter for the children in the area. There were always a variety of sleds but the best, and most expensive, was the American Flexible Flyer. I think it's still on the market. This sled was new then and had a wood cross bar on the front end which could be pulled in the direction you wished to go and the runners were flexible enough so they bent slightly in the direction of the pull. It helped, but if a turn was to be made the rider dragged the tip of his shoe in the snow to help steer it in the right direction. This was not good for shoes, it wore the tips out in a hurry. Lucy had a sled with the runners curled in front which I didn't like because it was a girl's sled and didn't travel very fast down hill. However, it was the only sled we had. I pestered Mom for my own, having the Flexible Flyer in mind.

One would think that a sled was a sled but, apparently, they were manufactured in masculine and feminine designs. So, one Christmas morning a sled was under the Christmas tree--no Flexible Flyer. I was disappointed again but by this time I was used to not getting what I asked for. The sled was red and made of wood throughout with round steel rods in grooves as runners. I turned it over and on the bottom was marked the figure 45. I knew this was the price of the sled--45¢. I realize that Mom, no doubt, didn't have the money and her budget wouldn't allow a Flexible Flyer which would cost about $4.50. It was another lesson--don't expect to get everything you ask for. It was also a good lesson in self denial and made one appreciate and value a gift. I never liked the sled, it was no good for belly-slamming and barely made it down a hill. In short, it was no damn good. However, I never owned another and made the best of it.

There was a toy I saw one time when I was with Mom which I wanted very badly. It was a wind-up one with a man climbing a ladder, depositing a bag into a container at the top and returning. I saved up about 10 pennies and Mom agreed to get it if it cost 25¢, she'd add the other 15¢. I waited in anticipation the evening she went to the store on 25th to get it. When she returned she had no toy--the price was 30¢. Too expensive. It was a cruel world. Believe me, I learned to be conservative. Perhaps it's a good habit--you're never rich but you're never broke either. I can understand Mom's point of view, she perhaps was having money problems and paying off the mortgage on our new home was number one priority and the income was not great. It amazes me to see what children get for toys when I see them in a department store--and they expect them.

We were taught to work, too. Every Saturday morning my job was to first dust the dining room and living room furniture and polish the stove if needed. Lucy was assigned other chores such as making beds, helping with dishes, and bread making. After I dusted the furniture I had to clean the chicken coop. This was dirty work which I didn't enjoy, you bet! Once in a while Lucy would help me but it wasn't her cruddy job. The fertilizer was spread in the garden and helped grow healthy vegetables. We didn't get paid for this, it was our job and it was done.

To earn a little spending money, Mom let Lucy and me pick weeds from our front and back yard at 2¢ per half bushel basket. The weeds never ran out, we had a new crop growing all the time. It was slow work filling the basket so we'd go to the field next door and add to it. However, it was a variety of weed we didn't have in our lawn and I guess Mom knew it when she inspected the basket but didn't say anything. The weeds weren't pressed down in the basket either but fluffed to make it look full. The two cents usually wound up in the candy store across the street. We knew just what candies we liked in the showcase and the ones we received the most for our money. There were "two-fers" and "four-fers"; then there were "likrish straps" and penny ice cream cones. The "two-fers" were chocolate-covered maple candy, two for 1¢. The "four-fers" were four chocolate covered carmel squares for 1¢. Watermelon candies were "four-fers," hard candy shaped like a watermelon with green and black stripes, four for 1¢. Let's not forget the jawbreakers, six for 1¢. Milk chocolate-covered almonds were 30¢ a pound and a pound of Lowney's assorted milk chocolate in an attractive red box with a pretty girl on the cover was 40¢. It was a good product and well-liked among those who could afford it. The candy store was run by two old maids who lived upstairs. The parents of one lived in a separate house in the rear yard of the store.

Mr. Redmond, the father, was a candy jobber who delivered candy in a closed wagon to stores around the west side. He had a nice matched team of bays, fast steppers, well groomed, which always ran at a fast trot. Since he was a candy jobber, the store always had a fresh supply being the only candy store in the neighborhood. Since it was across the street from the City Hospital (the old Poor House) it did quite a business, especially with the interns, nurses, and hospital help. Visitors to the hospital stopped by too. There was an ice cream parlor in the rear of the candy store where they served ice cream dips for 5¢ each with your choice of homemade flavor. A sundae was fancier than a dip because it had more things on it in addition to flavoring, such as nuts, cherries, whipped cream, etc. Now all dips are called sundaes. Banana splits were 10¢ or 15¢.

Let's sidetrack for a moment--soda jerks in drugstores made quite a show of mixing up a milk shake or malted milk. There were not electric mixers then and shakes and malteds were mixed by hand. I've watched many soda jerks and the good ones would swing the covered container over the head, shake it from side to side, up and down, near the right ear, near the left ear, and then ceremoniously pour it into a tall glass in front of the customer. Ten cents was the going price and if a customer wanted a raw egg in the malted--5¢ extra. Very nourishing--lots of cholesterol.

To get back to the ice cream parlor--it was equipped with wire backed chairs and heavy wirelegged tables. The fruit flavoring was in a glass covered bowl with a large gravy spoon to dish it up. Let's not neglect the ice cream sodas--5¢. Across from the candy counter was a glass display case with boxes of cigars and humidor to keep them fresh. Cellophane wrapping was unknown then. In back of the counter was a glass door cabinet with other tobacco items, such as sacks of Bull Durham for roll-your-own cigarettes, Sweet Caporals with (who smoked Sweet Caps in Custer's time?) Slogan, cut plug chewing tobacco, Copenhagen snuff in round boxes, as it still is, corn-cob pipes, clay pipes and more expensive briars. A cigar lighter on the counter was a must.

Speaking of the 5¢ ice cream soda reminds me of the time in the summer of 1913 when Mom and Lucy took the trip to Germany. One Sunday Pop decided to take me fishing in Rocky River under the bridge. I know now that he would rather have stayed home but he was a good pop and wanted to show me a good time. He put some cord in his pocket with a couple of fish hooks and we took the streetcar to the bridge. It was a hot Sunday, hot enough to singe the bark from a cedar post, and we had no lunch so Dad decided to return.

The Rocky River bridge, built about 1910, was touted as having the longest steel reinforced concrete arch in the world. Steel reinforced concrete was just beginning to be used in bridge construction at that time, so the claim must have been true. The bridge was approximately two city blocks long and about two years old at the time. The streetcar was crowded with standing room on the rear platform only. We were packed in when a man pushed and shoved his way through to the door at one of the stops. He had jostled Dad and I could see Dad was annoyed; however, the man got off and we continued on our way, and on reaching Detroit and 25th we got off to transfer to the 25th streetcar. Near the car stop was a drugstore, the building is still there, when Dad decided we should go in and have an ice cream soda. Dad didn't usually eat ice cream so the blistering hot day must have made him thirsty. He reached into his back pocket for his purse and found it missing with the two dollars it contained. Dad immediately suspected the man who had jostled him of having picked his pocket and I believe he was right.

We sat on stools at the soda counter and ordered two strawberry sodas. The druggist prepared them and set them before us. They were large, a beautiful pink, and I can still see them sitting there. Pop laid down 10¢, five cents for each and the druggist said they were 10¢ each. Dad picked up his dime and said to me, "Come on. We can get them anywhere for a nickel," and we walked out. Of course I was disappointed but Dad didn't let me down. We walked down the street a couple of blocks and bought two sodas for 5¢ each in a candy store. Pop wasn't about to be involved with inflation. We walked the rest of the way home instead of taking the streetcar and I assume Pop made up for the 10¢ by walking home.

To get back to the candy store across from our home, one of the ladies who ran it was a well-rounded person in a Schumann-Heink way. She was pretty in a hefty way, was not suffering from malnutrition, had fair skin, blue eyes, and black hair--no gray--pretty but well-rounded. One day I walked into the store to make a penny purchase while she was having a quiet tete-a-tet with a man leaning over the counter looking into her eyes with a more than usual amount of intensity. Quiet talks like that with the opposite sex didn't come her way too often, you see. Her glance towards me indicated more than a little annoyance at my intrusion and it was evident that she was extremely interested in their conversation, when I heard him say to her "You're just pleasingly plump." Moses on the Mountain! There is something about the truth that makes itself understood.

Once in a while a few of us kids would play a sneaky trick on the two candy store ladies. Lucy was in on it too. The store was on the corner of Sacket Alley and Scranton and we'd line up out of sight on the alley side. One of us would go in and the bell on the door would tinkle. We'd hear one of the ladies walking around upstairs, apparently doing household chores, and when she'd come down we'd buy a penny ice cream cone and leave. After a long enough wait for her to go back upstairs and start her chores, another one of us would go in and buy a penny cone. Each would take a turn until about the fifth time we could see she was beginning to smell a rat and by the look on her face could tell she was losing her temper so we'd call it off. She never said a word but we knew she knew, and she knew we knew that she knew.

There were stores which dealt only in tobacco and the needs of smokers. They were known as cigar stores and usually had a wooden Indian on the sidewalk with wooden cigars in one hand. This is where the expression "Quiet as a Cigar Store Indian" originated. I remember them very well. A cigar store Indian served the same purpose as a barber pole for the barber shop. Wooden Indians are now collectors' items. A regular cigar store was equipped with a cutting block and blade with which to cut a square of chewing tobacco from the large square of tobacco plug on stock. It was fresher that way. A brass spittoon was a part of the store fixtures as well as the gas and electric chandelier. Mr. Meier, whose sons I went to school with, had a cigar store near Dad's shop. His wooden Indian was quite decorative, the headdress had various colored designs.

Chapter 10

*I*t's surprising what the Health Department at that time let the handlers of food get by with. On the square we had the hot tamale man with his pushcart, the hot dog man, in the fall the chestnut vendors with chestnuts roasted over hot coals. In winter, butchers had dead rabbits with fur still on hanging outside. No one knew how long they had been dead. Live chicken handlers were common on market day. Many of the old timers wouldn't buy a dead chicken--or a dead goose or duck. There is many a housewife I've seen get on a crowded streetcar with a live goose or live chicken in a basket. The goose wasn't respectful of ankles or stockings either.

In summer we had the ice cream man who pushed a two-wheel cart along Scranton with a five gallon can of ice cream nestled in crushed ice and rock salt. Besides old shoes, a well worn cap and old clothes, he wore a dirty white apron. He'd push his cart along on a summer day while ringing a bell and sell you a penny or a five-cent ice cream cone. I never saw him make a larger sale such as a pint or quart. One afternoon I watched one of them from our front porch. He had stopped for three or four teenagers who each bought a 5¢ cone. This was a lucky stroke of business for him. Each one paid up as he was served except one who walked away, stood on the corner and laughed at him while eating the illicit cone. The ice cream man ranted and raved but there was nothing he could do since they had him boxed in. And he knew it. One of the bigger teenagers stood a distance on his right while the other two or three stood to his rear. If he had chased anyone or left his cart, the cart would in all probability, have been run down the street or dumped over. He finally went on his way without being paid. Diphtheria was prevalent for a while so the Health Department put thumbs down on the ice cream peddling.

Considering these small merchants must have walked for miles one way and back home again each day, they are to be admired. They made a living, sent their children to school with no complaint. When I think of the ice cream peddler, banana peddler, back peddler, scissors grinders, all raising families without free food stamps such as they have now, no assistance from Health and Welfare, no Social Security, my hat is off to them. This is what made America great-- determination and drive. When I look around today and see the advantages people have and the unsatisfied hippies, yippies, rabble rousers--well, I just better get off my soap box before I work myself into a tizzy.

Then we had the yellow, horse-drawn, waffle wagon with open sides equipped with a waffle iron and driven by a white-aproned man behind the counter. I was too short to see how the waffle iron was heated, but it was a hot fire since I could see sparks occasionally. There was no mistaking the wagon, the ringing of the bell and the wonderful aroma of fresh waffles. The price was 1¢ per waffle and six for 5¢. The hot waffle, straight from the griddle, was sprinkled with powdered sugar, placed on a piece of clean white paper cut from a paper roll attached to the counter and handed down to the customer. It was delicious.

While we're singing the praises of the small businessmen, let us not forget the city worker without whose services we would have been in a fix. They were hard workers, never attained fame or notice, sometimes ridiculed, but performed their work quietly and efficiently. I refer to the white wing and the garbage man.

The white wing was a man dressed in white who pushed a two-wheel metal container, equipped with broom and shovel, down the street each day. His job was to sweep up the horse manure and to sweep the gutters. When he had the container full he'd dump the contents in a pile at a certain point at the curb and it was collected by a city team and wagon. He did a good job and Dad took many a load of the horse manure and used it in the garden. For a little tip he'd

112

make sure it was all pure horse manure rather than mixed with other street debris. The only drawback was that the oats sprouted which had to be eliminated by hand hoeing.

The job of the garbage man was a bit harder. He'd drive down the street with an open iron bed wagon shaped like a long, large bathtub with a canvass cover. The horse took the street at a slow walk while the garbage man, carrying a large iron container on his padded shoulder, walked to the rear of each home and emptied the garbage into the container. When it was filled, he emptied it into the wagon. The horse watched his master and if it got a little ahead it would stop until the garbage man caught up. In summer the aroma was pungent but in winter not so bad. My hat is off to these unsung heroes. The dad of my friend Frank Pfister was a garbage man and a finer family I never knew. He belonged to St. Michaels, was well-dressed, something like a businessman, and led the singing in a deep base voice. There was nothing snooty about us bread-and-butter people.

We had a small "Heinz variety" mongrel dog named Trixie. This little mutt was quite a character and liked nobody but Dad. I believe he even hated himself. Pop had a way with animals. While Trixie was my companion on many jaunts to the valley, I never touched him without eliciting a growl or a snap at my hand. Dad could take a bone away from him without trouble, an unheard of thing with that mutt. All he'd do is lick Dad's hand. Old Dick was also attached to him. When Dad left the wagon he'd turn his head to see where Dad went and keep looking at the place until he returned. When Dad unhitched the hitching iron Old Dick would mutter and grumble while rubbing his head against Dad's chest.

Trixie was a good companion. On a Saturday morning, after completing my chores, I'd take my stick and start for the back fence. As soon as he saw this he'd yelp, bark and run down Valentine to the hill overlooking the valley I've mentioned before. It was a nice place then with a prairie, running streams, swamps, and the Cuyahoga river. Just before reaching the river was the B & O Railroad track running southward, perhaps to Mexico or Brazil--even. There were hills to the right of Jennings Road and woods extending. I do not know where. In my imagination the woods and fields were limitless and if one walked far enough you'd be in the Wild West. Of course, I knew that first one had to cross 25th on the west side. It was a great place for us kids.

Unknowingly, by observation, I learned a lot about nature, plants, trees, and insects. I knew the sassafras tree, the elderberry bush, blackberry, raspberry, hazel nut, and many others. I could tell the oak tree, the walnut, the hickory, the sugar maple and many others by the leaf or bark. I learned where certain flowers thrived and the time in spring or summer they blossomed. I learned how to sneak up on a bullfrog at the swamp by sliding my shoe forward along the ground instead of stepping with my heels. You see, the heel shudders the ground and the frog will usually jump at the vibration. It has large eyes too. I learned where to look for snakes and where to catch sunfish and bullheads in Riverside Pond. While lying in the grass I'd imagine castles in the white cloud formations drifting in the blue sky. It was a GOOD place for a boy. There were no factories in sight, except Staplers and the Masek Glue Works.

Today the fields and streams are gone and in their place are steel mills, factories, warehouses, you name it. The woods and farmlands on top of the hills are now residential. The springfed brooks had minnows which we'd catch and take home. Along unpaved Jennings was the east end of Riverside Cemetery. The property was quite extensive and had two large ponds, an upper and a lower. The lower pond was an excellent place for fishing. It had plenty of sunfish, catfish, bullheads and shiners with frogs and turtles at one end. At the east end of the pond was a large frame house of late 19th century construction with gables, verandas, many windows, and a carriage drive and barn. It was said to have been the home of the former landowner comprising Riverside Cemetery--this included the two ponds.

Trixie and I roamed the fields. I'd take along several potatoes for roasting, salt and pepper and, perhaps a small snack for the dog. I'd pick out a location to bake the potatoes, then I'd dig a shallow hole, gather twigs and wood and start a fire. After the fire had been replenished several times and there was a bed of hot ashes, I'd put the potatoes on the ashes, cover them lightly with dirt and start another fire over the spot. We'd then take off for an hour or so on a field mouse and rabbit-hunting expedition or catch frogs at the swamp. This was a lot of fun for us and Trixie would occasionally chase up a rabbit. I became quite adept at spotting field-mouse nests. They were made of dry grass and covered over to blend in with the surroundings. The inexperienced boys would pass them over every time and would stand right beside one and never notice. They often wanted to know how I could spot them so unfailingly. After roaming around we'd return and I'd have my baked potatoes. It, perhaps, wasn't the best way to bake potatoes but it worked for me, although they did sometimes have a hard black crust.

Then there were snakes, especially in springtime, sunning themselves around the swamp. One time I saw so many snakes at the swamp that I backed away. I didn't want to get tangled up with them. I don't know what species they were, presumably most were the harmless garden variety. There were long black snakes, some snakes with yellow stripes, some small, some gray and some brown. There may have been copperheads but I'm sure there were no rattlers. I'm of the opinion that some, at least, were harmless bull snakes but I wouldn't count on it. Another thing I learned is that snakes, gathered in quantity, have a cucumber odor. Take notice the next time you come onto a mess of them.

A bit south of Denison, east of the river was a remnant of the Ohio Canal. The canal has quite a history and there is no need going into it. It still had its towpath where the horses walked to pull the canal boats and it's said President Garfield pulled canal boats with horses in his youth on the Ohio Canal. One of our friends, a teenager, had a homemade canoe in a shed at the five-mile lock. He, Roland Miller, my next-door neighbor, and I would go out on a Saturday afternoon and paddle up the canal. It was all open country such as it always had been. The shed where the canoe was kept was just at the lock and under the supervision of a man living thereabouts. In the shed were more canoes owned by young people. Once in a while Roland and I would sneak down there, without the owner's knowledge, and borrow the canoe for a paddle up the canal. The last time we did this we ran into a sturdy twig sticking out of the water and poked a hole through the fabric just above the water line. We didn't know what to do about it but I had one of my brilliant mental flashes. I was chewing gum and stuck it over the triangular hole, on the outside, and it held. We put the canoe back and didn't say anything to our friend because we didn't want him to know we had been sneaking rides. It wasn't long afterwards he told us that someone had taken his canoe and put a hole in it and that the man at the boat shed said two young fellows had taken it out the last time he saw it. We didn't peep but he had a suspicious look and I'm sure he guessed who the culprits were.

In about the sixth grade, Sister was teaching us about minerals and, somehow, would come up with a piece of the mineral she was teaching us about, such as iron ore or copper. The morning after she had given her talk about coal and how it originated, Joe Uhelski came to school and put a large chunk of Pocahontas coal in the middle of her desk. I can still see her astonished look, but she kept quiet. She knew that Joe meant well.

One morning in spring she left the gate wide open--the subject was snakes. She didn't know it but some of us could have given her lessons on snakes. A group of us thought it would be a good idea to go down the valley after lunch, during noon and bring back live snakes for school. It shouldn't take long, Ed Stein knew where they were. We found snakes alright but how to take them to school was the problem since, in our enthusiasm, we hadn't thought of that in advance. One boy, perhaps better equipped in the Think Department, had brought along a two-quart fruit jar. The snakes we caught and held down with our sticks were aggravated. They hissed and spat--if one can say a snake spits. We finally put one in the fruit jar, covered it lightly so it couldn't escape, and decided to take along a couple of dead ones for good measure.

Like conquering heroes, we swaggered into the classroom, about an hour late. With great pride, like an offering on an altar, we put the snakes on the floor in front of Sister's desk. She was stunned speechless, by gad! What teachers don't have to put up with. To her credit, she kept a stiff upper lip and didn't reprimand us for being late. In a way we had her over a barrel. You see, she couldn't accuse us of skipping class because we had returned and she couldn't reprimand us for bringing in snakes since she was teaching about snakes and we had, so to speak, brought in samples for her to display. That ended the snake lessons. The snakes were removed that evening by one of the boys.

Trixie was a feisty little dog. He was about a foot long and 10 inches high. He'd tackle anything, any size. He was especially brave when he was with a member of the family. He'd tackle snakes and when the snake curled up and struck, he'd jump back just in time. Trixie would bark and snarl and go after it time after time. However, he never bit one nor did a snake bite him. Trixie would tackle rats, chase cats, and the size of the dog didn't matter. Opposite our home was the Gaeth residence. They had a large mongrel dog about the size of a collie with long reddish hair. Across the front of Gaeth's front yard was an iron picket fence through which Trixie and Gaeth's dog had a continual feud. Every time they'd see each other they'd run back and forth, barking, snarling, and creating a racket--all with the picket fence between them. I'm inclined to think they had a canine understanding between them since the gate was wide open and never would Trixie enter the yard or the other dog come out. They'd pass the open gate every time except once when Gaeth's dog came out and Trixie bit him. It was a mistake. Gaeth's dog grabbed Trixie by the head, shook him and dropped him. Trixie wasn't quite so porky with him after that. I was with him one time when a large, short-haired, dog ran across our front lawn. This was a no-no with Trixie so he tackled him. The stranger took Trixie's head in his mouth, shook him like a terrier shakes a rat and dropped him. When the dog turned and walked away Trixie ran after him and bit him in the leg.

There was only one time I saw him surrender. He tackled another large dog in our front yard. I could see this dog was really vicious and, I believe, Trixie realized it too. Trixie bit him and the dog shook him, dropped him and was about to maul him when Trixie lay on his back with his head back, throat exposed. This is a dog's sign of surrender, you see. The dog bared his teeth, growled and walked away without hurting him further. Trixie got up with his tail between his legs and headed for the backyard. I knew that Trixie had been taught a lesson this time and to see what he would do I followed him to the back porch calling "Yah, Yah, Yah, Trixie's afraid." He had his tail between his legs and wouldn't look at me. He acted as though he was ashamed and I believe he was.

His home in the kitchen was a rag-filled box between the stove and the chimney wall. Warm in winter. He had a habit of sitting up on his hind legs to beg for food when we were at the kitchen table and became expert at catching food in mid-air. His career ended when I was in my late teens. Apparently he had been run over by an auto and injured internally and one summer night he died quietly between our house and the neighbor's. I buried him in the backyard at age 8 or 10 years.

We had several dogs. One we had was a black water spaniel who, apparently, became separated from his master. He came to our door tired and hungry. We fed him, he adopted us and we named him Rover. Rover loved water and we'd take him down to the river where he'd pick up a stone, drop it at our feet and wait for us to toss it into the water. He'd dive in after it but never came up with it. He'd retrieve sticks tossed into the water and bring them to you. Rover had a bad habit of running under wagons and one day he dragged himself home after being run over. He was seriously injured and we had a policeman destroy him. Another dog we had for a short time also had the habit of running under wagons but with one difference, he'd bite the horse's hoofs. He was cured one day--permanently. He came home with his head a mess, missing one eye. The horse must have kicked him. He, too, was destroyed.

Then, we had a small black dog named Tippie by Mom. He was a nice little pooch and adopted us one day. He had a habit of following one of us wherever we went. One Saturday he followed Dad to the West Side Market and we never saw him again. It was about two years later Dad told us he had delivered furniture that day to a lady's home on a street off of Lorain Avenue. He saw a black dog which looked just like Tippie in the woman's front yard. Dad talked to him, called him by name and the dog jumped all over Dad, barking and wagging his tail. The woman said it was strange he acted as he did since he never acted friendly to strangers before. Dad asked her how long she had it and she said he came to her home about two years before all tired out and hungry and that they had fed him and he had stayed with them ever since. Dad told her that he was sure the dog was ours and the circumstances. The lady said he could take him home if he wished but Dad said he might as well stay where he was since he was being taken good care of. We decided that Tippie had followed Dad to the market and lost sight of him in the crowds; that he had mistaken Lorain for 25th and become lost. I believe that is how it happened.

When I think back, I appreciate what a good father Dad was. He bought me roller skates, he bought me a BB gun, he bought me, among many other things, guinea pigs. Dad came home with two of them for me one day. A large black papa and a large tan-and-white momma. He built a small hut in the backyard to house them and it was my job to see that they were fed and the hut kept clean. It wasn't long until they had a family and one of the traits of the baby pigs was to follow their momma in single file around the yard. While I enjoyed them for a time, especially the offspring, they and the care became a nuisance so Dad gave them away. I never became attached to them since they seemed more like tailless rats. Guinea pigs have no tails, you see. Rats are repugnant. I had much pleasure with the King BB gun Dad bought me. It was a single shot but quite accurate for a short distance. I was careful how I handled it and at what I shot. It was usually a tin can or some object out of line with a window. I never broke one to my knowledge nor was there ever a complaint from the neighbors. I might say it was good preliminary training in how to hold and fire a .22 rifle, with which I became quite proficient, in the valley during my teens.

One of the saintly things I did with the BB gun was to hide behind the front porch pillar and wait for a team of mules from the Statler Company to drive by with a load of dead horses. I'd take aim at the nearest mule's rump, either left or right, depending which direction they were trotting. I'd lead the rump a little, fire and hit a bull's eye every time. All the BB would do is sting since there was no power to penetrate the hide. The driver would be sitting quietly, perhaps thinking about the next saloon stop, when the mule would suddenly give a leap and lunge forward, trying to run. It didn't get very far since the other mule didn't know what was going on and didn't increase the pace. Then, too, pulling another mule and a wagon loaded with dead horses at the same time was a bit much. Add to that, a jerk on the lines by the astonished driver accompanied by a few salty swear words slowed him down in a hurry. Once in a while I'd ping a sheenie's horse but sheenie horses, not having much life left, just jumped a little. Most of them were old and ready for the bone yard and, I presume, the sting wasn't felt very much. More about sheenie's later.

As I mentioned before, the Statler Company was in the valley and had been there a long time. Their business was collecting dead horses, suet, and bones from butcher shops. What went on in Statler's and what was produced was a mystery to us. Actually, I believe it was fertilizer. Anyway, the story was that the horses picked up from various livery stables, companies with teams, were cut up, boiled and a mysterious something produced, most of it being glue. We kids believed, firmly, that chewing gum was made from boiled horse's hoofs. We never heard tell of chicle. Being on the main route to Statler's, wagons loaded with dead horses, legs straight in the air, were a common sight. Sometimes a horse would drop in the street for no apparent reason except a weak heart or old age. Other times they were hit by streetcars and had to be destroyed, or a horse would break a leg and be shot by a policeman. The worst livery stable fire, and the only one I ever saw, was McLeans Livery Stable. The papers said it was the worst on record around Cleveland. Many horses burned to death that evening and the kicking, stomping, and screaming of the horses was something I'll never forget. The livery stables on Woodland Avenue had plenty of horses which should have been retired to pasture instead of being hired out to rag peddlers and hucksters.

I've watched a few horses being killed by the Statler mule driver. I well remember school was just letting out for lunch when Brug's horse dashed into the alley off of Rowley Avenue across from the school, and collapsed. The Brug's had a milk depot diagonally across from the school and Anna Brug and her sisters went to St. Michael's. Brug's delivered milk in various neighborhoods by horse and wagon and, this day, the horse and wagon had been sideswiped by a streetcar. It could have been that the horse ran away and sideswiped the streetcar. The wagon was partially demolished and the horse, although badly injured, headed for home with part of the wagon still

121

attached to the shafts. When he neared the barn and half-way through the alley, he collapsed. I understand the driver was Brug's son and he was injured to such an extent he landed in the hospital. Old man Brug decided the horse had to be destroyed. This was excitement for us kids and we all gathered at the scene, some sitting on fences. I was dancing around sticking my nose into every angle of the scene. In a short time the Statler mule team and wagon backed into the alley. The driver was a husky fellow. He rolled up his sleeves, took a large sledge hammer from under the driver's seat, took aim at the top of the horse's head and struck. End of horse. The next thing he did was tie a heavy rope around the horse's hind legs, tilt the ramp against the lowered tail gate, unhitch the mules, block the wheels and through some pulley arrangement hooked the rope onto the traces and started up the mules at a slow walk. With the brakes set and the wheels blocked, the horse was dragged up the ramp onto the wagon. Exit carcass. I saw other dead horses in the street handled in the same way. Some had to be killed and some were already dead. What a dead subject!

One time, on Scranton across from our home, I saw a horse act odd. He had been pulling a light delivery wagon and the driver stopped for some reason. Came the time to get going, the horse wouldn't. He just stayed where he was. The driver tapping, coaxing, and clucking just couldn't get him to move. He got off the wagon, pulled on the bridle, examined his legs, climbed into the wagon again, whipped him and used strong salt-and-pepper sprinkled words but all it would do was jump a little and stay in the same spot. By this time there were five or six advisers gathered around and one of them told him to build a fire under it. While all this was going on , a buggy had stopped across the street with the driver watching. A few crumpled newspapers were put under its belly and lit. When the paper was lit the man in the buggy stormed over. He kicked the fire away and accused the man of cruelty to animals. It turned out he was an official, or deputy, of the Humane Society. After issuing a paper to the driver he drove off. I presume it was a court summons. It wasn't long after that the horse pulled away of his own volition. To this day I don't know what ailed it.

I mentioned sheenies before. I do not use the word in a derogatory sense. A man with a horse and wagon collecting rags, iron, and paper was called a sheenie and no one thought anything of it. We kids called him a sheenie-eisen-zack. He was also known as the Paper-Rags man because he'd walk his horse down the neighborhood streets calling "Pay-Pah Rakes, Pay-pah Rakes." (Paper Rags). The majority of these men were of Jewish descent. They were small businessmen and shrewd. In fact, some later owned their own iron and rag business. Mostly the horses and wagons used by them were rented from a livery stable on Woodland. The wagons looked a wreck, as though they'd been through a seven-year war. The horses were old nags and some poorly fed. One time I saw one which had collapsed in the shafts and couldn't have been gotten up with a hay fork. While the rag man was cogitating what to do, a well-beered barfly staggered out of a saloon. He said he could get him up and proceeded to bend and turn the horse's right rear hoof. Whether or not the hoof manipulation helped we'll never know but the horse staggered to his feet--momentarily. The horse was unhitched and I could tell the barfly was real proud and was just about to run around in front and kiss himself on both cheeks when the horse collapsed again--this time on him. He was pulled out from under and he headed back to the saloon. What became of the horse I don't know, since I left the scene.

Rag men apparently picked a route in neighborhoods to which they returned from time to time. Occasionally I'd see one return in the afternoon with a good load and pass one with a practically empty wagon. Apparently the one had poached on the other's territory and did a good business while the other man came too late. The peddler with the empty wagon would curse and carry on while the lucky one just laughed. There was competition in the rag business too.

123

We boys would save up old iron, bones, and rags wherever we could find them, to sell to the rag man. Burlap bags were in abundance then and the rag peddler had plenty of them. He used a spring hand-scale with a hook on the end for weighing. The clothing and rags were separated from the iron, put in a bag, the hook put through and the bag held up so the weight could be seen. We were sure the scales were doctored in his favor--and I'm sure they were. It was good business--for them. I noticed a trick with the scale when the bag was lifted, they invariably held the scale in a slanted position which jammed the pound pointer against the side of the scale, not giving a true reading. Rag peddlers were suspect anyway and, perhaps had an undeserved reputation.

I recall one time while in the Police Department we were called to a lady's home. She had been doing her spring housecleaning and, as was the custom, the coal base burner was removed to the back porch to be put in the shed for summer storage. A rag man came through the alley and loaded it on his wagon. He was seen by the lady who called us. When we arrived he had some cock-and-bull story concocted that he thought someone had just left it there to be hauled away by the rubbish man. Of course, we didn't swallow it and, since the lady did not want to prosecute, we ordered him to take the stove from the wagon and put it back where he found it. It was a job--but he did it. We didn't help him either. It was just a little instant justice for his thievery. However, despite some of their hanky-panky, they are to be admired. Many put their children through college and raised respectable families. Quite a few doctors, dentists, and professional men came from a rag man's family.

Chapter 11

One of my pleasures on a Saturday in spring was to go to the valley and pick violets for Mom. Mom loved them and I had the good places spotted. There was one hillside across the river which would be blue with them. I'd spend all morning picking and when one bunch was picked, I'd tie a string around it and put it in the river water to keep it fresh and secure it to the shore. When I'd have a large bouquet I'd take them home. In May I'd pick mayflowers, daisy time it would be daisies. I brought home plenty of goldenrod too--I didn't know about hay fever.

Mom was the one who enjoyed company, especially when we children were home on Sunday. Dad did too. However, Mom was the instigator in this direction and Dad went along for the good of the service. We had many friends and to name a few--there was the Raps family, first of all. Brother Al married Elizabeth and their children carry on the Stein name. Then there were the Radtake's, the Lamparyk's, the Springers's, the Adler's and many more. I'll wander away from the subject for a moment.

We had as friends the Baltz family who lived on a farm in Richfield, Ohio. The husband had died and Mrs. Baltz ran the farm with the help of her four children. They'd come to town in their fringed top surrey and stay overnight. The horses would be staked out in the backyard where they could eat the grass. One time Mom, Lucy, and I went back with them and stayed four or five days. It was about 1:00 p.m. when we started for Richfield. Mrs. Baltz and her daughter Myrtle had come alone that time and on the return trip Mrs. Baltz was the driver and her daughter assistant driver. The team trotted all the way until they came to what was then called Chestnut Hill, a part of old State Road. The road was unpaved and very dusty. At the bottom of the hill was a saloon, well-situated because it gave drivers a chance to breathe the horses before making the steep climb and, also, to clear their throats of dust with a schooner of lager. State Road, out there in the boondocks, was a one-track dirt road--you should see it now!

I recall, clearly, there was another buggy coming towards us and Mrs. Baltz wondered whether we'd be able to pass it. We did but each one had to pull as far to the edge of the road as possible to do so. Mrs. Baltz was thirsty by this time and went into the saloon to have a beer. Mom went with her and, knowing Mom, I'm sure she paid for it. I don't recall what the rest of us had to drink, it wasn't beer, so it must have been water. I wanted to ride in the front seat behind the team but it was too crowded so I stayed in back with Mom and Lucy. Under the seats and in the back of the buggy was the regular equipment, feed bags, hitching iron, bags with our clothes for the week, etc. We arrived in Richfield about 9:00 p.m. So, there was an eight hour ride in horse and buggy which, today, would take perhaps two hours by auto, at the most. We enjoyed Blatz's farm since it was something different.

One of my memories is Lucy and me being taken into the woods and shown an old shack called the Sugar House. It was used in early spring to boil sap into maple syrup. One day we had homemade ice cream. This took a bit of doing since the ice had to be brought from Richfield, crushed, salt added, the proper ingredients put in the cream, the turning of the freezer handle, and the rest. Another day we went to a Richfield town picnic. One of the attractions was a greased pig race. The squealing pig ran through the crowds and under the picnic tables and whoever caught it took it home. It was mid summer and Mrs. Baltz said there was danger of the well running dry because of no rain, so water was rationed for a few days and we all had to wash our hands in one basin of water. By the time it was thrown out it was inky. I'll tell you? Mrs. Baltz was a very frugal person, she had to be in order to feed and clothe her family. There was no thought of help from someone else. Welfare Agencies were unknown. It was root, hog, or die. You'd go a long way to find that sort of spirit.

To get back on the road again, New Year Eve was always a great time for a party at home with family friends. The day before Mom baked all sorts of goodies. Dad would have been to the West Side Market and brought home plenty of cold cuts, and other food. Mom would plan an old game she played at home in Germany. Small pieces of dough were shaped into symbols and baked. One in the shape of a ladder, one a key, one had a penny pressed into it, one in the shape of a skull. Each symbol was covered with a coffee cup and the guests gathered around and each picked up a cup in turn. The symbol uncovered was the fortune of the guest in the future. If a penny, you'd become rich, if a key you'd be lucky, if a ladder you'd go to heaven. There were other symbols I've forgotten. The skull meant death. When one group finished the cups would be reshuffled and the next group took its turn. Lots of fun. Try it some time! After the game we'd have lunch. More about this game later.

Memories keep coming in and I think I should not forget Euclid Beach Park and Luna Park. Euclid Beach had been started by the Humphrey family about the turn of the century. At first it consisted of a popcorn and taffy stand on the cliff overlooking Lake Erie on the east side at, roughly, the area 'round 165th Street and Lake Shore Boulevard. It was all country then and, I doubt if E. 165th or the built-up area it is now, was even dreamed of.

People used it as a place to go for picnics. Humphrey added a merry-go-round and attracted more business. Mom told me that at first Humphrey's had to be reached by means of a small ferry from Cleveland; later by train. You see, the streetcar line had not been extended that far into the country. Humphrey's popcorn, taffy and peanuts became well known through that part of Ohio. Euclid Beach

127

continued to grow until it was a full-grown amusement park, well kept, clean, with a good family clientele. At least once every summer Mom would pack a half-bushel basket or two with food, sandwiches, baked beans, and the like and we'd spend a day at Euclid Beach. In the evening Joe and Al would come from work and join us. Our family usually teamed up with the Raps family so Lucy and I would have Eda and Johana Raps as companions to walk around. We'd all eat together and afterwards Al would take Elizabeth to the dance hall.

My favorite place was the penny arcade where, for a penny, I'd stand on a stool and look into a picture machine. The pictures were animated by turning a handle on the side. Rides were 5¢.

The quality of the park remained for many years and it was not until after World War II that it began going downhill due to the change of clientele. It changed from white to mostly black and since it was a real change in the atmosphere of the whole place the whites stayed away in increasing numbers until the park necessarily had to shut down. I believe high-rise apartments are on the site now.

As for Luna Park, it was located at about what now is Woodhill and Buckeye, or Woodland Avenue. It was another large amusement park but, in my estimation, not of the quality of Euclid Beach park. I have been there many times and Dad took me there a few times the summer Mom and Lucy went to Germany. With Dad the money was a little more liberally supplied so, consequently, we went on more rides together. Luna Park was more on the honky-tonk side with side shows and shooting galleries and spin-the-wheel games. Then, too, it couldn't compete with Lake Erie at Euclid Beach. A rougher clientele was in evidence also. On the site now are apartment buildings.

It was New Year's Eve 1912--the year the Titanic sank--that we had a crowd of friends over to celebrate the coming of the year 1913. We were playing the same game when brother Ben picked up the cup covering the skull. I remember Mom's look at him and her saying "Bernard, du wirst nicht sterben?" (Bernard, you won't die?) About eleven weeks later Ben was buried. A coincidence. Mother never used the skull symbol again.

Brother Ben and I were not close as brothers should be. There was a disparity in age, he being about five years older than I. His interests were different from mine and he worked while I went to school. On the other hand, Lucy and I were close. There was not the age barrier, we went to school together and were home together.

Ben was a well-built and husky young fellow. He had light hair, blue eyes, and was about 5 feet 10 inches tall. Friends always remarked that Ben and I looked alike. I guess we resembled the Rogasch side of the fence. He left school to go to work about the end of the seventh grade. He was learning the sheet metal trade and worked at Boester's Hardware and Sheet Metal on W. 25th. I recall Dad got him the job.

Brother Joe and Ben were close. They'd travel together in the evening and there wasn't the disparity in age. Joe said Ben was a fighter and on the way home from school would fight at the first sign of being pushed around and that many times he had pulled him away. Apparently Ben had a temper but I don't recall it being in evidence at home. Sufficient to say, he didn't take a back seat.

One time Ben came home late from work. We were all sitting at the kitchen table having supper when he came in. He had a black eye, swollen cheek, and abrasions on his face. Dad asked him what had happened and the story was they were on a sheet metal job at a shop when one of the jokesters from the shop connected a live electric wire to the chain fastened to the tin cup at the water faucet. Ben picked up the cup to take a drink and he received a stiff jolt. The jokester laughed at Ben. Ben lost his temper, threw a hammer at him and they fought. They were separated and the fight was postponed until after work. They had their fight but I don't know who was the victor. Ben showed his marks and, I presume, so did the jokester. Perhaps it was a good lesson for both of them. Pop was wise, he never said a word in reprimand. He knew Ben had to kill his own snakes.

Ben was at the age when he wanted to be on his own and see the world. This is natural with teenagers, boys and girls, and part of growing up. They may have all the things they need and a fine home life but there is a wish to shift from under parental rules and make it on their own--a bird leaving its nest, so to speak. Ben saved from his pay and one fine day he didn't come home but left a note saying he was leaving. He was 18 at the time and, I presume, he preferred leaving the way he did because it was the easiest without creating a stir on the home front. A week or two later we received a letter, either from Ben or Navy Headquarters in Norfolk, Virginia, that Ben was in the Navy. At the time Navy regulations were that those under 21 years of age had to obtain parental permission. I do not know whether Ben misrepresented his age, as many adventuresome boys did, but Dad and Mom wrote to Navy headquarters that he was under age. That's when the britches starts to bind. Ben was let out of the service.

I recall the night he came home. It was Sunday and we had a house full of company. Dad was in the kitchen and I happened to be in the pantry, perhaps snitching a goodie, when Ben walked in the back door and said "Hello Pa." He said he wasn't feeling well and would go right to bed. I could tell Dad was a very happy pop to have his boy back. He never got out of bed again. The next day he complained of a severe headache, Tuesday the same; Wednesday the doctor was called and he was ordered to the City Hospital Contagious Ward. He had spinal meningitis, at that time considered incurable. Thursday I was on the front porch with Mom waiting for Father Peters who had gone to see Ben in the Hospital. When he came by, Mom asked him how Ben was and he said he's holding his own but one could never

130

tell what would happen. Mom later remarked that she knew Father Peters was alerting her, in a kindly way, that Ben was indeed critical.

In the meantime the City Health Department, as it was done those days, had tacked a card on the front of the house with the words "contagious--Spinal Meningitis." We were not permitted to leave the house until the sign was removed. It was a mild day and at the time Mom talked to Father Peters we had all been outside since the house was being fumigated and we could not re-enter until permission was given, which was late in the afternoon. This was the Thursday before Easter. About noon on Friday (Good Friday), a messenger from the hospital came to our door, we had no phone, and told Mother to come because Ben was critical. As Mom was getting dressed I saw Dad coming through Sackett Alley. He looked very serious and I knew things were not good. Dad had been notified by phone at the shop. Dad and Mom immediately went to the hospital but Ben had passed away at 1:15 p.m. This was Good Friday, March 21, 1913.

The next day, Saturday, dressed in our Sunday best and wearing black arm bands, we went to the rear of the Contagious Ward building. We were not allowed inside but a basement window was open where we saw Ben laid out in his coffin. It was a sad, sad experience for us, especially Mom and Dad. I heard Mom and Dad cry many times at home.

Because of the contagious illness the Health Department had promised brother Al that they'd furnish the pallbearers. We presumed they would be especially dressed or prepared somehow to conform to Health rules. Came the time to remove the coffin to the horse drawn hearse none had shown up. Reluctantly, hospital help carried it up. We then thought that the city pallbearers would be waiting at the cemetery--they never showed up. That left it up to Dad, brothers, Al, Joe, and Father Joseph Schafeld, brother of our parish priest, who was officiating at the grave side. It was a cold, dreary day and it was quite a walk to the grave. The next Monday Al went to city hall to inquire why the pallbearers had not shown but got nowhere. City employees are adept at sidestepping and passing the buck.

In retrospect I believe it would have been better if Mom and Dad had let Ben stay in the Navy. However, who is to judge? At that time military service was looked on with a jaundiced eye. I've heard the thought expressed that the Army was made up of nothing but bums and horse thieves. My personal opinion is that Ben "caught" the meningitis in the short time he had been in the service; that the doctors recognized it and released him. He surely had it when he arrived home.

Funeral carriages then were horse drawn by a team of well-groomed blacks or bays. For children's funerals, the hearse was white and pulled by a white team of horses. The carriages were shiny black with a door on each side beneath which was a small iron step to assist in entering. The inside was upholstered in black and the window curtains were black. There were two seats facing each other, each equipped with a blanket for comfort in winter. On the floor was metal container on which to warm your feet. I do not know what the container held but suspected it must have been hot water since hot coals would not have been feasible. To one, like myself, who was accustomed to ride in a wagon or buggy, this was luxury.

The carriage driver sat in the open and wore a black frock coat and high silk hat. Some had a small bright feather on the left side of the hat band. The whip in the socket was black. The carriages lined up in front of the church and the drivers remained in their seats or in close proximity until the service was over. On a cold winter day with the snow blowing it was difficult for the drivers to keep warm, the usual means of cover for them being a buffalo robe. However, at St. Michael's church they were a bit in luck since on the Clark Avenue side of the church, on the opposite side of the street, were at least two saloons, one of which was owned by Mr. Rohr whose children went to our school. Opposite the church on the Scranton Road side was another saloon and one block south at the corner of Rowley Avenue was another. The church was half-circled by saloons, you see. So, when inclement weather struck they had two choices, crawl under the buffalo robe or go to a warm saloon and "heist" a few, which some of them did.

The saloon at the corner of Rowley brings back the time when a few of us club members were playing ball on Scranton in front of the school when one of us batted the ball into the upper-story window of the braw-haus. The owner came out and we, having been raised as gentlemen, told him to have it repaired. He did and we collected enough money from amongst us to pay for it.

Saturday night was the time for the Salvation Army workers to make their appearance. It was usually in front of a busy saloon or in the market district. Twenty-fifth Street was crowded with shoppers on a Saturday, therefore, about six to eight workers gathered in a circle with their musical instruments and played religious hymns. One of them I remember was "Onward Christian Soldiers." It had good swing and rhythm. After playing a piece or so, one of the workers would give a short talk on being saved and another would pass around a tambourine collecting whatever coins they could. These are good, dedicated people. I admire them very much. Their reputation for kindness and good work among our boys at the front during World War I is well known. I've heard many veterans praise them for giving them food and cigarettes as a gift while other organizations charged them. During World War II, I became acquainted with a Captain Burpee McIntyre of the Salvation Army. He was a colored man who headed the organization in the colored neighborhood. He was a very fine person and I found him to be very helpful in dealing with the colored while I was assigned as Controller of Civil Defense Area No. 7 during the war.

133

The Salvation Army workers were not the only ones who preached on corners. The Public Square was a favorite place for the Jack Leg ministers. The term Jack Leg, Store Front, or Board Axe ministers was used among the colored. These were, sometimes, self-appointed, unanointed ministers who, one day, saw the Light and heard the Call to save souls and convert humankind. I don't know much about these ministers but I've heard them expound. Both colored and white. Some were downright spell binders and could talk fire into hell.

On the northwest corner of Public Square is a sandstone block which had been there many years. It was there when I was a child and it was still there when I retired from the Police Department in 1963. I'm sure it will be there for many more years. The block is about three foot high and the top reached by one or two sand stone steps. It had been the policy of the city over the years to allow anyone to speak from the block, on any subject, as long as there was no foul language used. Many ministers and so-called ministers used the block for preaching. If it could speak it would have interesting things to tell of the bygone politicians, preachers, Communists, anarchists, I.W.W.'s, you name it, who spoke from it.

On May 1, 1919, (May Day), the Bolsheviks, (they weren't called Soviets then) used the block for a speaking platform and really took a lathering from our returned veterans. Anyone wearing red, especially a red necktie, was chased and beat up by the enthusiastic veterans. The hospital emergency rooms were filled. I was working for the Lincoln Bonding Company, a subsidiary of the Lincoln Electric Company, when one of the drivers came in and said "They've got them stacked up like cord wood at the emergency room." It was an exaggeration, of course. However, the slogan for the day was "Down with Bolsheviks--Up with Old Glory!" The Reds never used it again to my knowledge. I read in the paper that evening that the officer in charge of the army tank on exhibition downtown had asked permission to ram his tank through the Red headquarters located

134

somewhere downtown. Of course, he didn't receive it.

Many Cleveland politicians and mayors made good use of the block during their election campaigns. Many started their political career there. It was a training place for speaking to crowds. The crowds, many times, had hecklers and this, too, was good experience for the ambitious young would-be politician. One man told me that when he went to college he'd mount the steps and spout off on any subject just to get speaker training before crowds. Sometimes there were large crowds and sometimes none. I well recall as beat sergeant I'd receive complaints from citizens for someone on the block speaking against the government. When questioned whether the man was using foul or indecent language the answer would always be "No." I'd explain the reason why people were permitted to talk and they'd leave satisfied. I think it's a good policy, lets off steam and does no harm. Citizens usually looked at the speakers with amusement and considered it a sideshow.

When I was a child there was no television and no radio so we depended on the newspapers for the latest news. In fact, it wasn't until I was 21 that I heard a radio. Dad and Mom had the German language Waechter und Anzeiger delivered each evening and either Brother Al or Joe brought home the Cleveland Press or Cleveland News. The News had the first sheet printed on green paper and the Press on pink paper. Newspaper boys were at the main street car crossing corners and the price per paper was 1¢. There was a continuous call of Extra, Extra, Ree-dall abaah dit." Some were quite inventive. A startler I heard was "Wuxtree, Wuxtree, Lake Erie's on Fiah." Then, in the morning, the newspaper peddlers downtown were men, or older boys. Some of the men had newspaper stands and regular customers. Their call for the Cleveland Plain Dealer or the Cleveland Leader would be delivered in a sing-song fashion--"Plain Deelah--Leedah, Plain Deelah Leedah." Corner newsboys had to be aggressive and, sometimes, had to fight to hold their particular corner against claim jumpers. There was no written contract holding a certain corner but a matter of who could hold it. The passive type was sunk. More than once have I seen newsboys settling their dispute with fists without benefit of the Marquis of Queensbury Rules.

Newspaper Extras were plentiful in summer when boys were on vacation. Usually it was just a scare headline with not much body to the article. I recall many of them and to name several: Jack Johnson's fight when he won the Wold's Championship, the "Japan Declares War" extra during World War I, the Titanic sinking, ""Pancho Villa invades the United States" and more too numerous to mention, especially during the war years.

I recall it was in summer, perhaps April, of the year 1912 when the extras came out about the sinking of the ship Titanic. There were large headlines in the papers for days describing the sinking in detail. It was a new ship and on its maiden voyage to the U.S. when it struck an iceberg with the resulting loss of many lives, among them were many prominent people. The ship was supposed to have been unsinkable and the newspaper artists gave full reign to their imaginations and drew sketches of the sinking with people dropping from spilled lifeboats. There was a scarcity of pictures since there were very few taken. Recently I saw on television a picture or two which were taken on shipboard at the time of the sinking. It was a disaster but there is no use recounting since the details can be looked up in any library. Perhaps one of the reasons I remember it so well is that the stories told how the ship's musicians band played "Nearer my God to Thee" while the ship sank beneath the waves. Also because of the piano sheet music published afterward about the sinking of the Great Titanic, or some such. Lucy played it on our upright piano and we all sang it. I can still remember part of the verse and tune. It was a mournful dirge.

Chapter 12

*P*ancho Villa was quite a Mexican revolutionary character. I followed his activities in the newspapers quite avidly. I was coming up towards my teens during his activities. The fact that he was portrayed as a bandit put him, in my mind, in the adventurer and daring-do class, perhaps with the Jesse James boys. Actually, Pancho was born a peon and a product of the times in Mexico. History shows his real name to have been Doroteo Arango. I don't know how he came by the name of Francisco (Pancho) Villa--perhaps he chose it himself or it may have been one of his aliases. However, Pancho is the Spanish nickname for Francisco. He was in his thirties when he was engaged in his revolutionary activities.

I recall the name of Mexico's President Porfirio Diaz and revolutionary Madero being linked with Pancho Villa. There were revolutions plus revolutions going on in Mexico then and Pancho was part of them. There was a Carranza revolution also along about 1914 and good old Pancho was in it too. The papers were full of Pancho, especially when he raided Columbus, New Mexico, in 1916. That's when Black Jack Pershing, later General of the Armies in World War I, led an expedition into Mexico to capture him. It was like the goose trying to outwit the fox. He never caught up with Pancho. You see, Pancho knew his territory and the natives were in his corner, having no general use for Gringos. The United States got into some verbal hash with the Mexican government about invading Mexican territory and the whole deal was dropped. Mexico's President Obregon, after whom a street is named in Nogales, Mexico, gave Pancho Villa a ranch and he behaved himself from then on. However, a few years later he was assassinated. I recall the picture in the newspapers of his body being brought in. He was about 46 at the time of his death--not a long life. In Nogales, Sonora, Mexico, across from Nogales, Arizona, is a cave in a hillside, now a restaurant called "The Cavern," where Pancho Villa stabled his horses while active in the revolution. The last time Leona and I ate there was with our son, Martin and his Jane.

About 1965 Lee Carlyle was a neighbor of ours in Tucson. He was on the sundown side of 70 and he'd tell us stories of life along the border when he was a child. His mother and dad had brought him to Arizona Territory in a stagecoach while a babe in arms. They settled in a small border town called Naco, Arizona. It was referred to as Naco-Naco because it was across from Naco, Sonora, Mexico. The town is situated a few miles west of Douglas, Arizona and Agua Prieta, Mexico. He told of there being no love lost between the Mexican rurales and the Americans. He'd watch the rurales take pot shots at buildings on the American side of the line until one time a detachment of U.S. Cavalry cleaned their plow. The cavalry was assigned to patrol our side and when sniping started, the officer ordered his men to dismount, pick a man and shoot, which they did. Several snipers bit the dust and that was the end of the sniping. While I'm off the track and still in Naco, I might as well tell you of another incident he related which he witnessed in Naco. It was a colored cowboy, he'd been celebrating something, was well-boozed up on tiger spit and shooting up the store fronts. The town marshall, who had no use for drunken cowboys and colored in particular, walked up to him and shot him in the head--exit cowboy--up with law and order.

I've wandered in my thoughts so, if you will, let's get back on Scranton Road. Those days it was against the city ordinance to keep a saloon open on Sunday. Saloons were cleaned up and closed at

138

midnight on weekdays, but on Sunday there were some you could get into through the back door. Duffy's was run respectably and I never heard of anyone complaining about its activities. Occasionally on a hot summer day Dad would like to have a glass of good lager with his supper and I'd be sent to Duffy's with a quart can. "Rushing the Can" is what it was called. Children were not allowed in saloons and I'd rap at the side door and tell the bartender to fill it up. The price was 10¢ for a full can--5¢ for half. The barkeeper would go inside with the can while I stood outside. He'd return with the beer and one or two pretzels for me.

Very seldom in years since have I tasted any quite as good. Perhaps my taste buds were keener. If the saloon keeper was willing, and he usually accommodated kids, you could buy a nickel's worth. This would be a dozen or more wrapped in newspaper, depending on the owner's generosity. When Dad had beer at home I'd be allowed a small glass at supper. My ration was cut off one day when he noticed I enjoyed it and asked for a second glass. Guess he didn't want me to become a drunk.

It was a man's world then. Women could not vote and were not allowed in saloons. For a woman who liked her lager or, perhaps, a short snort, there was a door on the side with a sign "Family Entrance" or "Ladies Grille" which led to a room in back of the saloon. It was furnished with tables and chairs and kids were allowed with their mothers. If the woman ordered a beer she'd usually order a soda pop for the kids.

Along about 1912 and 1913 we had Perry's Centennial celebration in Cleveland. I'm not sure of the year but it was in commemoration of Perry's victory over the British fleet on Lake Erie 100 years before. One of the Wright brothers was to give an airplane flight demonstration on the lake front as one of the attractions. Dad took

139

me along one afternoon and we sat on wooden stands erected for whoever wanted to watch. It was a rather chilly day and the wind was blowing from Lake Erie. The flying machine was wheeled out from under cover and headed into the wind. I recall a man sitting on the machine exposed to the wind and weather, no sides, no roof, nothing. I forgot how the machine was started but it took off over the lake, made a circle and returned. The word was that it was too windy for a demonstration. In cogitating about the year of the celebration, somehow the year 1909 seems to creep into my memory. We'll let it ride as is. I saw another one with Mom and Lucy at Euclid Beach park. It was a warm, sunny day and the flying machine took off from the beach and over the lake. The flight was a little longer this time. I suppose they demonstrated over the lake for fear of accident over land. Apparently it was okay to drown, but not to be killed on land.

Perry's Centennial celebration was the first of its kind I had ever seen. The carnival stands, sideshows, and the rest were set up along Erie Street (now E. 9 th). With the music, the barkers at side shows, the crowds, the gasoline torches, hot dog and popcorn, it was quite exciting. Pop was as interested as I was and took me into several side shows. The one which stands out in my memory is the one which had a large poster depicting a ferocious alligator, jaws agape, long fangs showing and slavering. The artist must have painted it from a nightmare. From the sidewalk we could see a large soup bone pulled up and down by a rope, accompanied by a roar. In order to see it one had to pay admission price of 10¢, climb a wooden stair and stand at a railing overlooking this vicious monster. Pop decided to go for it, he paid 10¢ and 5¢ for me and together we climbed the stairs. There were people coming down with smiles on their faces and Dad asked one what it was about and he just laughed and said "Go ahead. You'll see." When we got on the platform and looked down there was a small alligator about three foot long in a box and next to the box was a young man pulling a rope through a hole in another box making the roar. On the platform was a man pulling the big shank bone up and down on a rope in time with the roars but the alligator never moved. It must have been stuffed. I was a disappointed boy but Dad had his laugh. The exhibition did justice to Barnum.

When the circus came to town they'd pitch their tents on vacant land on Scranton near Wiley Avenue, and I presume the reason for the location was because of railroad facilities. It was very interesting to watch the tent erected by elephant and manpower. I'd wander around and take in the activities, one of which was watching stakes being driven into the ground. The stakes were for ropes holding up the tent. Circling a stake would be the roustabout, each one having a large wooden mallet with which the stake was struck in turn. It was done with such a rhythm that it seemed to be moving straight into the ground of its own volition.

I saw almost all the circuses which came to town because Dad and Al received passes from the circus press agent for allowing him to put circus posters in the shop windows well in advance of the circus date. Two of the largest circus companies were the Ringling Brothers and the Barnum and Bailey which, I believe later combined. However, there were smaller circuses in operation also. On the morning of the first day of the circus there always was a parade down a main street in the area. With the elephants, bareback riders, clowns, and calliope tooting, this was great stuff for us kids.

Buffalo Bill Cody (Wm. F. Cody) had his Wild West Show too. To rehash what is history, Buffalo Bill was born in Iowa, earned his name killing buffalo for food for railroad hands when the Union Pacific was being constructed through Indian Territory. Besides killing buffalo he spent some time with the Indians. Buffalo numbered in the millions on the plains and since his job was shooting buffalo he became known as Buffalo Bill which was fortunate for him. A writer from the east became acquainted with him, glamorized his name in fiction about his supposed exploits, true or mostly imagined, in the west that never was. The East ate up all the stories of "Way out thar in the West" and he became famous. I have read an article or two which quoted other frontiersmen at the time as referring to him as a fake, although he did serve as a Union scout during the Civil War and participated in Indian raids as many other scouts did. I also read that Yellow Hand, the Indian he killed in a knife fight at a river crossing, was a consumptive Indian. In ruminating about this I'm inclined to believe that Buffalo Bill, with all his handshaking, was mainly a fake, endowed with business sense and showmanship. This is perhaps putting it a bit strong but in looking back with a jaundiced eye, my boyhood awe and admiration of Buffalo Bill is dimmed. He had an impressive figure, as I well know from personal observation and was said to be a two-fisted drinker. He had, what is now called, charisma.

I'll cut out some of the telling about Buffalo Bill and go on to his show. He hired a few cowboys and Indians, bought a few buffalo and a tent and with a few rehearsals he was in business. As I remember, he was a man well over 6 foot tall (in his hat, anyway), had white, shoulder-length hair, a white moustache and goatee, and dressed in a fringed jacket and trousers. Boots and a white sombrero completed the picture. It was rumored that the Indians he had with him were from Custer's Last Stand at the Battle of the Little Big Horn and that Sitting Bull was among them. Recently I had the bright idea to write to the Cleveland Plain Dealer and to the Cleveland Public Library Reference Department asking them to check their records regarding this and the date of Perry's Centennial celebration. The newspapers

142

kindly referred me to the Reference Department of the library and Reference said researching this would cost $25 per hour. I said to hell with it.

It was either a Friday or Saturday evening that Dad took me to Buffalo Bill's Wild West Show. The passes Dad had were good for general admission which meant one had to sit on wooden tiers with your knees in the back of the person in front of you. The seats were long planks and not made with comfort in mind but were for those with general admission tickets and those with passes. The majority of the seats were reserved. This was a bit of a slick operation by the circus management since one must first pay general admission to get into the tent and once inside, one had to pay an additional price for a reserved seat. To some the show was not exactly inexpensive.

I can't apply the word "tent" to the enclosure where the show was held since it implies a roof overhead. Due to the shooting acts it had no top and the sky was visible. The show started with the fanfare of trumpets and performers circling the arena; then came the cowboys, Indians, and others in western gear, yowling and yipping and shooting into the air, chasing a small herd of buffalo. I'm sure the fired shots were blanks. The horses were running all out as were the buffalo. Then came an old time authentic stagecoach with passengers shooting out of the windows at the pursuing Indians simulating an attack. The arena was circled once or twice and the dust was heavy. With all the yowling, yipping, shooting, and drum of hoofs it was exciting. I don't recall Buffalo Bill in the action--he was the star of the show, you see--the piece de resistance. He didn't come out until the appropriate moment.

After the whoop-de-doo was over and the Indians, stage coach, etc. had left for wherever Indians and stagecoaches go during a show, there was a moment or two of no action. Then the band started up with a lively tune and, suddenly, Buffalo Bill dashed into the arena on his white horse. He cut quite a figure, I can tell you. I can still see him dressed in his western gear, waving his hat, white hair streaming and riding his horse as though he was part of it. He circled the arena at a gallop a couple of times, stopping occasionally to wave his hat at the audience. He then exhibited his ability with a rifle by firing at clay pigeons tossed to him by an attendant and hit them all but one. I don't recall him being very much in evidence after that since I was absorbed in the rest of the action in the show.

Not far to the north of Tucson is a town called Oracle. Buffalo Bill visited there one time and predicted it would be a large metropolis some day. Oracle is still a small town, bypassed by a concrete highway and, given time, will be absorbed by Tucson. As lives go, Buffalo Bill didn't live to be very old. He passed away at the age of 72.

Besides Buffalo Bill, there were other stories of famous persons or notorious bad men. I was familiar with stories of the Jesse James bank robbers, not only through occasional reference made to them by older persons who had heard tales from their parents but through the paperback books I read on the sly brought home by brother Ben. Mom frowned on this type of reading--it was a no-no. Jesse James and his brother Frank and their gang could not have committed all the things the wild stories credited them with although one, or both of the James boys, rode with Quantril.

One night Dad took me to a circus at the same location. We did many things together and I guess he enjoyed having me along. On this particular summer night the circus was let out about an hour early. We thought it was a short show and I was a bit disappointed. When we reached outside we could see the reason. The sky was red towards the north with flames and sparks shooting into the air in the

144

distance. It was the great lumber yard fire the like of which hadn't been seen before in Cleveland. The reason the show had been let out early was apparent, the burning embers floating in the air could set the tent on fire. At that time there were several lumber companies around the river and stacks of lumber were stored under bridges and a wide surrounding area. No doubt it was permissible and it proved costly.

Horse Drawn Fire Engine
Courtesy of John and Anna Kinnenun

Dad and I went to the fire. Pop was in the excitement too and followed the crowd. We climbed a hill, we climbed a fence, Dad helped me over. The top of the hill overlooked a valley of fire. The spot where we were must have been about where Abbey Avenue meets W. 14th Street. And where the W. 14th Street viaduct crossed the river towards town. It was a swing bridge; every time a ship passed up or down the river the bridge tender operated the machinery which moved the section crossing the river to a position parallel with the river, allowing ships to pass on either side. Prior to this maneuver the gates to the bridge were closed to traffic. The fire was tremendous. All the lumber stacked under the bridge and around buildings was ablaze. Soon the bridge started to burn. It was constructed of iron girders and the pavement and sidewalks were of wood. Since the pavement's first layer was of heavy planks topped by creosote or tar-soaked wood blocks, it didn't take long for the burning lumber under the bridge to set it on fire. We could see the flames flickering between the blocks when along came a fire apparatus. Many firehouses had converted from horse-drawn to motorized equipment by this time, which this particular apparatus was. Without hesitation they barreled across and made it. That particular section burned and collapsed amid a tangle of twisted girders. The bridge was closed for a long time before it was repaired and traffic flowed again. However, the next bridge was so constructed that it remained stationery and ships could go unhindered. The wind was just right to keep the fire spreading and a tremendous amount of damage was done that night. The story was that some wayfarer had started a small fire, perhaps to warm up coffee, and from there it had spread. It was getting late so Dad and I walked home. I would have liked to have stayed there all night.

When I was a boy, the horse-drawn fire engines with a span of three horses pulling the smoke belching engine at a gallop, the team pulling the hook and ladder and the horse with the two-wheel hose cart galloping behind was something to see. At W. 25th and Clark

Avenue was No. 5 Engine Company where I've watched the horses hooked up when the bell sounded. They'd dash out of their stalls, get in position in front of the engine and under the harness suspended by ropes and pulleys and when the harness was dropped on their backs and hooked up they'd take off at a run. Before they had sirens on the station house a warning bell was rung alerting traffic and pedestrians to get out of the way.

I was envious of my classmate Joe Uhelski. He had a job after school and on Saturday helping a farrier in his horseshoing shop on W. 25th south of Trowbridge. His job was to pump the bellows to keep the coals hot, chase the flies from the horse while the farrier was shoeing, clean the manure off the floor, and make himself generally useful. It was a good place to learn and to enlarge one's vocabulary of caustic swear words from teamsters who were experts in the field. Then, too, one soon learned the origin of life in clinical detail. The farrier or horseshoer as we called him, was always muscular, slightly stooped. Usually endowed with a strong voice and a choice of words not generally heard in church. He wore a divided leather apron which facilitated the shoeing when he put the hoof on his leather covered thigh to fit the red-hot horse shoe to the hoof before cooling it and nailing it on. I always liked the acrid smell of burnt hoof.

Some horses were passive but many were very nervous during the shoeing. There usually was an intermittent "Whoa, whoa, you son-of-a-bitch" by the farrier. The American language would be dull without the salty phrase "son-of-a-bitch." Joe chased the flies with a switch resembling a horse's tail with a wood handle and was also the recipient of a few cuss words. Farriers were not only good with horses but understood the treatment of various ailments. I watched a horse doctor (veterinarian to you) at Joe's place of employment one time. The horse must have needed some dental work. There were the veterinarian and his assistant. A leather thong attached to a wood handle was slipped over the horse's upper lip and tightened. Another one over its lower jaw. They were then pulled, one upward and one downward, causing the horse to open his mouth wide. The horse doctor then proceeded with his dental work, knocking out several teeth with a club. Perhaps he had been unsuccessful in trying an extraction by more conventional means but this is what I saw him do.

I recall one of Dad's horses had a problem with the two front hooves. The horseshoer suggested that Dad get a box of wet clay and let the horse stand in it for a few days. Dad made a wooden tray about three foot square, filled it with soft clay and let the horse stand in it. I don't know what the ailment was and doubt that the clay helped because the horse would not keep his feet in the box. After our first horse, Old Dick, every horse Dad bought was renamed Dick. Dad was good with animals but horse trading was out of his line. Dad had a few horses sold to him which he should not have bought. I was with him once when he was looking over a horse at a livery stable on Lorain. A bystander said to Dad, "That horse is alright except that he's got the lifts." Dad asked him what he meant by the "lifts." The bystander answered, "He lifts up his tail when he poops." Haw-haw-haw.

The two horses he got hooked with were the saddle horse which looked like an overgrown goat in the shafts and had no business pulling a wagon and the other one was a hard-working horse which never slacked off in pulling. I liked this horse but he had one trouble, every time he started to pull, he'd stumble. Mr. Ball, the man who teamed for the Pittsburgh Plate Glass, saw this one evening and told Dad the horse had a certain ailment, I forgot what it was, and advised him to get rid of it. Pop didn't have to because in the morning he found him dead in the barn. The price of a good horse then, for the type of work required by Dad, was between $125 and $200. Draft horses were more.

I enjoyed watching beer deliveries. The breweries had excellent draft horses hauling their wagons loaded high with kegs and barrels

148

of beer. They had to be good because of the weight to be pulled. Some wagons carried more kegs than others and required a span of

Horse Drawn Beer Delivery Wagon
Courtesy of Western Reserve Historical Society

three, and sometimes four. The delivery man had to know how to load and unload. This required quite a bit of skill and experience. The wagons were especially built so that the kegs lay in tiers with one of the keg ends to the street side to facilitate unloading. First he'd place a thick rope mat on the sidewalk at about the place he'd land the keg. The kegs were of different sizes from a half keg to a full barrel. A keg or a full barrel of beer wasn't exactly lightweight, you know. The delivery man usually wore a leather apron and when the keg was maneuvered into position, he'd slide it off the wagon and onto the rope mat. After that, it was a simple matter to roll it to the chute at the basement window and slide it down. Then, the empties had to be taken out and loaded onto the wagon. The job took muscle.

Since saloons were forbidden territory to kids, the goings-on inside were mysterious to me. I would peek under the bathing doors to have a look. There was always a cool, moist beer odor and all I could see were the legs of men lined up at the bar with one foot on a brass rail and hear a lot of man conversation. Spaced every so often at the foot rail were spittoons. The better equipped bars had a copper trough under the foot rail with running water--no spittoons necessary. Quite intriguing.

While helping Dad, he'd take me into saloons now and then, with the bartender's permission, and before having his lager at the bar he'd bring over a bottle of pop and a sandwich from the free lunch counter to me while I sat quietly at a side table. Pop never had any trouble with me , I knew what side my butter was breaded on. Lunch was free with a 5¢ glass of beer. One saloon I looked forward to stopping at with Dad was McFaddens at W. 25th and Denison, especially on Friday. Dad would pull in front and while I stayed in the wagon he'd go in and order his lager. At the free lunch counter he'd fix up a sandwich with fried fish and white bread and bring it out with a bottle of pop. The fish was deep-fried rather than pan-fired and, boy oh boy, was it ever good. I never forgot it. I prefer deep-fried to this day.

I was outside Duffy's saloon one time waiting for a horse to come along to be checked at the water trough when a man drove up in a buggy. The horse didn't need checking so he threw out the hitching iron, got out and went into Duffy's. The reason I remember this small incident is because when he opened the bat-wing doors he called out in a loud voice, "I just came from Strongsville." He was proud of his achievement and wanted everyone to know about it. Big Deal! Stongsville is about 42-50 miles from Cleveland and now can be reached in half an hour without any problem. Miles were longer by horse and buggy.

Chapter 13

Across from our home was a family by the name of Gaeth. I have previously mentioned their dog feuding with our dog Trixie. About that time there were small automobile manufacturers around the country trying to start into the auto manufacturing business without much capital and on their own initiative. Mr. Gaeth was one of these. He had his auto shop on Abbey Avenue east of W. 25th and I think it was called the Gaeth Automobile Company or Gaeth Auto Works, or some such. Every noon and evening he'd roll up in front of his house dressed in a linen duster, a large motoring cap with goggles and long leather gauntlets covering his hands. Apparently he hadn't overcome the exhaust problem since there always was a cloud of blue exhaust following him.

Mr. Gaeth was machinist and mechanic. He made the whole auto by hand with the help of one or two others. It was said that the engine, all nuts, bolts and parts were machined in his shop. I particularly recall the two-seater model. It was a shiny red with brake and gear control on the outside, alongside the driver. A shiny brass horn with rubber bulb to make it honk-honk were on the left side also. The windshield was plate glass (not shatterproof) and stood in a brass frame in an upright position. Shatterproof glass did not come into the picture until about 1925.

Mr. Gaeth was a respected man in the neighborhood and honest. The Gaeth auto had a good reputation for sturdiness and reliability and today would be prized as an antique. Gaeth finally had to give up because of competition. As mentioned previously, Ford and his Tin Lizzie were coming into the forefront, the Overland Company too--later the Willy's Overland. I do not know who absorbed it but for a time it was going strong. The name is still around. Boys could identify most makes coming down the road since body structure remained the same for each company several years in a row. The Overland auto had its name painted in small letters in a diagonal position in a corner on each side of the hood. Our neighbor Stroemple, the man who shot Mr. Ball in the back, owned an Overland. On a Sunday morning they'd start out on a picnic and on returning in the evening I'd hear the 16 year old daughter tell a neighbor that they had driven 45 miles that day and had five miles of bad road.

Mr. Laschinger, who learned his trade in Germany, was our organist and choir director at church. As a side line he taught piano and violin at home. The organ in the choir loft was pumped by hand and the boys in the fifth or sixth grade were picked for the job when the organ was required for High Mass or on special occasions. I was among the chosen pumpers. Over the pump handle was a gauge showing the level of air. It was a small weight which could be seen through a hole about the size of a dime. The hole was in a wood strip covering the channel through which the weight traveled. When one saw the weight through the hole there was enough air. If the weight passed the hole, downward, we'd better start pumping. There wasn't any time to horse around or let your mind wander since Mr. Laschinger would soon be yelling at you. It was quite a job for two boys to keep the wind up when he'd play "Grosser Gott wier loben dich..." (Holy God We Praise Thy Name) with a crescendo of sound. When the organ started to die out in a diminishing wail Herr Laschinger would yell, "Poompt-dah, poompt-dah, poompt-dah." It has been said that Laschinger wasn't averse to descending from his organ seat and kick the pumper in the pants.

Herman Fazer was the janitor for the school and church. As time goes by, names for jobs change through usage. Under the old title of janitor, Herman would now be referred to at least as custodian. To go one step further in giving Herman a promotion, the fact that he 1) fired the coal burning steam boilers, 2) watched the various gauges to keep the pressure up--or down, 3) gave at the good padre Schaffeld the nod when coal was running low, 4) the need for more glass for

St. Michael's Church--Courtesy of
Western Reserve Historical Society, Cleveland, OH

broken windows, 5) cleaned and mopped the school and church floors plus ringing the church bells, would now earn him the title of building superintendent or, perhaps, building engineer. Take your pick, the pay is the same. All in all, Herman Fazer was a good, honest and faithful worker. We had a lot of respect for him and I don't recall any of the boys ever giving him trouble. We always called him Mr. Fazer. A few of us boys who had enough heft would assist him in ringing the church bells during Sunday afternoon and evening devotions and on Wednesday and Friday evening during Lent. The time for ringing was during Benediction.

To reach the room where the bell ropes hung from the belfry we had to mount an open-sided steel stairs from the rear of the choir loft. This was a trifle scary. While the stairs had a low iron railing the distance to the vestibule floor was nothing to be sneezed at, should one be unfortunate enough to fall.

The big bell had two ropes, each one manned by one of us. Then there were about four or five other ropes controlling smaller bells. A door led from this room to a walkway over the ceiling of the church. In the arches of the church were small windows through which we could see the congregation far below. It was the job of one of us to watch when Benediction was given. At the proper moment, Mr. Frazer would give us the nod and we'd all pull the ropes and see who could ring the most. I enjoyed the largest bell, since, when we had it going good on its own momentum, one of us would grab the rope as high as we could when it was on the down pull side, hang on and let the bell carry us up in the air. When one landed back on his feet the other would go up. Lots of fun and noise. For this bit of service Herman gave us nary a penny, nor did we expect any. However, Herman would have been hard pressed to ring the bells by himself.

Every year one or two medicine shows appeared in the neighborhood. I particularly recall one which would locate in an empty lot on the northwest corner of Meyer Avenue and W. 25th. It had a portable stage, backdrop, gasoline lanterns, a tent for living quarters and a truck to haul the equipment. There were no seats for the audience, standing in the grass only. It was run by a slender middle-aged man and his buxom wife. He had a helper who helped

154

in selling and, with a generous stretch of the imagination, could be referred to as the actor. The merchandise consisted of painkillers, shampoos, snake oil (good for anything) and other nonsense in that line. To draw a crowd he'd have a different gimmick every night. One time it would be an act with stale jokes, another a beauty contest among the girls, then a minstrel show.

When selling his shampoo bar of soap he'd have one of the boys in the audience come up on the stage, sit in a chair and have his hair shampooed. This soap was something. I never did see a bar of soap yield so much white lather. Surprising, too, that the lather remained snow white considering that a boy would collect his share of dust in his hair during a normal day's activity in summer. I'm convinced it was a set-up. The showman was quite an expounder. His tongue was going all the time and, in time, could qualify for a place under glass in the Smithsonian. He bottled medicine for almost any aliment and corns could be cured without removing the shoe. His wife helped him nightly. She was well-stacked, especially in the upper three-quarter section and wore long, white dresses. Her forte was snakes--big ones. She had quite an act. The snakes were kept in a box and she'd refer to then as "Peizenuss R-r-r-r-reptiles." "I will now take these peizenuss R-r-r-r-reptiles and put them around my neck. One bite and I will be peizened." I believe them to have been big bull snakes, not poisonous. She'd drape them around her neck and torso and walk up and down in front of the standing audience while the snakes twined around her arms and shoulders much to the horror of the womenfolk. The master of ceremonies was quite a showman and did quite a business. The show remained at the location until the customers thinned, then he'd pack up and leave for another neighborhood.

On the shore of the Cuyahoga River, at the foot of St. Clair were boat docks. One for the D&C (Detroit & Cleveland) steamship line on which I took many trips with friends during my teens, and the other for the B&C (Buffalo & Cleveland) line. Mom took me along to visit Aunt Mary and Cousin Irma in Rochester via the B & C line, Lucy having accompanied Aunt Mary and Cousin Irma back to Rochester previously. The trip was at night, the ship shoving off the dock about 8:00 p.m. and arriving in Buffalo about 6:00 a.m. I enjoyed these trips very much. The interior of the ship was plush, virtually. The main salon was equipped with red plush upholstered cars and lounges. At each end of the salon was a red carpeted stairway leading to a railed gallery also carpeted in red, from which one entered individual staterooms. I enjoyed running around the gallery and looking over the mahogany railing to see Mom below. We didn't reserve a stateroom since it was an extra expense and the night was soon over. It would have been an extravagance anyway since I would have been up all night, prowling around and watching the ship's engine work from a lower deck vantage point. After debarking in Buffalo, Mom would hire a horse-drawn cab to take us to the railway station for a train to Rochester.

This brings to mind the steamer, Eastland, which had excursion rides to a few miles off shore in Lake Erie every evening in summer. It was mostly for young folk who danced to the ship's music, returning about 11:00. If the wind was right we could hear the music at home. The Eastland later operated out of Chicago on excursion trips. One day the crowd lining the rail at take-off time made the ship top-heavy and it turned on its side in the Chicago river, resulting in the loss of many lives.

By the time I reached the eighth grade the auto had replaced the horse almost entirely, although they were still around into the twenties. Fringe-topped surreys were relegated to storage or sold for junk and the livery stables had just about disappeared. The White Automobile company manufactured the White Touring car and the White Truck; Winton had a long-hooded eight cylinder touring car; Ford with his Tin Lizzie, Overland, Stanley Steamer and others. So now we were in the mechanized and motorized age.

156

We will now discuss long pants and get back to Commercial High later. Somewhere about the time I entered the first year of Commercial, I graduated to long pants. Prior to that we all wore what was called, bloomers which buttoned below the knee. With bloomers it was necessary to wear long black cotton stockings held up with an elastic garter stretched around the lower thigh above the knee. With long pants went socks instead of stockings. Much easier all around and more mannish. Yep! With your first pair of long pants you felt more adult, albeit a little uneasy when among real adults. One of the honors which went with long pants was that once in a while a small fry would call you Mister. Great day in the morning! What an important feeling. Also, some of the long pants occupants started to smoke. Cigarettes, even.

My first suit with long pants was purchased at Richman Bros., Ontario and Prospect Avenue. Mom helped me pick it out inasmuch as she was paying for it. It was a blue serge suit, one pair of pants with vest. Believe it or not, the price was right--$10. All Richman Bros. suits were $10. And made in Cleveland. It was a good company. I wore the suit for a few years until it became short in the legs and arms. It seemed it couldn't be worn out and, after a little aging, especially in the seat of the pants and back of the coat, it shined. There is nothing shinier in clothing than a well-worn blue serge suit. I learned how to press pants with this suit. I did my own pressing but sometimes one could tell a homemade press job from the professional. Fortunately, Mom had taught me to be neat and shined up so it wasn't often that the trousers looked baggy. I pressed the coat at times too but could only get to a certain point, which was the sleeves to the shoulders. Of course, suits could be cleaned and pressed for a nominal sum but a do-it-yourself job saved money. It left more spending money, too.

While we're talking about suits, I had help in picking out my second one.   I was working at Kleinman's then and brother Joe worked downtown at the Jones Optical. I preferred him to go along because I felt I was too big to have Mom along to pick it out. I wish I had. Joe was miffed. I could see. He was doing this on his lunch hour and he wanted to get it over in a hurry. We went to the Republic clothing store this time. I tried on a couple of suits and Joe let me do the choosing. What a waste of time. He should have stayed at work. I chose a gray salt-and-pepper, pinch back suit, one pair of pants. The damn thing never did fit right. Soon after I had bought it I was caught in a rain and it shrunk. Back to the blue serge for a while.

There were about nineteen of us who elected to go to St. Michael's Commercial High School after graduating from the eighth grade, the others having gone to work at one place or another.   Of the approximate 19 who entered Commercial High, 14 dropped out after the first year to go to work. I was among the five who stayed to finish. Of the class of 50 I went to grammar grades with there was only one whom I believe went on to public high school. I do not know if he finished or what became of him. That's the way it was. Young folks were expected, and wanted to, go to work and be on their own, especially where the family was large and the income limited. I had outgrown my job with brother Al and Dad in the upholstery shop, pay 25¢ a day, and only helped them when I was asked for some special purpose. I was very proud of my earnings of 25¢ a day--$1.25 a week during vacation time (5-day week) and brought it home to Mom every weekend. Mom would give me 25¢ spending money for my very own. By today's standards this may seem penurious on Mother's part. Not so! It not only taught one to respect ones' labors but to value money and be conservative. Out of the 25¢ and whatever else I could garner in running errands, I saved enough to buy Christmas and birthday presents, especially for Mom. That's one thing Mom taught us, remember the other members of the

Eighth Grade Class

family at the appropriate time. The presents were inexpensive, but the feeling was there.

In St. Michael's Commercial High we had good preliminary training in office work, shorthand, typing, bookkeeping, a few classics and, don't forget, religion. In the eighth grade we had algebra which everyone promptly forgot. We were not quite so militarized as in the grammar grades and treated more as apprentice adults. We were now in the same room with girls. Things were looking up.

As for the classics, we had a thin book titled *Julius Caesar* which we perused every day in class while the good sister who, perhaps, had just read it the night before, explained the various passages. I remember we should, by gad, "Beware the Ides of March..." I felt we had enough to beware of around us without worrying about the dates in an old Roman calendar. The *Leather Stocking Tales* by Cooper are said to be classics. I read them all. Such goody-good people. They turned me off. Somewhere in the dim distance I recall *Romeo*

159

and Juliet--"R-r-r-omeo, wherefore art thou R-r-r-omeo." Stone the crows! Actually, I believe I've absorbed a modicum of the classics, sufficient for my needs, through my avid reading over the past many years. Along this line, I'm all for education and wish I had more. Certainly, I do not subscribe to the idea that books rot brains, but among our friends and acquaintances the accepted norm was to get out and work and be self-supporting. A college education was looked on as something in the distance.

In 1914 came the rumbles of war. Archduke Francis Ferdinand of Austria and the Archduchess were assassinated in Sarajevo. There were headlines in the papers every day. One European nation after another declared war, and we had World War I. There was no radio or television so the newspapers had a field day in spreading the news--souped up. On her return from Germany in 1913, Mom told us that her brother-in-law in Kolberg had mentioned that there was a build-up for war and if it came it would be a good one. He was right.

I don't recall any particular war hysteria at the time since the action was far removed from our shores. It seems to me that sentiment was more on the side of Germany at first and the thinking was that England was looking for us to pull her chestnuts out of the fire. Came the sinking of the Lusitania by a German U-boat with the loss of American lives and the tide of sentiment changed. In 1915 the Germans began their submarine campaign, endangering all neutral shipping. They maintained that munitions were being delivered to the allies by the Lusitania at the sinking in the spring of 1915. It was a British ship of the Cunard Line. Actually, I believe that munitions were being shipped to the allies, all right, by manufacturers in this country to the detriment of the German war machine. So, who was making money and who was asking for trouble? These were thoughts being voiced at the time.

Inserted--(July 2, 1981--Today I read a few paragraphs about the sinking of the Lusitania which are enlightening. They are supposed to be facts and are contained in a book titled *A Man called Intrepid*, pages 267 and 268. The author is William Stevenson.) I do not know the truth of it and will leave it to my descendants to weasel out the facts from history books. I know that Germany did agree to respect American shipping, but another ship was sunk and they again resumed unrestricted submarine warfare. Whether the second ship was American I do not know. One of their sayings was "Spurlos Versenkt"--sunk without a trace. It was a mistake on Germany's part. The American people do not take to being pushed around.

Woodrow Wilson was President and not exactly popular in certain quarters. He was referred to as "Horse Face." He had been president of Princeton University and before the turn of the century had been admitted to the bar. Around 1910 he was elected governor of New Jersey, and in 1912 was elected to the Presidency when the Republican Party was split between William Howard Taft and Theodore Roosevelt. I heard the opinion expressed that he was an egghead and a dreamer. The word egghead was usually applied to a college professor. The Negro, Martin Luther King, said before his assassination "I had me a dream." I believe Wilson to have been a good President who had a dream, and one who did much good for the American People.

Dad and Mom's sympathies, naturally, were on the side of Germany at first, as long as it didn't involve their adopted country directly. However, when war was declared, Dad said America was his country and he stood by it. So did Mom. It was so!

Came Sunday, June 17, 1917, the day of my emancipation. With the other four male students and about ten female students I graduated from St. Michael's Commercial High. I have a properly inscribed gold plated medal to prove it. Whoever was responsible for the medal was on their toes. It was inscribed as St. Michael's Commercial Department. Up to that time we had called it high school but now it seemed we had only graduated from a Department.

161

In ruminating over this I believe the reason was that it really was not an accredited high school as such. Be that as it may, there we were, five callow youths and ten innocent virgins--I'm sure.

We were all dressed to the nines. In my blue serge suit, red wavy hair with the class colors pale blue and yellow pinned to my lapel I went to the alter of St. Michael's Church at afternoon vespers and received my diploma from Father John Schaffeld, Pastor. We were all very proud. Life was before us. The world was our oyster and we had the lion by the tail. The future was rosy.

After church we walked to Hudlett's Photography Shop on W. 25th and, with Father Schaffeld, had a group picture taken. Father Schaffeld was in the center of the front row and Ed Stein was somewhere in there too. We all held our diplomas in hand and looked as intelligent as possible. To this good day I don't know what became of the diploma and, as for the picture, I never ordered one. The only proof of my graduation I have is the gold-plated emblem with my name inscribed. Perhaps there is a record in St. Michael's archives.

Chapter 14

A couple of weeks earlier I had answered an ad for a stenographer and secretary at the S.H. Kleinman Realty Company, Garfield Bldg., E. 6th and Euclid. I presented myself in my blue serge suit, polished shoes and red wavy hair and landed the job. It was the thing those days to become a male secretary for some big corporation mogul, from there, work your way up through the company and finally become president yourself. The only thing wrong with that picture is that, everyone else was trying to work their way up until finally you're standing alone. The good sisters permitted this early work because they knew other schools would let out about the same time and there would be a scramble for jobs. For once they used their combined noodles. Actually, the ad information was a little long in the tooth. What the job amounted to was stenographic work for one of the sales managers. They glorified it a little by baiting the ad with the title secretarial. To grind it down to its proper level it was an office boy job with typing. I'll say this, I was a good, speedy typist, knew my spelling that was pounded into my head at school and didn't hedge when it came to work. At shorthand I was as good as the next one. I could also count to twenty with my shoes and stockings off. It was good training for a greenhand. There were eight sales managers, each with his group of salesmen.

I wangled a job at Kleinman's for Joe Hausman, one of the five graduates. Of the other three, two wound up at the Bauman Glass Company doing bookkeeping and office work and the other as a clerk somewhere. Of the five I always believed my choice of final employment was the most satisfying--rough but satisfying. One thing sure, you found out if you were a man or a mouse. Henry Schneider

(Bauman Glass) died in the 1918 flu epidemic. Ben Kastner (Bauman Glass) after the company ceased business held various jobs and, in middle age, joined the U.S. Post Office; Joe Hausman (Kleinman Realty) later employed elsewhere, transferred to Fort Wayne, Indiana, where he raised a fine family and has since passed away; Clarence Fastnacht, shoe salesman, since deceased. As for myself, in time, I joined the Cleveland Police Department and after 38 years experience in the seamy side of life, retired to Arizona. It was the most interesting and satisfying work but, at times, not without danger and risk. The experience was priceless.

The pay at Kleinman's was terrific. Eight bucks for a six-day week. During July and August we worked only half day on Saturday. I brought my pay envelope home to Mom every Saturday. Out of this she allowed me 25¢ a day for expense money and 25¢ over the week end for my own. My expenses during the week were 3¢ a street car ride to work and 3¢ back -- 6¢. Of the 19¢ I had left I'd go to the 5 & 10¢ store down town on Euclid and eat my lunch in their basement cafeteria--5¢ for a piece of pie and 5¢ for a cup of hot chocolate. I had a sandwich brought from home at the office. Occasionally I'd get a tip for running an errand for one of the salesmen. I learned the hard way one time to carry more money along when the property manager of Kleinman's took me along in the company's Tin Lizzie to go to one of the allotments in the country. On the return, it was lunch time and he stopped in a restaurant and I didn't have enough money to pay for a meal. I ordered bread and butter. He suspected that I wasn't exactly loaded with coin so he paid for the meal. I "learnt."

Sammy Kleinman was a smart businessman and go-getter. He was about 35 and unmarried. He had a room at the Hollenden Hotel with his regular home on the east side of town. He also owned a farm in Hudson, Ohio. The Hotel Hollenden was two blocks down the street and he stayed there some nights when he worked late. Once I was sent to the hotel with some contracts for Sammy to sign. It was about 9:00 p.m. and when I rapped at the door of his room a young, good-looking dame about 23 dressed in a gown, came to the door. I had heard he was unmarried, but assumed she was his wife. Sammy was in a rumpled pair of pajamas in the background. I was a little naive then. My boss just chuckled when I told him.

Sam had a peculiar grating voice. His private office was in front-closed door, naturally. Then came his bookkeeping and cashier office and then the large room with the sales managers and salesmen. In his private office he had his personal male secretary, in the cashier's office was a young man, Walter Kersten, as back-up secretary. Walter was a nice fellow, he jumped when Sammy Kleinman called and, besides typing, he ran personal errands for him. Sammy would call through the door--"Walter Kersten, a glass of water please." Walter would jump for the water glass. I became quite adept at imitating Sammy's grave voice. Sammy had an outside entrance to his private office so, sometimes the cashier's office wouldn't know he was there until they heard him. Once in a while I'd get out of sight near the cashier's office and call, "Walter Kersten, a glass of water please." Since Walter hadn't seen him come in he thought sure as hell it was Sammy calling him and he'd jump for the water glass. I'd come out laughing, much to his embarrassment. I noticed that the others in the bookkeeping and cashier's office jumped a little too and didn't take kindly to my joke, so for my general welfare, and before the hen laid an egg, I stopped it.

Samuel Kleinman was a shrewd operator. He'd buy a farm on the outskirts of Cleveland, send his surveyor out and mark off the streets and lots with stakes. The next move would be for the field crew to plow up the field into streets as marked by the stakes, grate it off, plow up the soil another three or four foot width about four feet from the edge of the so-called street, smooth it out and cover it with cinders. This was called the sidewalk. Next came small trees which were planted between the street and so-called sidewalk. A large billboard at the entrance proclaimed it to be, for example, Sheridan Hills or some other eye-catching name. A large tent with flags was erected on a corner lot in front of the new allotment and a full-page Sunday ad would proclaim free refreshments and a free ride to the allotment and return at no cost. Lots were sold with 10% down--no pavement, no lights, no water, no sewer, and no schools or transportation--only rosy promises in the booming future. Payments at a moderate interest rate were made to Kleinman and if it wasn't kept up the lot was taken back. Replevied is the word for this practice. People came for the free ride and free coffee and donuts--bit and bought. I stayed at Kleinman's about a year and a half. It was an eye opener. The experience was stored in my memory and has been useful since in examining golden promises. I heard Sammy committed suicide during the Great Depression.

This brings to mind the Florida Land Boom in the twenties. Some people made money and those caught at the collapse lost their shirts. I wasn't there at the time but remember all the publicity and talk. One of my friends who had been there and working in the building trade told me that prior to the boom, rooms could be had for $2 or $3 per day, which increased to $30 per day during the boom. It was an unheard of price then but now in 1979 is about average. The booms usually start with a few publicity items in the papers or by word of mouth. Certainly the real estate industry fostered it also by heralding the glories of the Sunshine State. People bought land in the morning and sold it in the afternoon at a profit. Prices spiraled. Land was bought sight unseen, some of it underwater, and the final owner holding the bag. Basically the cause was greed. And so it was.

After the declaration of war, patriotic fervor was tremendous. The American people were united as they always are in time of real

166

trouble. There were daily war headlines in every paper. The Germans were cartooned as Huns with slanted eyes and long fangs holding Belgian babies upright on bayonets. All pure hogwash. However, it did create hatred for the German, inspired a patriotic fervor to wipe out the Hun and hang the Kaiser from the sour apple tree. Hoon der Kaiser! Kaiser Wilhelm II of the House of Hohenzollern is said to have had a birth defect--a "withered" left arm. I presume "undeveloped" is the word. In seeing pictures of him in the past I noticed he had his arm in such a position that it was not noticeable. I seem to recall that the Queen of England at that time was the sister of Kaiser Wilhelm.

Any German with a business had to be satisfied with whatever business came his way and be careful of voicing the wrong opinion of the war or he'd find a rock through his plate glass window. About the only business which didn't suffer was the brewery business. They were mostly owned and operated by Germans but, you see, people liked their beer and to monkey with the beer business might shorten the supply. Colorful posters were all over the city and in streetcars for the U.S. Army, Navy, and Marines with Uncle Sam pointing "I want you." Sauerkraut was renamed Liberty Cabbage and sugar was hoarded.

There were almost daily parades downtown, usually at noon when the lunch crowd was out. When I worked at Kleinman's I watched many of them on my lunch hour. Bands blared, flags waived and the boys volunteered or were drafted for the service. Brother Al being married and having a child (Robert) was temporarily exempt; brother Joe was drafted and spent 1918 in training at a camp in Chillicothe, 32nd Company, 9th Training Battalion. I wanted to join the Navy but, being only 17, had to have parental consent, which wasn't forthcoming.

167

The drive for Liberty Bonds was on and some rationing was in effect. Mom, Dad, and I went with Joe to the Pennsylvania Railroad Station, E. 55th and Euclid Avenue the morning he left for camp. He had one furlough home, extent about five days, and it was rumored around camp that on their return they were to be shipped to France. This was in the fall and when Joe returned to camp the war was about over and he never did get there. There were many, many tears shed when the boys left for camp and many, many heartaches when a loved one was wounded or killed in action. Death notifications were telegraphed and when the Western Union messenger arrived at the door with a black arm band, one knew it was bad news.

I belonged to the Young Men's Club at St. Michael's and to a drama club. One of our members, Rudy Meicke, was drafted and spent his time in Germany. Another acquaintance was shot but recovered and there was one who left home to skip the draft and he was never heard from again; however, he had a sister and I'm sure she knew where he was. Small flags called Service Star Flags, were hung in windows. A flag consisted of a cloth about 15 by 12 inches bordered in blue with a star on a white background in the center. A blue star meant wounded in action and a gold star meant killed in action.

I watched John Philip Sousa and his band parade down Euclid. He was a short, stocky man, dressed in a white uniform and his martial music was a thing to remember. I saw France's French Blue Devils from the trenches march. And with other teenagers paraded down Euclid in the rear of Scotland's kilted soldiers from the war front whom the Germans called the Ladies from Hell. It was an exciting time and everyone was filled with patriotic fervor, especially we young people. Flags hung from all buildings and were in evidence all over the town. In one of the parades down Euclid the flag was carried horizontally, stretched from curb to curb, the edges held by volunteer women dressed in white. It was accompanied by martial music, before and behind. People were throwing money into the flag. I don't know what the hell for, but supposedly to help the boys "over there."

I was seized with sudden patriotic fervor too. With all the bands playing, cheering and flags waving, I threw in 50¢--a silver half dollar. Ye Gads! Two weeks, weekend spending money. I hope it bought a few packages of cigarettes for one of the boys. There was no radio or television then so wartime songs were sung with or without being accompanied by a piano. Dad and Mom had bought an upright piano for Lucy and, with a dim hope that I would become interested, partially for me too. I will speak of it shortly.

When we had company we'd all gather around the piano singing the patriotic songs which were going around then, such as "Over there, Over there, send the word to the boys Over there,"-- "There's a Long Long trail a-winding into the land of my dreams,"-- "It's a long way to Tipperary. It's a long way to go,"--"How you gonna keep him down on the farm after he's seen Paree,"-- "Belgian Rose"-- "I did not raise my boy to be a soldier," and many others. Lucy would be the pianist and start the song in good shape but about halfway through she'd invariably forget the left hand and play with right only. I loved to sing and so did brother Joe but, unfortunately, he couldn't hold a tune worth a damn. It came out off-key every time. However, I'd usually covered it up by bearing down with my voice box.

To get off of the war track for a minute and explain about the upright piano business, Dad and Mom invested in a piano with the hopes that Lucy would learn to play and, possibly, little Eddie. Almost every family then had a piano played by some member of the family. Lucy took lessons at first at Mr. Laschinger's but later switched to a Mrs. Lauer, widow, seeking out a living teaching piano lessons at two-bits an hour. Mrs. Lauer was a fine elderly lady living

169

upstairs in a home on Holden Avenue. I was also sent there to take up my musical career. I believe my schedule called for Tuesday after school and Lucy, Thursday afternoon. I never cared for it, you see it cut into my time. I was supposed to practice one full hour a day, after school. I usually dreaded going to Mrs. Lauer's for fear I didn't know my lessons well enough since I knew I hadn't devoted an hour a day to practicing. I finally got to the point where Mrs. Lauer let me play the "Fairy Waltz" and the "Teddy Bear Waltz," and simple pieces like that. Lucy was going along O.K., but not too happily either. Then, for a time she'd give me a percentage, 75% if I knew my lesson fairly well, 85% if it was better and 100% if I did O.K.

This worked for a while until one time when Aunt Mary was over I told Dad at the supper table, proudly, that I had received 100% for the "Teddy Bear Waltz." Cousin Irma was a good pianist and Aunt Mary knew something about piano lessons and was curious about this percentage business and asked Pop. I was always strong in the observation and reaction section and could see Dad was trying to evade a direct answer. He had a peculiar expression on his face-- unusual. He made some offhand remark and little Eddie Stein wised up that the sheep had been pulled over his eyes. Apparently Dad had gone to see Mrs. Lauer to check on my progress and they had connived and decided on the percentage business to perk up my interest. From then on I was a bit skeptical. I had trouble with the key E. I just couldn't remember it. By this time Mrs. Lauer was getting a bit impatient too. The climax came one afternoon when Mrs. Lauer perhaps was not feeling up to par--could be too many hot flashes, asked me to plink key E. I hesitated before making my final E plink and, in exasperation, she raised her voice, poked the E key several times and shouted, "E-E-E-E-E" with each poke. Then she said, "Get out of here--take your music and get out." Dogs' Bones! I wasn't all that bad. I scrammed--pronto!

Naturally I didn't tell Mom and when my next turn for the lesson came I didn't go. I wandered the alleys and byways until my hour was up and returned home. Lucy's turn came the next Thursday and when she came home she told Mom Mrs. Lauer wanted to know why I hadn't been back for my lesson. She may have been sorry for blowing her top and the loss of a two-bits an hour pupil. The cat was out of the bag. Mom asked me and I told her I hadn't gone. She didn't say a thing except that I didn't need to go again. Mom was wise. She knew there was no use forcing the issue. I never regretted not keeping with it. I doubt whether I would ever have made a halfway decent pianist since, when I matured, I had large hands and, it is conceivable, one finger would have invariably struck two keys. One thing I do remember is the key E and part of the "Fairy Waltz" and "Teddy Bear Waltz."

Now that I've disposed of the upright piano and my pianistic career, let's get back to the war zone. A common sight in the evening during the war was to see a car parked at a prominent street crossing with one or two people, male or female, exhorting the people to buy Liberty Bonds. Sergeant Blank of the Canadian Army who had been raised around the neighborhood of W. 25th and Walton Avenue had volunteered for service in the Canadian Army before our entry, and was one of the neighborhood heroes. He had been wounded and lost a leg, consequently walked with the aid of a crutch. He'd exhort the crowd too and was much in favor as a speaker. The trouble with invitations is that drinks usually go with it and, I heard, the good Sergeant Blank enjoyed his share. However, as the war progressed, his popularity declined and he faded from the picture.

The Germans were the first to have Army tanks, later copied and improved by the British and Americans. There was one U.S. Army tank on exhibition on the Public Square. In the interest of the Liberty Bond Drive it was decided to have a demonstration of the tank's

171

power, in the middle of E. 9th and Euclid intersection, during a noon lunch hour. It was high noon on a sunny day and the intersection was jammed with spectators--I among them. In the middle of the intersection was a sparkling new touring car, one of the better and more sturdy makes, which had been donated by the auto manufacturer for the purpose. Good publicity, you see. The object was to let the tank crawl over the auto and see if it could do so without flattening the auto. The tank rumbled up Euclid from the Square with the tracks clanking. The original Army tanks were diamond-shaped, allowing the metal treads to climb over or out of almost any obstruction. The tank rumbled up to the auto, climbed it and when exactly in the center--Wham!--the auto collapsed. Good demonstration.

We had coal-less Mondays. This was to aid the war effort and decrease the consumption of coal. It was tough in winter. Kleinman's had no heat so they let us off work after a half day with our coats on. I liked it! Instead of going home I'd go to the small moving picture theatre downtown and enjoy a movie. It wasn't as warm as usual but it wasn't cold either. Apparently enough heat had been retained in the theatre to keep the show going on Monday. William S. Hart was the favorite cowboy movie actor then, and I don't recall what the plot was about but the fancy title stuck in my memory all thru the years, especially since Hart was the good guy and the nemisis of the bad guys, usually rustlers, bank robbers, or the man who abducted his boss's daughter for his nefarious scheme such as blackmail and ransom. It was just recently when I was coming home from dinner with a group of friends from our condominium that one of the men, reminiscing, mentioned William S. Hart in "Blue Blazez Rawden"--bang-bang-bang. You could have knocked me over with a hoe cake. He was from Iowa.

Chapter 15

*I*n 1918 we had the worldwide influenza epidemic. I've read there were 20,000,000 deaths due to it. In this country many people died, the school and churches were closed and most people were apprehensive. It was passed on from person to person, but there really was no escaping it since the streetcars were always crowded during rush hour and there were crowds during the normal daily activity downtown. Two of my teenage friends passed away from it. Lucy had it and was a very sick girl for a time. Many business people who came in contact with the public, especially barbers, wore masks. I recall Calvary Cemetery couldn't bury the dead fast enough, and the coffins were stacked up and long trenches dug to accommodate them. I suppose I'm fortunate I wasn't a victim. I don't recall being too much concerned about it, but when one is young, one is usually too active to be worried about being sick.

The Public Square was the hub of Cleveland. All streetcar lines, except some crosstown lines, ended at the Public Square. People shopped at the big department stores. The main theaters and picture shows where one took one's date in the evening were downtown also. Most young people didn't have an auto, so transportation with your date was by streetcar. There were no large shopping areas on the outskirts of the city, so the Square was an active place with people going shopping or transferring to other car lines.

In mentioning street cars I'll go back to when I was a small child. Streetcar fares then were collected by the conductor who walked up and down the aisle collecting the fare by hand. Change was made from a change holder attached to a belt around his middle. After collecting the fare, or fares, he pulled a small rope arrangement attached to a meter in front which registered the fare, or fares, he had collected. The joke among the riders was that the conductor made more money on the side collecting fares than went into the coffers of the company. I believe it was true in many instances. The fare was 5¢ and small children were free. I recall my mother saying to me on the streetcar, "Mach dich klein." (Make yourself small.)

The new Superior-Detroit High Level Bridge with its subway was under construction, and the old Superior Viaduct with its swing bridge was still in use as the main west side traffic artery to downtown. The big beef then was that about the time office workers were going to work across the viaduct a ship would pass through, necessitating the shutting down of streetcar, and auto traffic so the center span could be swung to allow ship passage. A legitimate common excuse for being late for work, and I've used it, was "The bridge was swung." There were so many complaints about this that ships were denied passage up or down the river during rush hour. This helped the situation.

This descriptive business of downtown Cleveland may not interest our readers, but as long as I'm narrating about myself I might as well throw it in. It's part of my life. If any of my descendants are really interested in Cleveland, the Public Library downtown or the Western Reserve Historical Society is the place to go to get the straight of it.

I hung around the Public Square quite a bit, especially on half-day Saturday at Kleinman's during summer and, also, since it was my transfer point to get home. I was working, so as an adult my comings and goings were not questioned by Mom and Pop. More freedom now to be on my own and go places with my teenage friends without obtaining permission. Mom and Pop were wise, they knew I was growing up. Also, I knew they trusted me. I did usually tell Mom where I was going since I knew she'd be awake until I got home and I didn't want her to worry. If I was not to be home for supper or expected to be late for meals I'd call Mom and let her know. My coming and going didn't seem to worry Pop. He'd been around, you

174

see. He called them my "Flegel Jahren"--my fledgling years. He knew it was that time. Everything was new, life was rosy--wonderful years.

I particularly liked the activity at the southwest corner of the Square. There was no Cleveland Hotel, there was no Terminal Tower group, and the old buildings at that point dated from around the Civil War years. I recall the harness shop with its brown life-size plaster cast horse in the window; the Stein Alley leading to Champlain Street around the corner of which was a brewery; the saloon, the flea-bag hotel, the basement barber shop, the Greek candy store and, let's not forget Humphrey's Drugstore on the corner of Ontario and the Square, mostly devoted to large 10¢ ice cream dips.

Then, too, in the southwest section of the Square we had a pedestrian bridge over a goldfish pond with an old fountain. This bridge and pond had been there long before the turn of the century and was an attraction then. Now it was showing its age and during the twenties the pond was filled in and the bridge removed. When I took my examination for the Cleveland Police Department one of the questions was --"What bridge in Cleveland has the most pedestrian traffic?" It didn't take me long to figure that one out. It was the bridge on the Square.

I observed, enjoyed, and remembered. The northwest section, besides the Old Stone Church, had the Juvenile Court Building and around the corner at Frankfort and W. 3rd (old Seneca St.) was the County Jail. It's all gone now. The interurban cars had their terminal at the northwest section of the Square and I'd watch them pull in, unload the passengers and baggage, and take off with a new load. The cars were the Local, the Limited or the Express. Each one had its own colored flag in a holder at the front of the car. The name of the destination was shown by the sign on the front, such as Toledo, Detroit, Chicago; then for smaller towns were Akron, Canton, Columbus, Cincinnati, and so forth. Great distances to me. Up to that time I had never been to those places, so you can see the reason for the attraction. I'd stand at the station and observe the people getting off of the interurbans and I could make a good guess whether they were farm folk or small town folk. Sects like the Amish, wore their own particular style clothing which never changed. Later I rode in many interurban cars and enjoyed every trip. Within the city limits they traveled at a normal rate, but once the city was left behind they traveled on their own right-of-way and the motorman would open the throttle. The car would sway from side to side and with the wheels clicking over the rails and the farms and woods flashing by was very enjoyable. It was something like taking a chance on the shoot-the-shute in an amusement park--there was the chance the car might go off the track.

Gypsy caravans were still around and, every once in a while in summer they'd pull up at the southwest corner of the Square in their five or six colorful closed wagons. The wagons were their living quarters while on the road and usually had windows with curtains and a step in the rear to a closed door. The horses were well groomed and the harness flashily decorated. The men and women were usually dressed a little out of the ordinary in colorful clothes, the women especially wearing flowered long skirts. They were looked on with suspicion as sneak thieves and baby stealers, and there was always a fortune teller in the group.

About the time of the war there was agitation to prohibit the sale of liquor. There had been Temperance Societies agitating for prohibition for many years, the most powerful being the National Woman's Christian Temperance Union. I recall the advertisements in papers, on billboards and in streetcars. The theme was that without liquor there would be no more crime, jails would be empty and mothers and children would suffer no more from neglect by drunken husbands and fathers. It was the right time for this nonsense to go over. The Temperance Societies had finally come into their own.

Most of the boys were still in the Army and couldn't vote. The 18th Amendment was adopted in about January of 1919 and the Volstead Act, providing for the enforcement of prohibition, passed the same year. We had prohibition--14 of the most crime-ridden years in our history passed before its repeal. Into those years bootlegging, murders, and a great deal of corrupt law enforcement. I joined the Cleveland Police Department in the middle of it. So much for the Woman's Christian Temperance Union efforts. During that time, too, Women's Suffrage came into their own, with the passing of the 19th Amendment. Somewhere along the line I seem to remember that with our boys still being in the Army without a chance to vote and the ladies being allowed to vote for the first time, Prohibition came into being. Dates will have to be more thoroughly examined to substantiate this. However, it was the thought at the time.

The war finally came to an end, November 11, 1918. The Cleveland Press jumped the gun and had extras out on November 9 that the war was over for which they were much criticized. The jubilation and celebrations were tremendous. Everyone seemed to go downtown that night. I was there. The Square was jammed. There was much blowing of horns and singing and dancing in the street. I had taken Dad's cornet along which he had used in one of St. Michael's plays. Dad was not a cornet player but had bought it second-hand for two bucks from someone for the purpose of tootling it in a certain part of an act. I was caught in a jam at Ontario and when I pulled away the horn was bent out of shape. The streetcars couldn't move and the motorman kept clanging the bells. The saloon on the Square was packed to its batwing doors and a good time was had by all. I must have walked home that night since the cars just weren't moving. I do not recall the papers mentioning any broken windows or destruction of property.

The boys slowly started to come home from France. The early arrivals received the most recognition with parades and paper thrown

177

from office building windows. After a time those arriving did not receive this recognition because the newness had worn off. I recall one veteran telling me one time that the only glory he ever received from the whole thing was a parade down the main street of his small hometown.

With the end of war contracts and the return of our boys, work was scarce. I was working at the Lincoln Bonding Company and recall the line of young men in Army uniforms who applied for jobs. During the war I had joined the Young Men's Society at church and the Drama Club, whose director was Charlie Mueller. I was beginning to notice the girls more now, especially since I observed they were casting sheep's eyes in my direction. Casting sheep's eyes is an art known only to young women--no one teaches them, they're born with the skill. It's sort of an over and under, sideways swivel glance with a fluttering of the eyelashes and a small smile. Very fascinating to a young buck who didn't know too much about the handling of the feminine gender.

Being a member of the Young Men's Society and the Drama Club soon changed the picture. Bus rides and picnics with members of the Young Ladies Sodality, plus our popularity derived from taking part in plays of the Drama Club, bolstered our self assurance, consequently we could handle the ladies in a more suave and worldly manner without a wringing of hands, a tying of the tongue, and shuffling of feet. I was not unpopular due, perhaps, because I was always shined up and had the correct number of arms, legs, and so forth. The corners were now being rounded off.

The St. Michael's Drama Club was a group of young people picked by Charlie Mueller, who had acted in many plays in prior years at St. Michael's and knew his way around the stage. As I recall, the way he came into the picture was that the sister teaching us in the last year of Commercial had concocted a play for us to present at the auditorium that spring. I think she realized she just couldn't handle us big clods at this point and that it took a mature man with a little know how to get the show properly organized. She called on Charlie and he took over. I forget what the plot was but he had a nice personality and under his direction, the play was whipped into presentable shape. I was one of the participants and whether Father Schaffeld asked him to organize a Drama Club I do not know but there we were with a Drama Club and I was in it with a mixed group of boys, girls, and a few older persons of the parish who had been in previous plays. We had a heck of a good time.

I was working by this time and Charlie would purchase a suitable script and get the pastor's permission to practice on the stage with the idea of turning over the proceeds to the parish--which we did. The good pastor couldn't lose, it kept the boys and girls out of the alleys and brought a little cash into the coffers. We had one or two plays each year which we presented at St. Michael's. In between practice sessions we'd visit one of the member's homes, usually one of the girl participants who had a piano and we'd have a songfest, luncheon, and real good time. Not a drink was thought of. We branched out, too. We went to other parishes in the city and to outlying small towns such as Lorain, Elyria, and Ridgeville, Ohio--all on interurban cars. I was 18 and could pass for 21. Sometimes after visiting someone's home we fellows, with Charlie Mueller and a couple of the older men leading, would enter a saloon along the way home for a beer. We weren't questioned since we were with older people and, perhaps, looked of age anyway. We'd all have our beer or pop, nothing stronger, and go on our way. I enjoyed these little saloon visits because I was able to see the inside of various ones and observe the customers. The war and war work cut into our group, plus a natural drifting away to other things and the Butterflies, as the women members named the club because we flitted around so much, faded away.

179

The St. Michael's Young Men's Society was a club which one was expected to join after graduating from school. I don't know the minimum age limit, perhaps 16. Brothers Al and Joe belonged to it and you ceased being a member when you resigned or married. However, as one got older there was a natural drifting away to other organizations with older persons. We had our club rooms in the basement of the school. There were four pool tables, a candy stand, a side room equipped with easy chairs and a piano. It was a good place to go for young people instead of hanging around a corner, a pool hall or bowling alley. Here is where we had our meetings, made our plans for picnics and outings, and chose our friends to go with. It was open six nights a week and Saturday and Sunday afternoon--closed Monday.

Our club belonged to the Catholic Young Men's Association which was comprised of clubs such as ours from about ten parishes in the city. I was secretary and treasurer for our club. Almost each parish had its ball team, bowling team, pool champion and other clubs. Each had one or two elected delegates to attend the monthly meeting of the C.Y.M.A. during the year. I was fortunate to have been elected a delegate several years in succession. I learned a great deal in planning picnics, bus rides, and matches between the various teams. Once a year the C.Y.M.A. had a picnic for all the associated clubs at Cedar Point and as one of the delegates I had plenty to do.

There was a group of us who chummed around together and almost nightly met at the club rooms, played pool, sang, or played cards. I never cared to play cards and except for learning a little pinochle and a few fun games in self defense, I just wasn't interested. Shooting craps in an alley, or wherever, was another thing which never appealed to me. I was a spectator many times and wasn't holier-than-thou by any means, but always had the feeling it was a little low grade. Figure it out as you will, but that's how it was and I'm stuck with it.

Our group would go to the various parks, perhaps Euclid Beach Park, Luna Park or, over a holiday, take an overnight D & C boat trip to Detroit and cross into Windsor, Canada. Another favorite place was to drive to Conneaut Lake Park, Conneaut, Ohio and stay over a long holiday weekend and return. Frank Pfister used his Chevrolet touring car for this since the rest of us didn't have a car. Expenses were equally divided. During all this time one, two, or three of us dated girls and together we'd go to picnics, bus rides or to shows downtown. We'd take the gals to good restaurants among which were our favorites, the Mandarin and the Golden Pheasant specializing in Chinese food. I wasn't much for dancing but did dance the fox trot. We never attended the Botts Dancing Academy at W. 25th and Franklin or the Dreamland on W. 25th near Bridge Avenue. The tango was long past and the black bottom had not yet made its debut. Our favorite picnic spots with the girls would be Cascade Park, Allure, Crystal Beach on Lake Road, or the Vermillion River at Vermillion, where we'd row on the river or go to the beach. For almost a year the Hildebrandt boys and I squired three of the Schritz sisters from Olmsted Falls. The family lived on a farm, the parents liked us and we had picnics and good times. It was the years of good and happy days.

In the summer of 1919, at the Hall of Mirrors in the Palace of Versailles, the treaty was signed ending the war with Germany. One of the signers was George Clemenceau, called the Implacable Tiger of France, who had been in the Franco-Prussian war about 1870 and thoroughly hated the Germans. I have read that when the German Peace delegation came before them in the Palace he said, "The time has come when we must settle our accounts. You have asked for peace and we are ready to give you peace" and with that he threw the document toward them. The terms were very severe and history maintains it was basically the cause of World War II. One of the chief clauses of the treaty called for the formation of a League of

181

Nations. The U.S. Senate never ratified the treaty nor did the U.S. become a member of the League of Nations, so there went President Wilson's dream.

"Woody" Wilson became ill some time after his return from France. He wasn't a robust man by any means and the cares of his office didn't help. For quite some time he did not appear at the Oval Office but governed the country from his bed where he was confined. I do not recall the nature of his illness. It was talked around that the country was actually run by his wife who was at his bedside at all times and issued statements purporting to have come from the President. Political leaders became alarmed at his absence and visited the White House to see him personally to satisfy themselves he was still around. Much to their surprise they found him mentally alert and in good spirits. The ugly rumor floating around at the time was that while in France he had acquired a venereal disease. Pure hogwash!

Sometime in 1919 the saloons were to go out of business. There would be no more liquor or beer sold, the churches would be filled to overflowing and everyone would wear a halo from then on. I was on the Square the night before the closing--the beginning of prohibition. I felt this was a historic occasion, the beginning of prohibition and that I should be there. I was! It sure as hell began a new era, I'll tell you. All the saloons downtown, and I imagine wherever there was a saloon, were jammed to the doors. This was the last night to get a drink of liquor--there was to be no more. Drink Up! They did. Drunks were all over the Square, some had bought full bottles and broke the necks off on the curbing and drank it down. The police were around but could never begin to cope with the situation. Two thirds of the city must have been swizzled that night. If I had wanted a drink, I couldn't have gotten into a saloon. One fellow I recall leaning against a pole at the corner of Ontario and the Square with a jagged bottle of whiskey in his hand. He was gulping it down from the jagged edges. He must have injured himself when he broke the neck on the curbing since the blood was trickling from his elbow. There were plenty of people crowing around him to help but the last I saw of him he was sagging, and the distance to the sidewalk was getting shorter and shorter. I didn't stay around and often wondered what became of him.

The thought at the time was that if you had a bottle of liquor in your home the government had the right to confiscate it and arrest you. The saloon peekers were not quite so dumb. Long before the closing night they had bought all the liquor they could handle, trucked it to some hiding place, usually a garage or a barn in the country, and sat back and bided their time. The liquor and beer they had left after closing the bar the last night was also hauled away. So, now we were coming up into what was called the "Roaring Twenties," the flapper age, bootleggers, run runners, speakeasies, bootleg booze, bathtub gin and 3.2 beer called Near Beer.

It was in the early twenties that a few of my friends and I took a walk one summer night down Fulton Road. The area at that time was populated by Italians. We heard three or four shots and remarked that a black hander or someone connected with bootlegging has bit the dust. It was a remark made in jest and we thought no more about it.

A block or two down the street we found a man stretched out next to a picket fence. He was bleeding and it turned out he had been well shot up. We had seen a man pick up something from his side and cross the street into a house and then we noticed blood spots from the house leading to the victim. By this time the police arrived, followed the blood trail into the house and brought out a man whom we believe was the same one we had seen at the side of the victim. The victim had been shot dead. Being in an Italian neighborhood we felt sure he was the victim of bootleg or Mafia vengeance. It appears to have been my luck, or misfortune, to be around where things were happening. Then it may have been the wooly times or poking my snoot where it didn't belong. I could relate the time I witnessed the holdup and killing of a restaurant cashier downtown; the time in my teens I saw an auto thief shot near the Square and the time I saw a knifing, but I'll let it pass. This is no Wild West story.

About 1920 Warren Gamaliel Harding, owner of the Marion Star newspaper in Marion, Ohio, was nominated by the Republican Party as candidate for President. I think he defeated Democratic candidate James Cox and was elected by a large majority. He didn't do much campaigning but confined himself mostly to making speeches from his front porch in Marion. I don't recall him being much of a President, although he did do a few things like having the Washington Conference on arms limitation for the Navy, peace with Germany was officially established, participation in the World Court and a few other things.

As I recall the word was that he liked to gamble with cards with a few cronies at the White House and he picked a poor cabinet, a few of whom had their own pockets to fill. Two of the cabinet members, Albert Fall, Secretary of the Interior and Henry Dougherty, Attorney General, were involved in the Teapot Dome oil scandal. Teapot Dome was a Naval oil reserve in Wyoming which was leased, if I recall correctly, to a person by the name of Sinclair without competitive bidding. Fall was convicted and spent time in the penitentiary and Sinclair was sentenced for contempt of court. I remember parts of this because of all the publicity in the newspapers; however, the nitty-gritty of it I'll leave to you readers to look up.

President Harding took a trip and somewhere around San Francisco he died. At the time there was uncertainty about his death, some said ptomaine poisoning, some said apoplexy and the hush-hush rumor was that he committed suicide. Vice President Calvin Coolidge, known as "Silent Cal," succeeded him as President. He had been governor of Massachusetts. I don't recall anything important happening during his administration, perhaps just because there was nothing important happening. Some say that his remark that brokers' loans were not dangerous to the economy led to the stock market crash of 1929. "Silent Cal" just wasn't a talker but a cautious New Englander. There was talk in certain quarters about canceling England's debt to us but Collidge was indignant, remarking "They hired the money didn't they?" The story goes that one time he was officiating at a groundbreaking ceremony and after turning the first shovel he stood looking at the ground in thought. It was expected that he would say a few words for the occasion. He did--he was heard to mumble "There's a couple of good fishing worms there."

Came the time for Coolidge to run for re-election he made a mistake. He made the remark "I do not choose to run" and the newspapers latched onto it, made a big thing of it and his goose was cooked as far as being nominated at the Convention. The story was that what he intended to convey was that he'd take the job if nominated and elected, but that he didn't choose to push for it. I have read that when he learned he would not be nominated he lay on his bed and kicked his heels in frustration. I don't believe it.

Herbert Hoover followed Cal Coolidge. His campaign was "A car in every garage and a chicken in every pot." He was blamed for the stock market crash although it actually was not his fault. It was a buildup over the 20's which finally toppled. I was at the B&O Railroad station downtown the night he left after making a political speech at one of the hotels and saw him when he stood on the rear platform of the train. He looked serious and glum. I believe he was a good man and a good administrator but was a victim of the times.

Entering the twenties I was smart enough to realize that time was marching by; that I hadn't yet found a place where I could work my self up. I had come to the conclusion this Alger success story, *Up Business*, was for the birds. Jobs were not waiting to be plucked and the only thing I had going for me at that time, with the scarcity of jobs, was youth, willingness to work, and my share of horse sense. I landed a job with the Mechanical Rubber Company a subsidiary of the U.S. Rubber, as supposed secretary to one of the department managers. Since I am trying to keep the telling of my experience in more or less sequence, I'll speak of it a little later.

While traveling around with my group of friends from the club I was intrigued by a pretty little blue-eyed blond, a sister of Joe Touschner who was a member of our club. Leona is her name. At about that time I was experimenting with raising a moustache and when passing her home with my friends she'd be sitting on the porch with her sisters

Ed and Leona Stein, 1930

and call, "How's your moustache, Red?" I asked her to come to one of our bus ride picnics at Cascade park, Allure, and it is one of the shining, outstanding days of my life. It is so. I guess it was meant to be.

As was the custom, the girls brought the picnic lunch and at the park the truck was stationed at a spot convenient to picnic tables. We'd take off, either in a group or couple, and enjoy the day. I recall skipping with her, hand in hand, down the park paths and the elderly people sitting on the benches nodding at us with a smile. She was a cute little girl with a ready smile and laughter all that sunny, good, sweet day. From then on, no other girl really interested me. We had dates on and off, we saved our money for the Big Day, September 16, 1930, when we were married at Holy Name Church, Cleveland, and she had been my companion , my counsel and, the mother of our fine children and my helpmate for the past 50 years.

186

Chapter 16

I'll continue with the Mechanical Rubber Company. It is surprising the jobs they glorified as secretarial work. The details of the work doesn't matter but I was with them for three or four years, received several raises and thought I was headed in the right direction. After all, it was a big company and lots of room to work yourself up. Then I began to hear disquieting rumors--change in ownership or something.

An idea had been buzzing around in the back of my mind for some, time, I wanted permanence. Perhaps a Civil Service job where one couldn't be dumped at someone's whim.

To go on--with all the rumors I figured where there's smoke there's fire so I kept my eyes and ears open. Common sense told me something was about to happen and I had better jump. I did. Virtually onto a telephone pole of the Ohio Bell Telephone Company. Mechanical Rubber was phased out by the U.S. Rubber and jobs too. However, I had a job in the Cable Splicing Department of Ohio Bell. There I was--$22.50 a week, quite a big cut from what I was used to. However, I was going to learn a trade now other than what I had been used to. It was outdoor work, climbing poles, sitting on guy wires 20 to 30 feet in the air tying on work platforms (Look Ma, no hands) on which to stand and splice cables. It required working on cables in muddy manholes, too.

It was a cold job in winter and in windy weather we erected a tent so we could melt lead bars for soldering the sleeve on a cable after splicing it. At the end of each lead sleeve holding the splice was a large lead knob to seal the sleeve to the cable. To seal the sleeve was a tricky job and had to be done in such a manner that the dampness would not get into the splice or trouble on the telephone lines would result. To melt the lead bars in an iron pot required a small, about 15 inches high, coal oil-fueled furnace, therefore the tent in windy weather so the furnace would not be extinguished. I liked the scrambled egg sandwiches which Mom packed for me but in winter the sandwiches had to be thawed since they were frozen, having been in the cold all morning. That's where the furnace came in.

It was interesting work, it was healthy, the pay was lousy. I listened and I observed. The first thing I wised up to was that the picture painted by the employment office of the rosy future of the job had blemishes. I found Bell Telephone had no union (now it has), consequently there seemed to be a continual feeling of unease among the workers I came in contact with. I was cable splicer's helper, learning the work of cable splicing. The cable splicer I worked with was afraid of his boss; his boss was afraid of the superintendent, Mr. Shields, and so everyone seemed to be on tippy-toes. Added to that, the helper was lucky if his cable-splicing boss showed him anything and used him for more than a gofer. What a hell of a system to work under I thought. Then I learned that the pay of a competent splicer who had been with the company for years was $35 per week, less than I had received at the Mechanical Rubber. One of the club members had been working with the company as cable splicer helper for over a year before I arrived on the job and he quit to try bootlegging. I did some hard thinking. If I did become a full-fledged cable splicer and had to leave the company, what other company in town could use a cable splicer? It was a specialty. You were at the mercy of the phone company. No wonder the feeling of tenseness and unease. The phone company had the employee by the throat.

The idea of a Civil Service job became more appealing. A Civil

188

Service job seemed to be the thing to latch on to which offered permanence and a pension. I had the Post Office in mind; however, that seemed to be a slow hiring process with many applicants which cut down my employment chances. About this time, the City of Cleveland was advertising that applications were being taken for police officers. The city was enlarging its police force by several hundred men. The job was under Civil Service and pension after 25 years was available. I gave it some thought and decided I'd put in my application. I had no fear of the work, the change of shifts wouldn't bother me and if I should be lucky enough to pass the examination and appointed, I felt I would be better off in the long run. I was. As an example--the Great Depression came along and I had a job while others were out of work. A little planning ahead had paid off. I put in my application at the Civil Service commission, a birth certificate was required but a baptismal record was acceptable, so I went to St. Michael's Parish House where they fished out my baptismal record from a large dusty book. There I was, Edward John Anthony Stein. I found I had another name--John. Now I had two second names. Whoever heard of two second names but there it was. What's in a name? After all these years I kept Anthony and stored John in my memory bank. I heard tell later that I had been named after Edward John May, a friend of the family.

Along this line, it may have been for the purpose of the police examination, I acquired from the Bureau of Vital Statistics my birth certificate. The certificate did not give my name but referred to me as "Sex-male." I was told that it was not valid since it did not give my name. Therefore, I can assume that officially I haven't been born.

In due time, came the day to take the written examination. Most

189

of the questions were about the locations of streets, buildings, and hotels downtown; the location of parks and crosstown lines. Arithmetic was not bad with a few "thinker" questions. The downtown section and the parks were duck soup for me. I had been around in my teens and knew all the hotels, buildings, and byways.

Then came the physical ability test held in a hall somewhere downtown. I was in good shape after a winter outside. I was young, had good muscle from climbing poles and pulling cables, I was ready to tackle anything. At the examination I had to run, jump, chin myself a required number of times, and so forth. Not hard for me. I felt sorry for a colored applicant, he weighed over 200 pounds and when it came to chinning he couldn't lift himself once. End of applicant. Now the NAACP would yell discrimination.

Next we had to report for a physical examination to Dr. O'Malley, Police Physician, whose office for the department was at the 8th Precinct, W. 29th & Detroit. Dr. O'Malley was a good and understanding man and well-liked. He was the department's physician for quite a few years. He was a veteran of World War I and had been decorated. He did the usual chest thumping, the usual stethoscope listening--"Breath deep--now breath normal." He took our weight and measured our height. I well remember one of the applicants, Alphonse Toomey, was a small slender fellow. He barely made the height and couldn't make the weight. It was just before lunch time so Dr. O'Malley told him to report back after lunch. Alphonse was no dummy, he could read between the lines. For lunch he stuffed himself with bananas and drank all the water he could hold. He passed the test. As Tommey grew older, like all of us, he became heavier. He was a good officer and a good man to have beside you in a pinch. I should know. He and I fought a gang on a streetcar on the Public Square one afternoon.

I felt I had done reasonably well but you're not sure until you get the results. The Police Department was being enlarged by 500 men. With this amount I should have a chance. I did. It was a great day when I received the result by mail--I had passed. Glory alleluia! I was 105th on the list. My character had yet to be investigated by the Police Department which didn't worry me since I knew I was okay with the neighbors, had never been in the slammer, and had no arrest record. I was in. Actually, as I later calculated, and I don't think I was wrong, I should have been within the first 50 on the list of 500, but that's a political story I wasn't wise to at the time. I went into the examination innocent as a newborn babe. It was a time of waiting now, I was still up on poles or down in holes. I hadn't told my bosses and thought it was time enough when I was called to be officially sworn in as an arm of the law, albeit a very green arm. I was one for playing safe--don't count your chickens before they're hatched. Who knows about these Civil Service shenanigans? My notice came one fine day so I told my boss and his boss. They congratulated me and things of that sort and I noticed a note of respect in their voices. I supposed they thought this guy is now going to be a policeman--we can't order him around anymore.

The day of the official swearing in the City Hall Council Chamber came. Others had been sworn in a day or two before. There were about 50 of us besides Chief of Police Jacob Graul, Safety Director Edwin D. Barry, members of the press and Edward Stanton, the Director of Law who swore us in. One of the new appointees was late. He had apparently just come from work. He was an ice man and still wore the heavy blue wool shirt which ice men wore winter and summer. Perhaps he had the ice wagon parked in front of City Hall. He received a thorough dressing down before the whole group.

I knew Joe throughout the time I was in the department and he was a fine officer. I had started a new lifestyle and was now Patrolman Edward Stein, Badge #1171. It was a new number which never had been used before since the force was increased by 500 additional men and new badges had to be made. From now on I was to see the other side of life, you bet!

In about 1920 Mom and Dad had sold our home on Scranton Road and built a two-family home at 10608 Bernard Avenue. Brother Al lived with his family at 3401 W. 100th Street. After the First World War, brother Joe moved to Youngstown, with the Jones Optical company, which was later bought by the American Optical Company. Joe married and had several children and lived there until he passed away at the age of 84. He had married three times, two of his wives passed away and the third is still living. Lucy was married about 1924 so that left me with Mom and Dad on Bernard Avenue.

The day of my appointment I was told to report to the police school at the 8th Precinct Police Station, W. 29th and Detroit at 1:00 p.m. The class was from 1:00 to 5:00. Then at 7:00, I was to report to the 9th Precinct, W. 25th and Althen, where I was to work until 11:00--a total of 8 hours. Police school then was a far cry from what it is today. Now they have a new name for it--it's the Police Academy. Their method of teaching is entirely different, it's more diversified. There is no comparison. It's much better. However, the actual learning is out in the street. The hard, indifferent street where you are alone. I know, I was there.

Our afternoon class was conducted by Captain John Kadel, a veteran of about 28 years, he must have been appointed about 1900 or before. I suspect that it must have been a pain in the neck to Captain Kadel. His method of teaching was to read ordinances from the city ordinance book. Once in a while he'd ask a question. In between we had a go at state laws, felonies and misdemeanors. His voice droned on and on throughout the hot spring afternoon. Remember, he had another class in the morning, 8:00 a.m. to noon with the same ordinances and laws. This was for one solid month. We learned zilch. I acquired my knowledge of state laws and city ordinances by studying them on my time off at home.

The day of our appointment we had been furnished our equipment which consisted of a night stick, a day stick, a police box key, a fire department box key, a whistle, and a book of rules and regulations--the bible of the Police Department. Then came the big item--a 38 caliber Smith and Wesson Police Special revolver plus a dozen rounds of ammunition. These revolvers are very good and still used in many departments and, at that time, was new equipment purchased to replace the revolvers many of the officers had used for years. I doubt that police now equip new recruits with revolvers the first day. However, that's the way it was done in 1925 and, probably had been for the preceding 25 or 30 years.

As I see it now, the way of doing things then was a holdover from before the turn of the century and no one thought of changing it. However, equipping a greenhorn police officer with a revolver the first day of his appointment seems to me to have been asking for trouble. Many of the men never had handled a weapon before. In fact, one of them, a few days after his appointment, shot himself in

193

the leg, while trying to draw it from the holster. Anyway, that's what he reported. Perhaps he's lucky he hadn't pulled the trigger while looking down the barrel to see what was inside. As for myself, I had a healthy respect for a firearm, having owned two .22 caliber rifles with which I practiced down the valley during my teens. In fact, one of them is still in the possession of my son Ed. As for revolvers, I had also handled one or two. I wasn't a firearm expert by any means but I knew enough to respect them.

Captain John "Darby" O'Brien was our instructor in the use of firearms. He knew his business and he made a study of it. "Darby," unfortunately, didn't have the proper equipment to teach the rookies that he would have liked to have had. In the basement of the 8th Precinct, the same building where we were attending police school, was the Police Target Range. It consisted of a counter to lay our ammunition on and at which we stood when firing at a bulls eye target about 50 feet in front of it. Darby instructed us how to hold the pistol, how to aim, hold our breath and squeeze the trigger. We all had our turn at banging away. One of the rookies apparently never had handled a revolver before--he closed his eyes each time he squeezed off a shot. I don't think Darby knew it.

I'll give a brief description of the equipment. There was the night stick (billy club to the layman). It was two feet long, of hickory wood with a braided leather strap at the holding end; then we had a daystick, two feet long, made of hard, mahogany colored cocabolla wood at the holding end of which was a heavy red cord and tassle; then the police box key which fitted all police boxes in the city. It was a very necessary key used for ringing into the station when on the beat and for calling patrol wagons for arrested persons, also in time of trouble when help was needed; then a fire box key in case we discovered a fire; then the police whistle. It was used for direction of traffic, the calling of attention of other officers, the movement of pedestrians, and so forth. It was a useful item. I was told by veteran policemen that it was used by the beat man at night when summoning help of the adjoining beat man in case of trouble. The three blasts for "Help" and two answering blasts for "I'm coming."

Personally, I never used the whistle for this purpose for the reason that there weren't enough officers to allot to each beat, so a blast would have been useless. Also, we were usually assigned to three or four beats at a time. I can well understand the use of the whistle for this purpose, the shrill blast carries far on a quiet night. Last, the Book of Rules and Regulations. It was a green paperback book approximately 5" by 7" in size. It was THE book. It laid down rules for the highest ranking officer down thru the ranks to the lowest--from the Chief of Police to the last appointed rookie. It covered the conduct, deportment, dress, actions, you name it, of the members. I don't know how long this book of rules had been in existence but from all indications it was a long time. Some of the rules may have been alright at the turn of the century, but for the enlightened year of 1925 some were downright asinine.

One rule always gave me a chuckle, perhaps because Dad had a horse or two and I did know a little about them. The rule was for the men in the Mounted Unit--it went approximately like so-- "They are not to leave their horse unless it is turned over to someone familiar with the proper care and handling of horses." What nonsense! The average person in the city knew nothing about a horse--automobiles, yes--not a horse. So, theoretically, if you were called into a building by someone in case of an emergency you couldn't leave the horse because there was no one around who was familiar with its handling. It follows, you either rode the horse into the building or didn't answer the emergency. You were in violation of the rules and regulations either way.

And so it was with other rules--you were damned if you did and damned if you didn't. I was in the department a few years when a new, up-to-date book was published. However, this new book wasn't born without its hassle. There were two or three officers, in the higher echelon, assigned to rewrite the rules. Years later, while I was assigned to the Chief's office, I reminisced with an Inspector of Police about the old rules. He happened to be one of those assigned to create the new rule book. He said that the three of them couldn't come to an agreement on what should and should not be in the book with the result that the book they presented for approval was thrown out--it was a hodge-podge. The job was then given to only one man who didn't have to compete with two others, consequently the final book was acceptable.

The things we learned from the old-time beat men were good. I stored them in my memory and they helped me over some rough spots. However modernization was creeping up on the old timer and as their 25 or 30 years in the service came up they faded into retirement.

The officer on the beat, was referred to as a "brick pounder," by us. We fell heir to many of the police terms and they were part of police jargon. When asking someone what assignment they had for the day the answer would many times be "on the bricks" if it was a beat. Some would say "pounding the pavement." Apropos, don't you think? I doubt if any policeman today would know what the term means. Then, too, each police department usually had its own jargon. Generally they were synonymous.

At the time of my appointment there were four shifts, the 6:00 a.m. to 2:00 p.m. called the day shift; the 2:00 to 10:00 p.m. called the half and half; the 7:00 p.m. to 3:00 a.m. called the dog shift and the 10:00 p.m. to 6:00 a.m. called the night shift. The dog shift was later eliminated and all the starting times of the shifts pushed one hour ahead.

We worked the eight hour day, six days a week, with the same day off each week for a whole year. Days were assigned to us by the lieutenant; therefore, theoretically, if you should be assigned to a Monday, it would be seven years before you had a Sunday off. Of course, one had Sunday off during the two-week furlough time and, occasionally, a Sunday could be finagled if one had overtime coming. Also, much could happen in seven years, such as transfers, reassignments, and so forth. There was the possibility that when one reached the Sunday vacation day, you were reassigned to another precinct and your vacation day could very well be changed back to Monday. Myself, I believe I worked about a dozen years before I had regular Sundays off, due to reassignments. None complained, it was part of the job.

As for the two-week furloughs, it went by the seniority system. The latest appointee almost always received a late fall, winter or early spring vacation. It was a slow process and took years to work yourself up to a late spring or summer vacation. Once you were in the summer category you stayed there due to your seniority.

197

There was a bit of injustice in the department way of drawing furloughs in some of the precincts. Due to the location of the parks and heavily traveled intersections there were men from the traffic division and the mounted troops assigned to a few precincts who, at furlough drawing time, drew with the regular precinct men. After the drawing was over, these traffic and mounted men were reassigned by their superiors to a late spring, summer, or early fall furlough if they desired so, due to seniority, summer furloughs could not be had by some of the precinct men. We grumbled but didn't voice our complaint--it wasn't done--you accepted. We were in a semi-military organization. Keep your mouth shut. Years later we had a five-day week, received an extra day off to compensate for each holiday during the year, the method of furlough drawing was changed and more furlough time allotted. This was a big improvement and obtained through the Fraternal Order of Police efforts. The F.O.P. was started some years after I joined the force and it has been instrumental in bettering conditions for the police officers of the department. Prior to this, the uniform ranks had no one to speak for them and the administrations just coasted along as long as no one complained.

It is impossible to recall or relate all the happenings which occurred in my 38 years on the force. In fact, I was tempted to skip the whole thing and close down my narrative were it not for it being down in my promise book.

Chapter 17

*A*ny police department has its spectacular and bizarre episodes but to picture this as occurring continuously through the 24 hours of each day is stretching the imagination. Actually, much of the work is quite routine.

During the month we attended police school and we had our measurements taken for a summer uniform and a winter uniform. The police tailor shop was on the second floor, over the jail, at the 8th Precinct and supervised by Jim Krejci, a police officer who had been a tailor prior to joining the force. His title was Superintendent of Police Tailor Shop and he received a salary commensurate with that of a higher officer, perhaps a captain. He supervised six or eight other tailors and two or three women. He was a nice fellow and while measuring us he'd give us advice about the job we were about to undertake, what to expect, and so forth. He came up from the bricks too, you see, and he knew whereof he spoke.

For the month we attended police school we reported for duty on the dog shift--7:00 p.m. to 3:00 a.m. Having attended school for four hours that day we only worked until 11:00 p.m. Besides myself there were about four other rookies assigned to the precinct. Since there were 150 new officers appointed we had, as yet, no uniforms, so we reported in our civilian clothes. Later I learned the uniform was referred to as a harness, regular clothing was referred to as plain clothes or street clothes and a policeman was referred to as a "Bull" or "Harness Bull." The police emergency was referred to as a wagon, and the garage where the Emergency was kept was referred as a barn. All holdovers from horse and buggy days. To the end of my police days, out of habit, I referred to them as such. I'll bet the new rookie thought me an ancient old timer when he heard these expressions.

Came the first day of street duty, I reported to the lieutenant in civilian dress clothes, my gun holstered on my hip, my police box and fire box key, plus a notebook, pencil, flashlight and small street directory. A blackjack was also part of the equipment which officers purchased with their own money. On the day shift flashlights were usually dispensed with. This made quite a bulky load in the back pockets or inside jacket pocket. They were all necessary items. I had taken along the night stick, but since we were not in uniform it was kept in the lieutenant's office. We were to wait in the roll call room which was a large square room next to the office and had a podium, opposite which was the stairway to the locker room upstairs. We heard men talking and walking around above us and in a short time a bell rang and policemen came down the stairs. These were the men who had the dog shift that month and each of us rookies was assigned to one. Reminiscing, all the rookies who reported with me that night have since passed away. When we were all lined up the lieutenant came to the podium and had roll call. We all know what roll call is, as each name was called there was an answering "Here" or "Yo." If a man was absent he'd better have a good excuse for being late. After calling the names, the policemen were each given their assignment of the beats they were to patrol. Every precinct was divided into beats and each beat had a number.

After this the departmental orders of the day were read; then came the list of the crimes committed in the past 24 hours, description of suspects, and the license numbers of stolen autos. The last thing the roll call officer said was, "Keys and Guns" which I'll explain a little later. The dog shift was also used for distributing warrants, prosecutor's notices (called Jew warrants), notices of complaints to be answered or taken care of on your beat and many other things in the line of police work. Now warrants are handled differently-- usually two men in a car make the arrest and the prisoner is put in the back seat and locked behind a heavy screen, then driven to the station. In those days we made the arrest alone and walked the prisoner to a police call box.

About the last thing we did before leaving the station to go to our assignments was to synchronize our watches with the station house clock in the lieutenant's office. "Spiking" our watch is what we called it. The reason was that each beat man was given a time to report in. Reporting in had to be on the exact minute, either by phone or by police call box. Not much variation was allowed. The small handle which, when pulled down, would "ding" the box number. Let me explain that the call boxes were made of heavy metal and painted blue and usually attached to a telephone pole.

The call was registered through the police telephone exchange and to the police station where it came over a ticker tape. The time the ticker tape punch came in was compared with the station clock. Of course, there were times when the patrolman was in a situation where he could not report by call box so when he was through with whatever police business he was engaged in, he'd call the station by phone and explain. This keeping record of the patrolman's calling time served a good purpose. Not only would the lieutenant in the station house know where he was located but if he missed several calls in a row his brother officers would be out looking for him in case something had happened to him. Further, if the station house officer had a complaint for him to answer, or a job for him, he would be "dinged" back.

The patrolman then picked up the earpiece recessed in the call box next to the handle used to ring the station house and talked to the station house direct. Some of the call boxes were used infrequently which was evidenced by the spider webs and other insects lodged in the box. I recall one call box on the north and very end of W. 65th, overlooking Edgewater Park which I used when I was on the beat. It had apparently not been used in years since it was in an isolated spot. The door was hard to open and on the inside the earpiece was covered with dust as well as the "ding" handle. Other debris was collected in the crevices also. The reason I recall this particular call box was that I carried a nickel-plated inexpensive watch with me. It was the kind which Mr. Epstein gave me with a suit years before. They could be purchased for $1, and were called "dollar" watches. They kept accurate time and were suitable for my purpose since I didn't want to carry my gold Illinois-make pocket watch because of the chance of it being lost or damaged in case of a fight or scuffle. I had made my call on the night beat and later missed it, presuming it had fallen out of my watch pocket or the

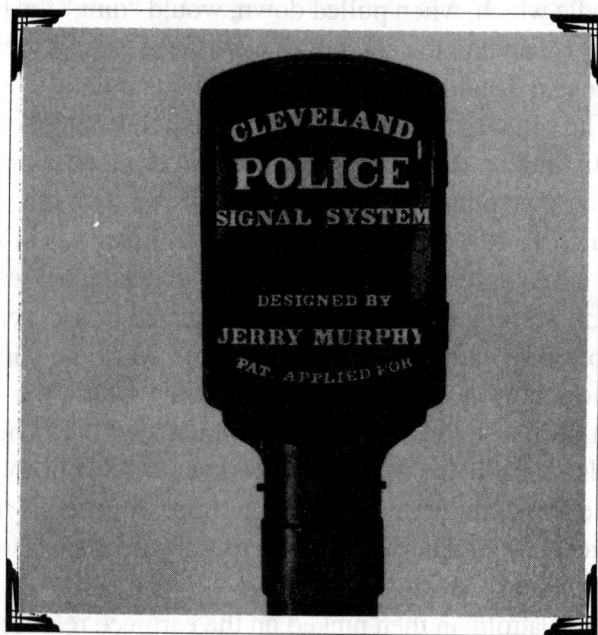

Call Box
Courtesy of the
Cleveland Police Historical Society

black shoe string to which it was attached to my belt had worn out. I had the same beat the next night and on a hunch shined my flashlight around the base of the pole to which the call box was attached and there, face up in the grass, was my watch still ticking away although it had rained quite heavily that day. They were sturdy watches and easily lasted several years before having to discard them.

The call box was not only used to report your time and location, but was used to call the emergency patrol (wagon) when an officer needed it to transport a prisoner. The handle was then pulled down twice and the operator in the exchange would "ding" back to let you know the call had been received. Sometimes the waiting was quite long because the wagon had other calls to make prior to yours. If one had a troublesome prisoner who was belligerent and in a fighting mood and the officer had trouble holding, he pulled the handle down three times which meant "trouble" to the police exchange and perhaps a wagon from another precinct or a cruiser was immediately dispatched. All these nice little things made up the police job, especially before radio equipment was in use.

I do not recall with whom I was assigned my first day but I remember it was in the area south of the 9th Precinct where I had been raised--Scranton Road, City Hospital, Schwab's butcher shop, and so forth. I felt at home--not quite so useless. Things were quiet that night. We walked, we talked, I received information on what to do in certain circumstances; what to look for, how to call on a police box, and try doors (shaking doors as we called it). It was very interesting. At 11:00 p.m. I reported back to the station and was dismissed. I took the streetcar home.

As I have mentioned I joined the force innocent as a newborn babe. On one of these dog shift nights I received an inkling of what the hell went on behind the scenes in the political arena when the officer I was with asked me what I had paid for my job. I was astonished. I told him I had paid nothing. He said, "The hell you didn't." My

203

protest was quite vehement so he asked me how high up on the list I had been . I told him 105th. He said, "Well, maybe you didn't but others did." It's the first I knew. I thought everyone in city hall was honest. From then on I was alerted. I listened. I heard and began putting two and two together. Somewhere along the line the Civil Service examinations weren't on the up and up. The questions and answers could be had for a price. Promotional examinations were the same. This was not only in the police examinations but examinations for other city jobs. Understand, there was no proof, no one mentioned names, it was all quiet gossip and like a mist in the air--but it was THERE. A closed mouth was one requisite of the job anyway, so we had no trouble with a loose tongue. In police work one might discuss things which occurred at work with other officers and sometimes must necessarily be discussed; however, to tell a layman some things is poor business since a policeman is quoted, misquoted, and the telling stretched out of shape to such an extent that it has no resemblance to the original occurrence. This is especially so with reporters who will slant and color any occurrence to suit themselves just to make a good story. We learned fast.

In this semi-military organization I was in now I learned to do as I was told and not to deviate because I thought it should be done differently. This was brought home to me on my first day in uniform. On the fourth of July night, at the Brookside Park stadium, the city had arranged for a display of fireworks, preceded by a play of some sort. A policeman had been stationed there for several nights as protection against theft of property and vandalism. The end of each month was quick changeover day for the shifts. This means that the man on the night shift, the night before, had to report for work at 2:00 p.m. giving him eight hours layover instead of the usual 16 hours. The previous evening I had been ordered to report to the stadium at 6:00 a.m. July 1st and relieve the night man on duty so he could get home as quickly as possible without reporting to the station. Of

204

course, no one told me the reason. I was told to do it by the lieutenant and that was it. I guess doing exactly as I was told hadn't been impressed on my mind as strongly as it should have been during the month I had attended police school.

On leaving the station the night of June 30, one of the policemen with several years service under his belt asked me where I was assigned the following morning. I told him I was reporting at the Brookside stadium. Apparently I hadn't made myself clear that I had been ordered to do so and I'm sure he meant well when he told me the place to report first would be for roll call at the station. This was to be my first day on the job in full new police uniform and being new and fresh, with a willingness to do the right thing, I thought this was good advice since the whole previous month I had reported for roll call--then came the awakening. I reported for roll call at the station the morning of July 1st. We were lined up with the lieutenant calling roll. He must have seen me and called my name and that's when the feathers hit the fan. I was told in no uncertain terms that I had been ordered to report to the stadium and that's where I should be; that the sooner I learned to do what I was told the better off I'd be, and on and on. All this in front of the whole shift. I had sense enough not to open my mouth, certainly not to tell him that a patrolman had told me the place to report was at the station.

Then the lieutenant said to the wagon crew, "Take this man to the stadium and relieve the night man." They drove me there and the driver, "Peanuts" Gayneau, told me that the lieutenant wouldn't have been so mad if it hadn't been change day. I didn't blame him, after all I hadn't done what I had been told to do. I had "learnt" a lesson that day which I never forgot. I was embarrassed to have been corrected in front of the whole platoon but I also learned that this did not mean a thing to them. They were used to corrections at roll call since this is where they were corrected if they had committed an error. They also knew that their turn might be next. The purpose was two-fold--1) the error was impressed on the officer's mind and he was not apt to commit it again--2) correction in front of the other men served to alert them not to make the same mistake. Personally, I felt it was a crude way of correcting anyone and that it should have been done in private. However, I could see the value of it and we all soon developed a thick hide and let this type of correction roll off like water off of a duck's back. The superior officers, or bosses as we called them, were mostly old timers and that is the way they had been trained. Considering that we could be placed on charges before the chief for almost any mistake we made, this type of correction, naturally, was preferred. We had bosses who were martinets although I never worked for one but I've heard of a few. Generally, we had fine understanding superior officers.

Another part of roll call was inspection of our general appearance before going on our assignment. Ordinarily, the bosses weren't too tough but if they noticed certain members were a little careless in not keeping up their appearance, such as shoes not shined or clothes not pressed, they were soon told about it and that would correct the matter. Some officers were naturally neat and shined up and never needed correction, they took pride in their appearance. Then there were a few who had to be watched and kept after occasionally. One wondered how the hell they were raised.

As I mentioned, the last thing the roll call officer said before leaving roll call was, "Keys and Guns." At that we'd all display our keys and our guns to show we had them with us. Frequently he'd inspect the revolvers to see that they were clean and properly oiled. One time Old Barney, who was from the Auld Sod, for some reason had to stand roll call with the regular platoon. He had a school-crossing assignment and was not required to report at the same time with the regular shift, consequently he rarely stood roll call and was not subjected to the regular routine but noted the crimes and other pertinent information in his notebook before going to his school

206

crossing. It didn't make any difference whether he noted the information or not since he never looked in his notebook anyway--he was just THERE. To his surprise, at this roll call, the lieutenant had gun inspection. It seems that the last time Barney's gun had been inspected was in the dim past since the revolver was covered with dust and in the barrel the lieutenant found popcorn. We can see the value of gun inspection. I recall one time an unusual thing happened to Barney. A holdup had been committed and a passing motorist had seen it and was following the car which the holdup man was driving in his getaway from the scene. The passing motorist saw Barney at the school crossing and told him. Barney couldn't get away from his particular sworn duty to uphold the laws of the great state of Ohio and got into the car next to the driver. Give Barney credit, he was preparing for a shootout with the holdup man and in drawing his revolver from its holster, shot himself in the leg. End of chase.

It was some time in the summer of 1927 that a young fellow by the name of Charles Lindbergh was headlined as having taken off in his plane to fly across the Atlantic to Europe. I had never heard of Charles Lindbergh before but there he was, the center of news. It seems the country at that time needed a hero and Lindbergh was it with his memorable flight at the right time. I do not believe young Lindy had any thought of being a hero nor that he sought publicity. He seemed to be a quiet and shy young man and just did what he felt he had to do--cross that ocean in a plane. As I recall, he seems to have had his flight expenses underwritten by a businessman or large corporation. We can call it drive, ambition, the call of adventure or what you will, it took courage and all credit to him. I believe that he was surprised at the furor he created. After a great to do in France they had a parade and tickertape reception in New York for him and he was in great demand by cities throughout the country that wanted to do him honor. There is much written about Lindbergh, the details of which can be looked up in any library. He received much publicity during his life, some tragic, such as the acceptance of a medal from Hitler or Goehring of the German Reich before World War II. All in all it tended to make him extremely shy of publicity. My own feeling is that he was a great American.

I remember it was about the summer of 1928 that Cleveland's turn came to honor him. By this time, he had received so much publicity that his adventure became somewhat stale news. It was on a hot, blistering day that fellow officers and I were assembled at the Cleveland Airport to handle crowds awaiting Lindbergh and his Spirit of St. Louis. The airport at that time consisted of a few small buildings and was considered "way out in the country." I recall it well since the day was so hot it was a foretaste of hell and I was spit thirsty with no water around. A kind person in the crowd offered me a bottle of water and I had just taken a couple of healthy swallows when my lieutenant, "Snapper" John Stanton, came by. "Snapper" was one hell of a guy, always growling but esteemed by us all. He asked me where I got the water and I told him. My mother having raised her son to be, hopefully, a gentleman and to share the good things of life, I thought it only fitting and proper that I offer to share it with him. I did. He accepted. I expected him to take one or two slugs and hand the bottle back but, instead, he upended it and down the hatch it went. There I stood, cut off at the water line and still thirsty. A rookie officer with any sense does not argue with his boss. The lion is not judged by the jackal, so to speak--no brownie points there. You see, bosses were likened unto Jehovah.

Then, flying low from the east, came the Spirit of St. Louis. (Leona and I later saw it at the Smithsonian Institute in Washington.) It was low enough for me to see Lindbergh in the cockpit. I did not witness the ceremonies at the field but, with other officers, was shifted to Euclid Avenue to handle expected crowds on the street waiting for Lindy to come by in a parade of autos on his way to a reception. There was no crowd of spectators when we arrived. Some time elapsed and I was still thirsty. I thought it would be a good time to find a drink before activities started, so I looked around for the handiest open building. A porter from one of the buildings came out with chairs and lined them up at the curb for expected onlookers. I entered the building and had my drink at the water fountain and when I came out the porter was removing the chairs. I asked him why he was doing that and he said Lindbergh had just been driven by--two cars. Big parade! That was the end of my day with Lindy.

We had a melting pot of nationalities in the police department and on the west side, where I worked, it seemed that the Irish predominated. In the 6th precinct, the Broadway section, it seemed the Bohemians predominated. It didn't matter to the regular rank and file what the nationality or race of any policeman was since they were, so to speak, all brothers in the same line of work. It was, and still is, a purely democratic way, promoting social equality in this respect. This brotherhood, if we wish to designate it as such, was also an unconscious protective measure drawing them together in time of trouble or stress. This was evident by their reluctance to have anything to do with reporters who, many times, misquoted occurrences out of all semblance to facts and slanted a happening in whatever direction they chose.

As a small example--it brings to mind the time I had a call of an injured man in one of the large and high old-fashioned homes on Euclid, west of E. 55th. I had been there a short time previously on complaint of a fight. It wasn't a fight but just a heavy argument. A family consisting of the mother, two daughters, and a stepfather were living on the second floor and this was the wedding night of one of the stepdaughters. During the course of the small festivity the stepfather had an argument with the groom. I forget what it was about but recall there was something not quite right about the whole thing. I was streetwise long before this and it appeared to me that the stepfather was jealous of the groom, was infatuated with his

209

stepdaughter and didn't take kindly to the marriage. I quieted the argument and left.

A short time later we received a call of an injured man at the same address. When we arrived, we found the stepfather lying on the front sidewalk leading from the front porch--dead. From my investigation and observation it was evident that he had jumped from the second floor porch to the sidewalk below. To this day I'm convinced I was right in my assumption that he had committed suicide because of his stepdaughter's marriage. I could see no reason for making the jump other than that and the family wasn't talking. Of course, we could say he fell off of the porch but there was no evidence of a fall, especially in view of the fact that he was sober at the time I spoke with him on a short time previously and the porch had a high railing which was undamaged as it would have been if someone fell through it. In the early 30's my report, from my investigation and observation, may have read suicide but now my report was headed, "Dead Body Found." The reason for this was that the insurance companies based their claims on the investigation reports of police, consequently not paying claims in some instances, leading to lawsuits. The department, therefore, changed it's heading of reports to dead body found and left the decision up to the county coroner, whose say so was official and final. This left the department off of the hook and was what should have been done in the first place.

Now, to get back to reporters, the next morning the *Cleveland Plain Dealer* had the story in the paper but with the added attraction that Sergeant Stein stated it was a suicide. It was a downright lie because I had made no such statement, merely giving the barest facts that the man was found dead. What surprised me was that I knew the reporter quite well, also his father who had been a reporter before him, and didn't think he would misrepresent facts and use my name to lend his statement authority. Members of the fourth estate are tricky. Anyway, while assigned to desk duty the following day I received a

210

phone call from the new groom vociferously objecting to my statement that his stepfather had committed suicide. I had quite a time explaining that I had nothing to do with it and invited him to come to the station and I'd take him to the reporter and find out who was responsible for the statement. This quieted him down and he never showed up. I wish he had. It was some time later I talked with the reporter but received no satisfaction.

When I was sergeant assigned to a zone car (prowl car to you) or, for that matter, when I was detective sergeant, and had a seriously injured person lying in a hospital emergency room, I was usually bothered by phone calls from reporters wanting to get the gruesome details so they could have the story ready to go to press. This was especially so in the late evening or early morning hours, particularly if there was a homicide involved. It was an annoyance since, many times, they would make continuous repeated calls and I didn't have all the information concerning the happening and, obviously, couldn't make any statement. I developed a system of my own which worked for me--I'd tell the reporter that I didn't have the complete information at the time (true), but that he'd have to wait till I called him. Somehow I never had the time to call him back. These were little things we learned by hard experience.

To return to my early years in the department, arriving at the station in time for 6:00 a.m. roll call wasn't exactly convenient since I had to get up about 4:15, eat my breakfast, walk about a quarter mile to the streetcar, walk three blocks to the station and arrive early enough to put on my uniform, see that I was shined up and ready to go. I had no automobile at the time and sometimes the streetcar was late, also its schedule at that time in the morning wasn't always up to par. This getting up business was not bad in the summer months but a nuisance during the spring and fall rains and especially during winter. Sunday morning was another story altogether. I had to hustle to arrive in time for mass at St. Michael's Church which was about four blocks from the station. I'd leave right after communion, practically trot to the station and get there in time. What helped on Sunday morning was that roll call was always about five minutes late due to having what was called "School." The platoon would go back up to the locker room after roll call and wait for the lieutenant or desk sergeant to come up and hold "class." Sometimes we'd have roll call right in the locker room without going downstairs first.

This so-called "school" was a good thing. We'd sit around at ease while the officer read laws and ordinances, explained them and we'd have discussions of what to do in certain circumstances. We'd discuss happenings of occurrences during our tour of duty, what we did, and so forth. It was a good place to hear other opinions from streetwise men. We exchanged information, learned about hoodlums hanging around the corners and pool rooms, learned who to be on the lookout for in certain neighborhoods, and what establishments were easy targets for crime. It was very good training, kept one well informed and helped immensely in the protection of citizens and property. It was not all dead serious--there was plenty of humor too.

I recall the time one of the superior officers who had held classes, told when he had asked a veteran officer what he'd do if he found the door to Kelly's saloon open on his night beat. The old timer said, "If I found the door open I would first search the first floor to see if anyone was in there; then I'd go to the basement and search there; then I'd come back up, open the front door and look up the street, then down the street and if I saw no one coming I'd lock the door, go behind the bar and draw myself a beer out of the wood." It was so, the old timers liked their beer and drank plenty if a brewery was on their beat. Now we had prohibition, there was supposedly no more beer.

No beer? Practically every homeowner was his own brew master. There were stores all over town selling the necessary items to make beer, such as hops, yeast, bottling equipment, and the rest. It was a thriving business during prohibition--and legal. Recipes for making beer, corn liquor, and various wines, could be had from almost every other neighbor. Dandelion wine, elderberry wine, raisin-jack ,and gin made by distilling grains with juniper berries could be bought at the right places. A friend of mine told me he had received a good recipe for making corn liquor and had tried it. The directions were to fill a small keg a quarter full of regular field corn used for feeding cattle and poultry, fill the rest of the keg with water and bury it in the ground for three months. He did. After three months he dug it up, uncorked it and the aroma would knock down a horse. No corn liquor--just a mess.

It seemed that about two homes in every block in the Polish settlement, called the south side, were dispensing liquor. When working half-and-half shift and assigned to the south side, we'd return to the station about 7:00 p.m. and pick up warrants and prosecutor's notices, called Jew warrants by us. A prosecutor's summons was merely a notice to appear before the prosecutor to answer a complaint made by a person. It was not a warrant and was not an arrest summons as such. If one failed to show up at the prosecutor's office it, many times ended the matter. However, it could result in a warrant being issued. The reason they were called Jew warrants was because frequently Jewish business people relied on the prosecutor's summons to scare people into paying their bills. However, the notice served a good purpose too. It was sent out when a complaint had been made by a citizen against another person, for example, an injury, accident, or assault cases. In order to hear the other side of the story the prosecutor issued a prosecutor's summons and on hearing the other story would take action accordingly, many times settling arguments or claims without going to court.

In delivering the notices to various homes or apartments in a building we'd always go the rear door if possible where we'd listen to hear what was going on before knocking, particularly in the Polish neighborhood. This was a protective measure. On the south side the conversation was usually in Polish but occasionally we'd hear a fight or argument going on. Frequently, during the bootleg days, we'd hear the voices of men, clinking of glasses and movement. We'd rap at the door, prosecutor's summons in hand, and there would be a dead silence. We knew, in all probability, that liquor was being sold on the premises. Then someone would call, "Who Dere? Wat you want?"

We'd call out, "Po-o-o-lice." There would be a second or two of dead silence and then a scurrying and scrambling around inside. The door, of course, was locked. We'd hear glasses being emptied, water running from the faucet, and a lugging. We'd repeatedly rap and finally the door would be opened by a white-faced man or woman. In the kitchen would be the reek of white mule and at the kitchen table, acting innocent and unconcerned would be anywhere from three to six men staring blankly at the wall. We'd hand the person the summons and leave without a word. We knew what had happened. They had dumped all their liquor down the kitchen sink drain which was not the ordinary goose neck variety with a water trap opening on the bottom which could be unscrewed for clean out purposes, but a 4 or 5 inch diameter drain which ran from the underside of the sink directly into the sewer. No evidence, you see. We had seen no liquor being sold, we had seen no liquor, we knew the evidence had been dumped and that was as far as we could go. They did, however, pour away their supply of liquor and we had our laughs. We weren't anxious to make this type of arrest anyway since we had a liquor detail in citizen clothes to whom we'd report our suspicions and it would be their job to check it out.

Some of these illicit dispensers of liquor were widows with children to support or men trying to supplement their wages to raise their families and the customers were usually hard-working neighborhood family men who not only felt sorry for them, but also felt the need of a shot of whiskey which they couldn't get any other way. When one is used to a shot or two a day it's hard to do without.

214

I had no use for the big-time bootleggers who made a big business of it and cared not how the law was violated. I never came in contact with them anyway. I only knew them from the stories in the papers. I did not condone the violation of law but my sympathy did lie on the side of these small dispensers of liquor not only because they were trying to support a family but also because I, perhaps, was a little saloon-minded, having been brought up in the saloon era and, I might say, had fond memories of "rushing the can" for Dad and the wonderful fish sandwiches which he brought to me from a saloon's free lunch counter. The saloon pretzels may have had something to do with it too. I wasn't in favor of the law anyway and few people were. I consider myself fortunate that I was never assigned to the liquor detail. However, it was the law and it had to be enforced and our personal feelings couldn't enter into it. I believe most officers, if they have been in police work for any length of time, feel sorry for the person they must arrest on a warrant or otherwise from time to time but, necessarily, go through with it.

Some of these home-liquor dispensers, or bootleggers as we called them, gave the police a rough time. I particularly recall the time I was working on the south side when I was called to meet the liquor detail at a certain address. Since the detail was always in civilian clothes it was advisable to call in the uniform man to accompany them so there would not be the excuse that the bootlegger did not know it was the police. This particular time the liquor detail had received many complaints of liquor being sold by a widow in a tenement, or beehive as we called them , in the Polish neighborhood. I recall the detail consisted of Sergeant Perrell, later lieutenant, with whom I worked closely during the war, Alred "Skip" Hones an officer and one other officer. I accompanied them and by the time they were admitted to the apartment the Polish widow (for lack of the right name I'll call her Aggie) had disposed of the evidence by pouring it down the kitchen sink. This time the drain had the standard goose neck with a clean out opening in the trap which could be unscrewed.

One of the detail men proceeded to unscrew it to obtain the liquor contained in it as evidence when Aggie, who had been standing quietly on the side and not saying a word, suddenly lunged for the coffee pot on the stove, swung it towards the sink and poured the coffee all over the officer. Whether she had aimed it at the sink or at the officer was hard to tell. She was the quiet type and one couldn't tell what was going on in her Polish head. But there was the officer with his hair and shirt soaked with warm coffee. It was done so quickly and unexpectedly that no one had a chance to stop her. Aggie still didn't say anything and we restrained her from further action. After drying himself with a towel the officer proceeded to complete his task and put the evidence in a bottle. There was enough liquor to permit a test. Aggie was left home until the chemist had made the test and certified the alcohol content of the liquid and a warrant was issued for her arrest.

Several days later I was assigned to the scout car for the south side and I was given a warrant for Aggie for liquor law violation. I was on the afternoon shift then and went to Aggie's home to serve the warrant. She must have seen me coming. After a time, my knock was answered by a white-faced boy about 10. He said his mother was not at home. I knew by his action that he was lying and also knew that kids of bootleggers had been taught to lie at an early age. While standing in the hallway trying to find out from him when his mother would return I noticed a slight movement of the bedroom door leading from the kitchen. There was no breeze and since the apartment was on the first floor I became suspicious. I crossed the kitchen and opened the door and there was our Aggie, dressed in hat and coat, with one leg over the window sill ready to jump out the window. She was an agile gal about 40. I had her lift her Polish leg back into the bedroom and told her I had a warrant for her arrest. I asked her if she had anyone she could leave the boy with and she jabbered something to him in Polish which, I presumed, was for him to go to a neighbor or stay put. Still not saying a thing she walked into the bedroom and picked up an infant which was sleeping on the bed. Due to the darkness of the bedroom I had not seen the infant and was surprised. I then knew that her plan had been to jump out of the window, wait around a corner until I had left and then come back to her flesh and blood. It was a bit of a puzzle--there I was with a prisoner but what to do with the baby? Touchy! We couldn't put the baby in jail and she wasn't about to let go of her offspring. I didn't blame her. She was no dummy, she had me temporarily outfoxed and she knew it. She was a slick hen and had been through chicken coops before.

My brain worked a little overtime and I decided to take her and the baby along to the station. I could have left her at home and returned to the station with the warrant but it was not the thing to do since Aggie could very well fly the coop and I would be criticized for not bringing her in, especially since I had her in custody. The boy left the home and we arrived at the station. The bosses puzzled over this too and made a wise decision. They didn't want to put a baby in jail either--or send it to the Juvenile Home. She was told to go home with the baby and arrange for bail before coming back. I believe I drove her home. This was a sensible decision and I was in the clear. A boss can make these decisions without being criticized but a young officer better leave it to him. She arranged bail and had her hearing but I don't know the outcome. There's always something new cropping up in the police line. You think you've seen or heard it all but there's always something new.

217

Joe Filkowski was a Polish boy gone bad. I didn't know him personally nor did I ever have contact with him except in a general way when a house, in which he was thought to be, was mistakenly tear gassed. Joe was born and raised in the Polish community east of W. 14th. He became mixed up with the law in his teens and, possibly, as a juvenile. He came of good parents and had, as I remember, at least one sister. He became notorious through newspaper publicity because of his illegal shenanigans and holdup activities and they kept him in the limelight and worried at him like a dog worrying a bone. I firmly believe that no one is all bad and that everyone has their good points and Joe must have had his too.

Corner gangs were common on the south side in those days and I scattered many of them. It was there that much of the skullduggery was hatched among the young element and that is where Joe may have got his start. It reminds me of the time I was walking the beat down there one dark night when I spotted a young man standing in the doorway of a store. It was unusual since the street was deserted-- it was long after midnight and no traffic around. When I came near I heard an iron object drop on the cement and on investigating found a large, heavy, monkey-wrench lying in the doorway behind him. He denied ownership and I had no proof. Was he waiting to tap someone on the head or was he going to break into the store? I never did find out.

Joe, it seems was a product of the times and, I'm sure, the bootleg days contributed to the shaping of his outlook on life. By the time he reached his twenties he was an experienced holdup man and slippery. He had narrowly escaped the law several times, did a little shooting and became a bit of a hero in the eyes of the younger southsiders, something like Jesse James.

Two of my friends on the force, good policemen in every way, received a tip that Filkowski was to come to his place of lodging on a certain day. My friends were in the detective bureau at the time. As I recall the homeowners left the premises so the police could wait

218

for his arrival. Both officers had sawed-off shotguns. Joe came home, saw the officers and headed for the door. To prevent his escape, the officers intended to shoot but in the tension of the moment one of them forgot to release the safety catch on the shotgun and the other officer didn't want to shoot for fear of hitting his partner, so Filkowski, in that instant of hesitance, escaped. The papers did a lot of cackling and the two officers were suspended from duty, had a hearing before the Civil Service Commission and were fined the loss of a number of vacation days. It happens. It was one of the risks of the job.

One summer evening we received a call to assist detectives at a house on W. 11th. When we met we learned they had received a tip from a person, who supposedly knew Filkowski, that he had seen Joe enter his neighbor's home. A group of us surrounded the house, staying in the shadows as much as possible in case Filkowski should come out shooting. The detectives hailed the darkened house, shouted that they had it surrounded and that Joe should give himself up. There was no response, just a dead silence. After repeated calls and no answer, a couple of tear gas containers were lobbed through windows and the smoke and fumes poured out but no action from inside. After a time, when the fumes had dissipated, the detectives opened a rear unlocked door and entered a hallway at the end of which was a closed door which, for the time being, was left alone. A search of the premises showed no one there so it was thought Joe could be hiding behind the closed door. With guns drawn the door was opened and there was a man in there alright. He was sitting on the toilet in a confused and befuddled state, obviously from imbibing too much liquid grain, and hadn't noticed the tear gas fumes. He was a boarder in the house and the man the neighbor mistook for Filkowski. So much for hot tips.

Clyde Metal and Clarence Banks were two veteran, experienced detectives whose territory was the west side which also included the south side. They knew all the bad boys and Filkowski too. They made a good team and had their own little system of interrogation which gained results. Metal and Banks were both in their forties. Metal was medium height, slim and serious looking while Banks was short, stocky and fatherly looking. Metal assumed the bad guy attitude, speaking roughly to suspects, while Banks showed a fatherly concern and voiced his objections to Metal's harshness, with the result that many times the suspect confessed to Banks rather than not at all. It was a good act and brought results.

Detective Metal, momentarily, came into the Filkowski picture. One day through a tragic incident, I don't know what precinct or district I worked in at the time nor do I know the nitty-gritty of the occurrence; however, there was a young man by the name of Fortini who worked as route manager for one of the newspapers. It was said he resembled Filkowski in a general way. A detective sergeant, whose name I have forgotten, received information that Filkowski could be seen in a certain area at a certain time almost every day. The sergeant walked this area on the lookout for the supposed Filkowski and one day he spotted him. The man was Fortini. Through later investigation it was thought that Fortini apparently knew he was being tailed by the police; that he apparently was amused and, on purpose, acted suspiciously--a little hide and seek. When the sergeant finally approached him to question him, Fortini is said to have had his hand in his pocket, pulled it out and the sergeant, thinking he was about to be fired on by Filkowski, shot Fortini dead. There is, perhaps, more accurate information to the story, but that is the way I remember it.

Metal was called to make a positive identification of Filkowski and it was then found the wrong man had been shot. The sergeant was suspended from duty, tried in court for manslaughter, or some such, but the jury found him not guilty. The sergeant was returned to duty in uniform. Filkowski was eventually captured and spent many years in the penitentiary. On his release, I understand he married and, if he is still among the living at this writing, he must be in his seventies.

Chapter 18

*T*here is a difference between liking a shift and liking a beat. Because one liked a particular shift to work on does not mean that one liked a particular beat in the shift. I'll talk a little about shifts first and get to beats later on.

Each shift had its good and bad sides. I like them all, perhaps favoring the morning shift. It was hard to get up in the morning hours but it was nice to be off duty in the early afternoon. Then, too, on the first shift one usually did not run into the troublemakers one did on the other two. Things were quieter, people who normally drank in the evening, hung around beer parlors and became troublesome, would be at work. It was daylight and crime was at a minimum; however, it was a time of burglary and housebreaking reports since many business people found their store burglarized when they opened for business.

I liked the afternoon shift because it gave me time to work around the house in the morning, eat lunch at home, and take off for work. The bad side of this shift was that I came home late at night, didn't have a chance to enjoy my two fine children in the evening while they were growing up; however, I tried to make up for it on the other two shifts and on my day off. Also, coming home late at night I'd be wide awake and didn't go to bed until 1:00 or 2:00 a.m. Leona always had a light lunch laid out for me if she hadn't stayed up until I came home. This was usually a good-size sandwich with a bottle of beer or milk in the refrigerator. Afterward I'd read and hike to bed. Those men who had working wives saw very little of them during the month, except for their days off. Social activities were at a minimum and Leona and I experienced this in particular during the years she returned to work to assist in the education of our children. After 20 years at home, Leona returned to work to help put our sons through high school and one through college and medical school. It was a hard job to work and keep up the housework, shop, and prepare meals. Luckily we had two good, understanding sons, which helped immensely.

I enjoyed the night shift because of the action, the absence of traffic, and the quiet of the streets. However, Friday and Saturday nights were rough due to brawls, accidents and some persons letting themselves go all-out for a good time on weekends. In some respects it was a time of greater risk, greater trouble, and a time when one was often absolutely alone in circumstances where there was no help, especially if on a beat. Working one's way out of difficulties built confidence and made one streetwise. One matured in a hurry and soon learned there are two sides to every story one heard and one soon became adept at sizing up a situation from the actions, the nervous glances, the shifting of feet, and other body language. I read somewhere that there are three sides to a story--yours, his, and the truth. Police work also has a tendency to make one cynical and suspicious. A streetwise officer is usually a good judge of character. You see, he's usually dealing with people who either want something or complain about something; he's dealing with the hoodlums and criminal element almost daily, who are usually evasive and tricky and an officer who has been around can usually pick out the lies in a statement, although he may not voice his suspicions.

The bad side of the shift was coming home and attempting to sleep in daylight. It threw your whole system out of kilter for one month and it usually took me three weeks to get used to it. Try sleeping in the daytime on a hot summer day. I tried wearing black cloth eye shades which tied in back of the head and were advertised as inducing sleep. It kept me awake. There were no suitable electric window coolers then, such as they have now, so all I could do was pull the shade and turn on the fan, which only blew hot air.

222

Another bad feature of the night shift was that if one made an arrest and had to go to court the next morning, he'd usually arrive home about noon, dead tired. This happened often. If we arrested the ordinary intoxicated person where the charge was just intoxication and no other violation was involved we had a choice of sending him to court or placing him on the Golden Rule Book. Where it got the name I do not know but placing him on the Golden Rule Book meant that he would be held until he sobered up, perhaps about 6:00 a.m., when he would be allowed to sign a waiver and he'd be released without court action. Many times drunks were in fights, accidents, and assaults, where this would be out of the question and he'd be sent to court--women too.

The old timers told us that when they were rookies they'd ask one of the officers, perhaps appointed before the turn of the century, what the difference was between being drunk and being intoxicated. They had a good explanation for those times; an intoxicated person was one who could still navigate, although a little weavey and knew pretty well what he was doing, whereas a drunk was a man who had to be hauled to the station in a wheelbarrow.

At the time I was appointed there were 15 police precincts in the city. The dictionary defines a precinct as "A subdivision or district of a city patrolled by a unit of the police force." Each precinct had its own headquarters building and jail under the supervision of one or two captains, subject to the orders of the chief of police whose headquarters was the 1st Precinct Police Station, or Central Station, on Champlain Street downtown. Now the Terminal Tower group of buildings on the square is on the site.

The captain was sort of a king in his own domain, looked up to, respected and sometimes feared. He was the one who decided whether charges should be preferred against a subordinate. He had the power to have a subordinate transferred to the boondocks and, if one incurred his disfavor, he could arrange the most miserable details or assignments for you if he was so inclined. Fortunately, they were all fair men, having come up through the ranks. However, the department did have one or two who were considered martinets and looked at with a questioning eye. In the main, we received a fair shake all around and were satisfied. Every department, as with any organization or large business in private life, has its bad apples. We had them too, one way or another and they had to be disciplined or rooted out. The fire department had them also. However, they were not given the publicity in the papers the police were. You see, unfortunately, the police in trouble made better and more interesting reading. We were supposed to be like Caesar's wife--above reproach. Then, too, many citizens considered an officer only a necessary evil, a man who gave out traffic tickets, a man who could restrict your liberty. It's an American trait, it seems, too many times people resent laws and its representatives. I do not class every citizen in this category, far from it, but the feeling does exist in many, albeit buried. It has been my observation that those who criticize the most are the ones who call for help the loudest.

I don't know who named the period between 1920 and 1930 the Roaring Twenties since there didn't seem to be anything roaring about them at the time, less so than during the war years of World War I and II. People lived and went about their work the same as always although the big bootleggers came into being and perhaps a more frequent and bizarre type of killing was invented by them, such as cement shoes where the victim was murdered and his feet encased in a bucket of cement and thrown in the river or lake to sink and never come up. We had gangsters and bootleg kings. Movies portrayed the bootleg gangsters wearing white felt hats with snap brims and a double-breasted Chesterfield overcoat with velvet collar. Chesterfields were the style then and I wore one too. The stance of the gangster was supposedly hands in pockets, a sneer on his lips and a big cigar in his mouth or a cigarette dangling from his lips. Don't forget the yellow kid gloves and white scarf. It wasn't only the bootleggers and mobsters who dressed in that fashion--it was the style then and many men wore that type of clothing.

The Leonardos and Parellos of Murray Hill were the kingpins of the trade around Cleveland. I don't know which one of the two tribes they were after, and I cannot tell you who I mean by "they" but four or five of them were in a barber shop on Murray Hill one fine day and were gunned down--dead. A corner which earned a bad name was about E. 26th and Woodland. It was called the "Bloody Corner" because of the bootleg killings committed there. Newspapers are good at naming things.

I wandered a little afield there. Being the rookie policemen we were, using an old sailing day term, "below the salt." I read that the term was used by officers of a sailing ship who applied it to the lowest-ranked officer sitting at the captain's table. Since the salt was in the center of the table and the youngest officer was at the end and least experienced, he was "below the salt." In other words, we weren't experienced enough nor had we been around long enough for the veteran officer to fully trust us in certain directions. Their conversation was, many times, guarded in our presence. We had to prove ourselves as it were. I knew this was part of the job and, like the rest, put up with it knowing it would pass. That phase soon cleared up.

I recall with amusement one time when two experienced officers and I were walking to our beats. We were only allowed to walk two abreast, therefore, being "below the salt" I walked in the rear. The area to which one of the men was assigned (Brookside Park) could be reached by walking past his home. In fact, we could have all three walked past his house without being off our route to our assignment.

He was a regular imbiber of home brew so when we reached the corner of his street he said to the other older officer, "Come on home. I want to see if that extra overcoat I have will fit you." Stone the Crows! Who did he think he was fooling? They were going to imbibe in home brew. At the time of my appointment all complaints received were answered by the patrolman on the beat, the patrol wagon (emergency), or if big trouble or crime by the cruiser known as the Flying Squad. There were no police radios and the Cleveland Police had still to install radios and radio equipment in their cars, consequently complaints were slow in being answered due to the time it took to relay the information. Heavy crimes called into the precinct station were phoned to the Information Bureau at Central Station who waited for the cruisers to phone them. They were supposed to call the Information Bureau every 15 minutes but many times they ran into situations where there was no phone available or the job they were on booked no interference, so there would be a delay.

The city started to furnish some of the precinct stations with Model-T Ford touring cars, referred to as scout cars. The 9th precinct was one of the lucky ones. I remember the first time it was used. It was a shiny black and the going price for that model at that time was about $500. One man was usually assigned to it on each shift and, sometimes, two men on the night shift. I recall one morning I was assigned to it and was on the south side. I had called into the station and was given a complaint of a knife fight. At that time Cleveland's traffic laws gave the right of way to all east and westbound traffic so it behooved the driver traveling north or south to watch the intersecting streets where there were no stop signs. The complaint was in the Fulton Road area and I was headed west on Starkweather Avenue. A call like this usually was given to the cruiser to answer, but it must have been busy on another call.

226

I wanted to get there in a hurry and knew I had the right-of-way over north and southbound traffic, so when I came to W. 10th I kept going. It was a bit of a blind corner and suddenly another car loomed in front of me headed south, the driver of which had not used caution at the intersection. I'm sure if both of us would have used caution the accident would not have happened. It was a touring car driven by a man. I hit him broadside right behind the driver's seat and drove him against a telephone pole. Before hitting him I had turned the wheels to the left in order to avoid him but the impact turned the scout car over on its side. There I was with the windshield (not shatter proof) broken in pieces, the contents of the car, seats and all, scattered on the street, an accumulation of report forms blowing down the street and me crawling out of it. Luckily I was unhurt. I was shook, naturally, but knew what to do.

I surveyed the wreckage of both cars, called the Accident Investigating Unit and waited for whatever was going to happen. The accident attracted a crowd, pictures were taken by our unit, the cruiser had been notified and appeared on the scene and we took the other driver to the station while the tow truck was called to clear things up. Lieutenant Schwenk was my boss that morning and Sergeant Kalina was on the cruiser. Schwenk asked Kalina when we came in, "Is the car damaged bad?" and Kalina said "Hell, it's a pile of junk." It was. One of the wheels had been sheared off, the radius rod was dangling and it was a mess.

The other driver was a businessman and the owner of a building material company. He was covered by insurance but the traffic violation, under the circumstance could not be overlooked. Consequently, I wanted to hold him for court. He told the lieutenant that he was a friend of our traffic commissioner and asked that he be allowed to talk to him. Instead Schwenk called Commissioner Donahue and it was decided that a traffic ticket for the violation would be sufficient instead of holding him for bail. It was a good decision, the insurance company paid for the damages and the man paid for the ticket. He was a satisfied man, no one was hurt and the damages were paid. In a few days I received an estimate of the cost of repairs from our repair department and the bill came to $100 even which I collected and turned in. I would like to know what damage of that kind would cost now!

The driver's job on the scout car was to answer minor complaints which did not require a cruiser. His job also, sub rosa, was to run errands for the boss in the station, get a sandwich for him from the restaurant, plus a pitcher full of coffee. The pitcher was part of the station-house equipment. Money from the boss always accompanied these errands to pay for the purchase. Sometimes a restaurant owner would throw the coffee in free.

The scout car man also served warrants and sometimes put the prisoner in the back seat while he drove to the station. Putting a prisoner in the back seat required common sense. An older person with a minor charge against him was usually pretty safe. Although one could be fooled too. A younger man sometimes was a bit chancy. We had to judge. One could say they could be handcuffed but that wasn't always practical. In seating a prisoner in the front seat there was always the possibility that he'd grab the steering wheel and head for a telephone pole so he could make his escape. Their minds were always working for a way out. Seating him in the back seat presented a problem too--he could throw his arm around your neck and choke you while driving. It happened to a friend of mine. So you see, caution and suspicion was always uppermost in ones mind. The first thing I learned about handling a prisoner was to never, never, let him get behind you. Have him walk in front of you with your hand holding his belt. Not his coat--his belt. A coat could be shed quickly while walking and you'll find yourself holding a coat instead of a prisoner.

I remember the time when assigned to the 8th precinct. I was working on the scout car one summer morning. It was Sunday, the day we usually served warrants left over from during the week, due to people not being home or just plain dodging the police. We usually found them home resting in bed on Sunday and it may be because they thought the police weren't working that day. This time I had a warrant for a young man charged with a misdemeanor of a minor nature. He had been hard to locate and was always somewhere else when the police arrived. I had long ago become streetwise and acquired my allotment of suspicion, cynicism, and know-how but sometimes it isn't quite enough. It was about 10:00 a.m. when the door was opened by the father of the young man. My inquiry from the father elicited no information but I could see he was uneasy so I suspected the young man was at home, likely in bed. He was. I had him dress, made sure he had no weapons and, holding him by the back of his belt, followed him downstairs. Papa seemed relieved and I suspect he had trouble with his boy all along and was glad to see him in custody.

Of all the days, this is one time I had forgotten my handcuffs although I don't think I would have used them. Everything was going along smoothly with no objections or conversation from the young man. I was alert to the fact that when persons are in custody their minds are very active in considering how they can "beat the gap" or escape. As it turned out, his was too. The front yard of the home was enclosed by a fence with a gate. In holding him by his belt I tried to stay as far back of him as possible since he could make a fast swing with his elbow and strike me in the stomach. I had him open the gate slowly and just as he stepped onto the front sidewalk he gave a quick jerk to the left, causing my arm to strike the fence and loosen my hold. He ran down the sidewalk and lost himself in the maze of houses and

229

backyards. I could have fired a few shots at him but there was the possibility of the shots striking someone in a house and I didn't think it was worth it anyway since, sooner or later, he would be picked up. He was. This was just a minor incident but points to the fact that we had to be very careful and continuously on the alert when handling a prisoner.

Fourney Haas was an acquaintance assigned to the Motorcycle Division downtown. One day he stopped a young motorist for some minor traffic violation on Euclid in the vicinity of E. 40th. The young motorist could not produce his driver's license and said he had it up in his room in the rooming house in front of which they were parked. Fourney, trying to be fair, allowed the young man to go to his room to get it. His room was on the second floor and Fourney was behind going up the stairs when the man turned around and shot him dead. The question is, did Fourney Haas search him before allowing him to go to his room? There were no witnesses but I'm inclined to think that Fourney did, considering he was no rookie. However, sometimes weapons can be missed in a search by the best of us. It happened to me. The man was later caught and, I believe, executed. There is a saying among the criminal element, "Never kill a policeman or a reporter." It's a truth. The reporter is protected by the newspaper for which he works, who give it all the publicity they can, offer rewards and spare no expense, often hiring their own investigators. As for killing a policeman it's an affront to every policeman. They know they may be the next victim. The teams working on the case follow the slightest lead, work all hours and no expense is too great or distance too far. I have yet to see a police killer, in my time in the department, escape although sometimes quite a while elapsed before they were caught.

It reminds me of one summer evening when cruising around the east side, when in the detective bureau. We received a call to go to an address on Kinsman where a policeman had been shot. Nearing the address we heard the roar of shotguns and pistols being fired as though a war was on. On arrival we found a mass of people lining the curb opposite the storefront office, which in the rear was a warehouse containing lumber and supplies. The police, although under cover, had the place surrounded and, facing the store, was a line of police with shotguns and pistols. As in all shootings, the detectives are called to make their investigation as to the whys and wherefores and that is why we were sent there. At the shooting of a policeman, higher-ranking officers also arrive at the scene, such as perhaps a captain, the inspector of detectives and, many times, the chief of police. This time one of them was Inspector of Detectives James McArthur for whom I had worked while in uniform and who was now my boss.

I learned that Sergeant Beasley of the 5th District had received a call of a burglar in the place. While examining the premises for entry and trying a side door he was shot and he crumpled to the pavement. A call for assistance was radioed to headquarters by the driver and soon plenty of police arrived and Beasley was taken to the hospital. Someone saw a shadow and movement in the office and believed the culprit was still inside. Tear gas canisters were thrown through the windows but no one came out and it was then the officers lined up in front and opened up with their shooting irons. The office and contents was shot to ribbons and not a pane of glass was intact. Inspector McArthur and I went in but there was no one there. At the time we were puzzled because we were convinced the shot came from the inside and there was no way the party could escape because the place was surrounded. The next morning the puzzle was solved when the day crew, searching the immediate vicinity, found a rifle lying in a truck parked in an alley directly opposite from where Beasley had been shot. It was apparent it was a false call made by a person who wanted to kill a policeman and had thrown the rifle away and took off when the police arrived.

Sergeant Beasley had been shot in the leg and limped for the rest of his life. The last time I saw him was in Municipal Court. He had passed the Bar examination, practiced law after his retirement and was defending a client. To my knowledge, the person responsible was never caught and the city paid for the damages. I'm sure that all the shooting was partly due to anger of the officers because of a brother officer having been shot and they were determined the one responsible shouldn't get away--one way or another. It could have been a subconscious wish for execution without benefit of trial.

Patrol wagons (emergency wagons) were not the only ones to convey prisoners. In addition to the scout car, we also had a motorcycle with side car during the daytime. This vehicle was manned by a motorcycle man stationed regularly at the 9th precinct. His job was to answer minor complaints, issue traffic tickets, and the rest throughout the precinct. Minor warrants were also served by him and it was amusing to see a man in the sidecar of the motorcycle being driven down the street. It wouldn't happen now.

Chapter 19

*O*ccasionally a rag peddler's horse would walk away with the wagon loaded with old iron, bedsteads, bedsprings and rags while the junk man was busily engaged in a business deal in someone's back yard. When the driverless horse and wagon was reported by a citizen, the emergency would be dispatched so one of the officers could drive the wagon to the station until it was claimed. It was an amusing sight to us and to the good citizens when this happened.

Twice a year we had uniform inspection--in the spring and in the fall. The purpose of the inspection was to see that each man had a uniform in good repair and presentable. If this wasn't done, some of the men, on the careless side, would wear a uniform until it was a disgrace. Old uniforms were allowed on the night shift when it was dark and the work was rougher and the rougher element was encountered, especially by the emergency crews. We were notified of the inspection about a week prior to being held. In the meantime it gave us a chance to have our uniform cleaned, pressed and the buttons shined. We'd shine our badges until they sparkled and the peak of the police cap was shined also. I had a board with a slot into which I could slide about five buttons attached to the uniform. This made for easier shining and prevented the cleaning material from rubbing or showing on the cloth.

In spring we had inspection of the winter uniform and in fall inspection of the summer uniform. We'd be lined up, if the weather was dry, in the station driveway or on the front sidewalk and the captain would walk down the line and carefully inspect each man's clothing. He was accompanied by a sergeant who would mark down the pieces of the uniform the patrolman was told to replace. If shoes weren't shined or one's clothing looked a little well worn, the captain would warn you. If, in his opinion, the uniform needed replacement, you were told to get a new one and it better be done--or else. Having come up through the ranks the captain knew all the tricks and the cover-ups. Some times he'd have a man turn up his cuffs, the bottom of his trousers or turn down the waistband to see how worn they were. I recall one time we had winter uniform inspection. Our overcoats were made of heavy blue material, more like a felt, and lined with blue corduroy. I had Mom press it the morning of the inspection. When my time came to step forward in front of Captain Harwood he called my attention to the shiny imprint of Mom's iron in the middle of my back. It was a bit embarrassing but I couldn't be faulted for my good intentions.

Uniform caps were always made by the Opper Cap Company although there were other uniform manufacturing companies around town. It was rumored among us that the company was paying off someone to have the business thrown their way but there were always rumors floating around so I can't vouch for the truth of it. It could be they were better equipped to manufacture police caps. However, I did wander one time when Captain "Gunboat" Smith had uniform inspection. I had on a practically new uniform cap, peak shined and the cap was spotless. It had been used only a few times. Captain Smith ordered me to get a new one. You don't argue with the boss so a new one was purchased. The hat section was sent to the uniform company and they proceeded to make up the hat from the size indicated on the inspection sheet, so we had no choice in the matter. Yep! We could be heroic and object; we could make a written request to have our uniform reinspected which, in all probability, would result in being ordered to buy a complete new outfit on the grounds that something had been missed on the first inspection. We could also hint that there was hanky-panky going on with the uniform company but then one would be labeled nuts and a troublemaker.

The accepted and sensible thing was to say nothing. We didn't. Shalom aleichem!

A lieutenant, the name doesn't matter, had a few acres out in the boondocks where he raised a few vegetables and such. He had a small Model T Ford pickup truck. By today's standards the truck was really small. It amounted to a box about 4 by 6 feet mounted on a Ford chassis behind the driver's seat. Sides were installed in the box to lend it height. At the 9th precinct barn (garage to you) two horses from the mounted unit were stabled for the mounted men assigned to Brookside Park. When the stalls were cleaned the manure and straw was put aside in the manure box until the city was notified to haul it away. The lieutenant was a conservative German and knew good, fresh manure when he saw it. Also he owned those fertile acres way out there. So, when the manure pile got to a sufficient depth, he'd pull his pickup truck into the barn next to the manure and it was filled by one of the wagon men. There apparently never had been an order issued by him for the pickup truck to be filled by the policeman but it was always done. You see, ordering a policeman to shovel manure was out of his line of duty as a policeman so if a wagon man, or any other policeman assigned to the wagon on manure day, didn't read between the lines and shovel manure that day there were subtle ways he'd find out that the boss was displeased. I shoveled my share of manure too. I didn't like it, but I shoveled. Having shoveled plenty of it for Dad it wasn't all that bad, except that it was an affront to my dignity as an arm of the law. Besides, one carries it around on his shoes and smelled of manure.

The barn crew consisted of the emergency driver, the emergency rear-ended man and the cruiser driver. They were permanently assigned and were never shifted to outside beat work and kept the same superior officers. Some of the cruiser drivers would help make reports which piled up at the end of a busy day but some were hoity toity and wouldn't lift a finger. They were drivers only--in their own minds. Come my turn to hold down the back seat of the cruiser this attitude didn't bother me. I was used to office work, could run a typewriter like nobody in the whole station and reports came easy to me. And--most important, I kept my mouth shut.

I had noticed that some superior officers hated to operate a typewriter and used the hunt and peck system in making reports. A patrolman was usually assigned to the office to help out in answering phones, keep tab on the beat man reporting in from the call box and he was the sole man in charge of the station when the lieutenant or other superior officer had to leave on an investigation. It wasn't long after I had gained some experience that I was frequently assigned to the station office when the regular man was off duty. Experience in office work was noticed and paid off a little in the line of being inside on a rainy day or in the cold weather.

I liked the cruiser assignment since, when it was called, the action was usually of a different nature. The cruiser wasn't sent unless there was a felony committed or in the time of more than usual trouble, such as holdups, knife fights, brawls, shootings, break-ins, and the such. When we were out on an assignment or on a cruising night, since there were no car radios, the sergeant called the Information Bureau every 15 minutes for assignment. A slow process but that's the best which could be done under the circumstances. Every third day was cruising day, which meant we had the entire west side to cover from Cuyahoga River to Rocky River Drive. The cruiser, or flying squad, was a Peerless touring car which seated the driver and sergeant in front with one man occupying the back seat. Actually the car could hold seven passengers since two collapsible folding seats were part of the back seat arrangement. Hanging by straps in the back of the front seat was a shotgun in a leather case and on the floor in back was a box containing tear gas canisters, and ammunition.

We had never been taught to fire a shotgun or to use tear gas at that time and the use of it was left to the officer in charge of the cruiser

236

who, usually, didn't know much about it either. I had used a rifle and handgun but not a shotgun although I knew its general operation. Years later the new appointees were taught how to handle weapons, tear gas, Tommy guns, and shotguns, when the Arms Unit was established. We older officers took a training course also although it should have been included in our original schooling.

When the station was notified of a holdup in progress the sergeant or lieutenant on the cruiser for the day would ring the barn bell three times, which meant a serious crime was in progress, a policeman in trouble, or things of an important nature. We'd jump into the cruiser, the motor started and the lieutenant or sergeant would come running out of the station and we'd be off with the siren wailing. If a holdup was supposed to be in progress we'd be careful with the use of the siren because the sound carries and could scare the culprit away. Usually the officer in charge would say "Get out the shotgun" if it hadn't already been done, in which case the rear man removed it from its leather case, checked to see that it was loaded and at the scene jumped out ready for a shoot-out.

This may seem exciting to my readers but, actually, it was routine. That is the way it was done. Usually the officer in charge would enter the building with gun drawn and sometimes the man with the shotgun, depending on who got to the door first. The shotgun was not always used and depended on good judgement. The driver covered the front or back of the establishment, depending on which side the officers had entered. If they had entered the front, he'd cover the back, for instance. The detective team would also have been notified by headquarters and they were not long behind.

If the establishment had been full of customers at the time of the occurrence there was either near silence or a jabbering, especially women. The first one we'd interview was the victim as to the description of the culprits, weapon used, car used, and direction of flight. It was usually a haphazard description because the victim had only seen the gun or other weapon, was frightened at the time and had not thought to size up the culprits as to height, weight, clothing, or looks. It's understandable. However, we'd phone the information to Headquarters where it was relayed to all precincts.

Now, with radio, it's much quicker. In questioning witnesses it's surprising the various descriptions received. This is understandable, too since persons are not prepared for the happening and are caught off guard. Color of car varies also. Once in a blue moon someone has presence of mind to notice the license plate number; however, the car or license plate number is usually found to have been stolen. Sometimes the questioning aids in the escape of the culprit due to the time consumed in obtaining the necessary information from a hysterical victim. Instead of staying with the questions asked them they'd wander off on another angle of the happening which had nothing to do with the description so necessary in the apprehension. Therefore, the time consumed in obtaining the proper description to phone to headquarters aided in the escape of the culprit. With the coming of the car radio this method was much improved.

It was seldom that a holdup was actually found in progress because by the time the victim called the police, the holdup man had already left the premises and by the time headquarters relayed the message by phone to the station and we arrived at the scene the culprit was long gone. I never cared to handle the shotgun, perhaps because I was not familiar with it and it was cumbersome but preferred to rely on my Police Special Smith and Wesson which I knew and could use. I have been asked on occasion if I was afraid when answering these calls and I can honestly say that I never actually gave it a thought. We were too busy getting to the scene. Rather, we had an eagerness to get at it and "get the so-and-so." I firmly believe all officers felt the same way in time of possible action. We had a contempt for the criminal, you see, although not to the point where caution would be forgotten. I never heard an officer express fear although he may have had it, which is only human in certain situations. I suppose we all have it on occasion but the idea is not to let it get the best of you. As I see it, it was also a matter of training, the result of almost daily contact with miscreants and the knowledge that it was our job. This combined to make a good policeman. Anyway, that's the way I saw it. In reminiscing I like to think that when the chips were down I came through when it counted.

I didn't intend to get on a stump about this subject but while we're at it, let's go a little further. My thought is that, perhaps, the word bravery and cowardice should not be a part of the English language. I may be entirely wrong and looking through the wrong end of the telescope but, actually, who is qualified to judge? We're all born of a long line of ancestors and each one of us carries a bit of the good and bad of each. Someone said that each one of us is like a train, every so often one of our ancestors stick an arm out of the window and that is either one of their good points or one of their bad points which we have inherited and there isn't such you can do about it. The seeming coward may be brave as a lion under different circumstances and the seeming hero may be a coward under certain circumstances. Also, the seeming hero may not have brains enough to feel fear. As I see it, fear is a protective measure too and if you're born without the brains to have fear you're in a sad way. My thought is that there is a mixture of both in each of us and given the right combination of circumstances either one can show up. I've often wondered who deserved the medal, the man in the trenches who knew he had to go over the top and, in all probability would die but went over anyway, or the general who was in the rear directing operations from a shelter who received the medal. During World War II General George Patton was known as "Blood and Guts Patton." The GI's serving under him said it another way, "His guts and our blood."

Occasionally we'd receive a call of a policeman in trouble. This meant that the policeman was having a battle on his hands, perhaps surrounded by angry citizens and fighting to keep from being beat up and, perhaps, for his life. Fortunately, this wasn't always the case but I've seen it happen. When a call such as that was received we went all out to get there. With siren screaming we'd barrel down the street, through traffic lights, on the wrong side of the street to avoid collision, around the wrong side of streetcars--anything to get there in a hurry. A man in such a spot does not have time to call for help and the call is usually made by an alarmed citizen. It's a fact that many citizens enjoy seeing a policeman take a beating and will not assist him in his dilemma. Usually we'd find the policeman fighting one or two men and surrounded by citizens, perhaps egging on the culprits. The policeman was usually out of breath, perhaps his clothing torn and just hanging in there and doing the best he could.

It's one heck of a situation to be in. I know--I was there! It happened like so: As a sergeant assigned to the car covering the Polish territory where, as a patrolman, I had walked a beat, we received a call one evening of trouble in a beer parlor on College Avenue. I had Patrolman Harley Kinney, driver, with me and patrolman John Becker, in the back seat. We later found out that we had been called by the woman bartender. However, she never told us personally for fear of reprisal. The barroom was filled with about a dozen men and the two who gave us trouble. They were both young men, in their early thirties, steel workers from McLaughlin Steel and in their prime. They were all well-liquored and in belligerent moods. They had been creating a disturbance, threatening the patrons and looking for a fight. The three of us entered and I engaged the youngest one in conversation while Kinney and Becker talked to the older of the two. We tried persuading them in a nice way to leave the premises but they cursed us and called us names which we overlooked since we always found that the easiest way was the best and we wanted to remove them from the premises peacefully.

We finally had to take them by the arm and escort them out of the beer parlor. I believe that some of their belligerence came not only from alcohol but because there was a crowd around whom they wanted to impress with their disregard for the law. The police car was parked in front of the beer parlor and it was our intention to put them in the car and drive them to the station to be locked up until they were sober. It would have been poor business to merely remove them from the premises and drive on our way since, in all probability, they would have returned to the parlor and resumed where they had left off. When we neared the car, the older man started to tussle with Kinney and Becker, who had a hard time holding onto him as they were trying to put him in the police car. When the man I had saw this he turned on me and tried to pull away. Right there I knew we were in for a bit of a rough time since the beer parlor emptied of customers who circled us. People from the neighborhood heard the commotion and started to add to the crowd. The prisoner I had was trying to pull away from me and was pulling and punching at me at the same time.

Kinney and Becker were having their hands full and unable to reach the microphone in the car to call for help. In the meantime, the crowd was getting larger and screaming and yelling to the two men to "give it to them" and encouraging them in Polish. It was the spring of the year and we were still dressed in our heavy winter overcoats with our gun, blackjack and handcuffs underneath and unable to reach them during the action anyhow. We were so busily engaged that I don't think any of us thought of them and if we did and used a weapon, the crowd would have screamed police brutality. With all the karate and judo displayed on TV I wonder if in actions such as this, which we encounter from time to time, it could have been used effectively.

While hanging on to my prisoner so he couldn't escape and during the pushing, pulling, and slugging, I lost my hat and my glasses, both of which were picked up by a citizen who later returned them to me.

241

We fell to the muddy ground between the curb and sidewalk, he was determined to escape and I was determined to hang on to him. He was under arrest and he was all mine. We rolled over and over, clawing at each other until I finally got on top of him with his head over the curb and my hands on his throat. I was out of breath, encumbered with my heavy overcoat, and expected the mob to jump us. By this time I didn't give one good damn if I killed him because it was either him or me and it was a fight to keep from being hurt in addition to keeping my prisoner. I started to strangle him. Out of that whole yelling, belligerent mob there wasn't one person who helped us. While this was going on, Kinney had been lucky enough to reach the "mike" and call for help.

Just about the time I had my prisoner's wind choked off over the curb and he was struggling with both hands to tear my hands loose, I heard sirens in the distance and knew help was on the way. When it arrived our trouble was over since they took care of the rest. My prisoner had sucked in enough air when I released him to still be belligerent, and it took five officers to put the two into the emergency wagon. Needless to say they went to court, were fined, had to pay for a new uniform for me and were sent to the Workhouse for a month. A small piece about the affair, with their names, was in the paper the next morning and they lost their jobs at the steel mills too.

One time before that, in my earlier days in the department, I was knocked to the pavement by a mob while trying to protect two prisoners in the squad car. It was the only time I had to resort to the use of my club to protect myself. Would any of my readers care to be a policeman? If you think this was a glorious and heroic adventure, you better have second thoughts. I wouldn't wish such an occurrence on anyone. It was a living--I had a lovely wife and a fine five year-old son to support.

I've been knocked to the pavement on the north side of the 2nd district; I've been kicked in the stomach in a house on the east side of the 2nd District; I've been punched in the jaw in a house on the south side of the district and, given a little thought, I might remember something which happened to me on the west side of the district. Of the three, the third incident was a bit unusual. It was the night shift while assigned to Zone Car 210 with Bill Bonness, the driver, when we received a call to go to a home on a street off Broadview on a report of a woman beaten. With an elderly couple in the kitchen of the home was a small woman sitting in a chair badly beaten with blood streaming down her forehead, lacerations of the scalp and both eyes almost swollen shut. She was barely able to talk. She was a small, fragile woman in her seventies and weighing no more than a frail woman of her age should. It was a pitiful sight. The couple told us that she was a neighbor and had run away from her husband, who had beaten her, and came to their house for refuge. I had the lady conveyed to the Pearl Road Deaconess Hospital by the emergency crew and then went next door to investigate.

The front door was unlocked, the lights were on and the place was a shambles. All the dining room furniture was broken, the bedroom furniture was overturned and smashed into kindling and in the kitchen was a small, wiry man tearing up paper into small pieces and throwing them towards the ceiling and dancing under the falling confetti and yipping. Something like a war dance.

I later learned he was 73. I believe, that evening he went slightly nuts. We had a hard time holding him and he kept repeating, "Where's my glasses? I can't see." Thinking I might find them and he'd then see we were the police and quiet down, I searched the battered rooms and found the undamaged glasses on the bedroom floor among the wreckage. In the meantime Bill was having a time

243

with the little rooster. He didn't want to hurt him and was being pulled around the kitchen. When I put his glasses on for him he said, "Oh, I see," and the next thing I saw was a fist flash in front of me and I received a stiff punch in the jaw, straight from his shoulder. I was momentarily jarred but luckily didn't go down. My instinct was to hit him back but I didn't. I realized that if I hit him I might well break his neck and I'm glad I didn't. Although I was okay my neck and jaw did hurt for a few days thereafter. I'm of the opinion that the man was basically mean by nature and drink had set the fuse.

We handcuffed him, closed the house and took him to Deaconess Hospital to be examined in case he'd later claim he had been beaten by us. His wife, who refused to prosecute, had been admitted. The emergency crew was still there and after warning them to be on guard for his belligerence we left him in their charge. I left instructions to have him charged with intoxication, assault and battery on me and to lock him up for the next day's court. I was later told that while lying on the examining table he suddenly heaved up and kicked one of the policemen in the chest with both feet. The next morning in court he was still argumentative and belligerent with the judge who fined him and ordered him to serve thirty days in the Workhouse.

The lady had a married son whom I contacted and I learned from him that this was his mother's second marriage; that he had wanted her to live with him but she wouldn't and had married instead. He had no idea the man was that sort of person and that now he would see that his mother would live with him whether she wanted to or not. I advised him to look after the house and make sure everything was secure, such as gas, water, and electricity and that's the last I heard of the whole affair.

Chapter 20

We had a two-car garage on Bernard Avenue, the one side housing Mom and Dad's Model T Ford sedan and the other side was for whoever lived upstairs. Dad wasn't much for driving so when they wanted to go to the German Farm, as it was called, on State Road I did the driving. The German Farm was a German organization to which Dad and Mom belonged. At the time it was out in the country, had a dance hall and a few booths where refreshments could be bought. The language spoken was mostly German and Dad and Mon enjoyed being there. After bringing them home, I was free to use the Ford for the rest of the evening.

I was courting Leona at the time and since her family had moved to E. 93rd in Garfield Heights, and I had no car of my own, Mom and Pop's Ford came in handy. The streets leading from Garfield Boulevard were unpaved at the time so I had to park at the corner in rainy weather. The first Sunday afternoon I called on Leona in the new Model T Ford it had rained all morning and the street was a quagmire. I decided to show off our new Ford and drove down the street. The mud was plentiful and the ruts deep. The wheels were spraying mud and water on each side and it must have been quite a sight. Leona told me later that her dad had said "Here comes that redhead in an old beat-up ford with brass headlights and radiator." Of course, he was joking since Ford had long since discarded the brass on Fords.

One Sunday morning I bought a small basket of blooming pansy plants which had caught my eye. I thought it would please Leona and that Ma Touschner could plant them in her garden. Not having the Ford that day I used the streetcar and when I entered the house I was greeted with smiles and laughter. I didn't know what was funny but, it seems, Pa Touschner had spotted me coming down the street with pansies and had teased Leona about me bringing a peace offering for being late. No matter, they were always laughing and joking anyway.

That Model T is almost a story in itself. In order to check how much gas there was in the 10-gallon tank situated under the front seat one had to lift up the front seat and lower a graduated-by-gallon stick into the tank. The

Leona Stein

sedans had the front seat in two parts so that only the person accompanying the driver had to get out while the tank was being filled. In wintertime this was a cold business since not only would one's feet be cold from the wind blowing through the floor boards, especially around the pedals, but the door had to be opened to allow the gas hose to be put into the tank. The Fords had no car heaters, you see.

246

I usually calculated the number of miles driven to a gallon but it was not always accurate and quite a few times I ran out of gas as a result. I well remember one evening when I took Leona, her mom and dad somewhere, perhaps for a ride, when I ran out of gas on Schaaf Road hill, known as Skinners Hill. It was a dark night on Canal Road and not a gas station around except at the bottom of Warren Road hill. The Fords at that time had no fuel pump such as they have now but gas was fed to the carburetor by gravity, consequently when the Ford sputtered to a stop I knew the gas was low. I was half way up Schaaf Road hill and had to back down to get to a level spot at the bottom of the hill where I could turn around. The gas station at the bottom of Warner Road hill was closed but I knew the owner lived in the rear of the station and it being only about 8:00 p.m. I thought I could get him to come out. I hammered on the door and he came out in his nightshirt. He wouldn't open the pumps and shut the door. So there was only one thing for me to do and that was to back up Warner Road hill until I reached Garfield, which I did. I didn't live that down for a long time.

To start the Model T was a tricky business in itself, especially if it had been out in a cold garage all night in winter. It was not unusual to find it necessary to pour hot water over the manifold to help it start. We all had alcohol in the radiator during the winter but it had to be cranked by hand and the oil would be stiff, so it would be necessary to turn over the motor with the crank handle--quite a job. Remember, Fords had no starters then, it had to be done by hand cranking. The procedure was to first pull the spark lever, situated under the steering wheel about halfway down; then one set the gas lever about one third of the way down. The hand brake would be on or you'd get run over if you weren't careful. Next would be to stand in front of the radiator,

247

grasp the crank handle in the right hand but remember not to enfold it with your thumb because, many times, the motor kicked back and a broken thumb could very well result.

After having grasped the crank in the prescribed manner one sort of took a stance with spread legs so effort could be put into the upward pull of the handle. On the left side of the lower part of the radiator was a wire with a loop which lead to the carburetor and which one had to hold between the thumb and index finger of the left hand. Now that we were in the classical position we were ready to start the motor. The crank handle was shoved in to lock and while making a quick heave in a clockwise direction, the wire to the carburetor was pulled at the same time to feed it gas. If the motor was warm, usually in summer, perhaps it would start on the first try. If it was cold you might wind up swearing and kicking the tires in frustration. After the engine had started, one quickly ran to the steering wheel and pulled down the spark lever to give it more spark to keep it going and, perhaps, raised the gas lever a bit to idle it down. If it was a cold day perhaps a little more lowering of the gas lever was in order. In the meantime the car was shuddering as though it was going to shake itself to pieces and the noise could be heard for a block until you had the gas lever and spark lever adjusted to the position where it would run evenly. This was learned by experience. Larger cars had the same problem unless equipped with self-starters, as they were called.

During this time I was studying criminal law, city ordinances, city traffic laws, the book of rules, fingerprint identification and quite a few other books preparatory to taking the sergeant's examination. There was always a strong rumor floating around that the Civil Service examinations weren't exactly on the up and up; that if you wished to get high enough on the list to get the promotion one had to grease the right palms. There were no names mentioned, no proof but the rumors were there and where there's smoke there's fire. Rumors would predict who would be on top of the list and they were usually quite accurate. I knew of some who were promoted from the high end who, in my opinion, were so uninformed they couldn't find the end of their arm. However, I kept at the books and figured it wouldn't hurt to try and the knowledge I absorbed would be for my good. The rumored price for a Sergeant's job was about $300; for a Lieutenant about $600 and for a Captain about $1,000. Eddie Stein wasn't about to pay anything. I took examinations and got zilch. The others on the list who were ahead of me all seemed to be smarter.

In the late 20's some boss in the detective bureau must have heard of my ability with a typewriter so I was transferred to the Auto Theft Unit. I kept records, typed, answered phones, and such. There were three or four of us assigned there with Detective Ralph Imhoff, an old timer, and sort of supervisor of the office staff. The unit was commanded by Lieutenant Harry Weiss, a fine fellow, whose father was Captain Weiss of the 1st Precinct. Captain Weiss spoke with a slight German accent, having come to this country in his youth. He was witty and kind and respected by everyone. His son Harry was much like him. Many detectives then wore a sort of uniform, one might say. It consisted of a dark suit, a chew of tobacco in cheek, and a black derby hat slightly tilted. Willing or not, they acquired a certain walk too. Anyway, Ralph wore a derby and when I first worked alone at night he'd come in, ostensibly on some police matter, derby and all. He didn't fool me--he came to check on me to see if I was on the job, sleeping or what have you. I didn't mind, Ralph was only doing his job. There wasn't time to loaf anyway since the phone was ringing all the time, especially on a rainy night when accidents were many and police phoned in for verification of auto ownership and check on possible stolen autos. The work was confining, the continuous answering of phones was a nuisance and I missed the outside. I requested a transfer and eventually received one to the 8th Precinct where I worked in an area mostly comprised of Romanians, Angle Irish, Gypsies and other nationalities. All good citizens.

The Gypsies were in a class by themselves, the majority not being able to read or write, they stayed among their own kind and one couldn't, many times, make head or tail of their excuses. They lived by their own rules and by their wits. Some were night people and roamed the bars at night with their fiddles making a haphazard living. They had a peculiar way of loud talking and could be heard for a block at night. The ladies made a living by telling fortunes by day-- or night and some by picking pockets. Gypsies have a private whistle which they use when trying to attract another on the street. I learned it and for my amusement used it many times when in back of a group of them who'd stop and turn around to see who was whistling for them but never connected me with it since I was a Gadjo--a non-Gypsy.

There was a settlement of Gypsies around W. 24th and Franklin who were said to be from the Slav tribe and another small settlement around W. 28th and Lorain who were said to be from the Hungarian tribe. I doubt if either knew where their forefathers had come from and only knew themselves to be Romany. For a time we'd receive complaints from the male gender that while driving home late at night they had been flagged down at Superior and the High Level Bridge by two women. The women were always in pairs and on being picked up asked to be driven home--to W. 24th. On the way the driver would be persuaded to stop at their home for a drink as a sort of reward for the lift. The car would never be told to stop in front of the home but to park quite a few doors down the street. These young men, perhaps having a little booze in their systems to begin with, thought they were making "time" with these pleasant girls and had other things in mind than talk and a shot or two of booze. The result was that the next morning they'd find themselves lying in an alley around W. 24th St. and Franklin without money and with less clothes than they had on at the time they had picked up the Gypsy ladies the night before and, occasionally, with no clothes except socks. A Mickey Finn had been added to the booze. Having been in the dark of the night they could never identify the house and being befuddled, the women either. Would they have been able to identify these sweet Gypsy ladies it wouldn't have done any good since there would be denials and two against one would knock out a chance for a warrant.

When I used the word Angle Irish I refer to those living in what was called the Angle, which is an area north of Detroit, a name given to it many years before, perhaps because the streets met each other at an angle. Many of our politicians came from there and many held high, respected offices at city hall. The old-timers were immigrants from Ireland and worked on Whiskey Island unloading ore from the ore boats by wheelbarrow. Whiskey Island was so named because the Cuyahoga River cut it off from the shore. In the early years the island was reached by, as told by old timers, a row boat or small ferry which they had to take to get to work. The island was without water so, it is said, whiskey or beer had to be drunk when thirsty. Take it with a grain of salt, if you please, but that's how they say the island received its name. I do recall, when I worked in the 8th Precinct, the abandoned brick building at one end of the island with the wording

John Dare--Saloon. The story was that Dare had a donkey and when it became thirsty it would stick its head in the window and Dare would give it beer. We can believe all this or not but I heard it from several sources and I believe that, mainly, it's true.

Large cities and small cities have their quota of crime and Cleveland had its share too. There is usually the same type of crime in all cities but the amount of crime is usually in proportion to the size of the population. For a time we were troubled with gas stations being held up and every so often, one gas station was held up more than another. It may be that it was so situated that the culprit could make his escape more easily than at others.

I recall one gas station in Brooklyn which was a frequent target during the evening hours so a patrolman was detailed to conceal himself on the premises to capture the holdup man. I took my turn at these assignments like anyone else. This particular station was a small one-room station with the only place of concealment being the small washroom. We'd be assigned there from about 6:00 to about 10:00 p.m. closing time. I never was quite sold on this assignment because of the close quarters. Sitting on the throne in uniform, peeking through a crack in the door to observe everyone coming into the station was a tiresome and boring job. Thoughts entered my mind as to how best to go at it in case of a holdup. I figured angles of approach, how I should open the door, jump out and surprise him without getting shot and, at the same time, not shoot the attendant. I made it a practice to keep my gun in hand and decided if the time came, I'd throw open the door and come out shooting. These plans are okay but too many "ifs" entered into the picture which one couldn't forsee. Possibly the tension would be so great that your shots would go wild. We were subject to apprehension too, at times, just like any normal person. However, we were on the alert which was half the battle. Fortunately a holdup man never showed up when I was on the assignment. It must have been his night off.

When I worked in the 8th precinct there was a drugstore on Detroit at about 54th. Like all drugstores the druggist was usually in the back room working on prescriptions. The back room was reached by walking behind the counter and entering an open doorway on one side. The opposite side of the drugstore had the same entrance arrangement through another open doorway. This druggist was a young fellow in his thirties and he had been hit so many times in succession that he reasoned the holdup fraternity took him for a sucker. He devised his own method of putting an end to this business so he'd stay in the back room until a customer entered and look him over through an opening in the wall partition and if he looked okay he'd wait on him. On three occasions after he started this system a holdup was attempted. The druggist told that he'd see the man come in and stand at the counter with a gun in his hand, waiting for the druggist to come out of his back room. The druggist would come out but from the opposite side and behind him. He'd make his presence known and when the holdup man turned around with the gun in his hand he'd shoot him down. He killed three in three years.

When I entered the department and until they changed the police precincts to police districts, the area around Central, Scovill, Woodland, Orange Avenues and thereabouts, was in the 3rd Precinct and called the Roaring Third by an enterprising reporter. The name stuck as in the case of the 1920's which is nationally known as the Roaring Twenties. The 3rd Precinct police station was on E. 37th, south of Woodland and housed in what was once one of the better class homes before the turn of the century. I was detailed there from the 9th Precinct on the night shift when they were short of help. I was told that originally the population in the area was mostly German with a mixture of other nationalities; however, in time it became populated by blacks. For some years it was considered a punishment to be transferred to the 3rd Precinct and, indeed, policemen who misbehaved on the job and violated too many rules and regulations were transferred there now and then. The reason it was considered a place of punishment was because of the work load; more crime, more fights and shootings, and cuttings were frequent. The system of transferring the erring officers to the 3rd precinct backfired because the work was so interesting and plentiful that the boys, once there, hated to be transferred away and, actually, requests to be transferred to the 3rd were received from time to time. I had one of the officers tell me that he was glad when his furlough was over so he could get back to work.

Chapter 21

*M*uch of the black population in Cleveland had its start at the time Mayor Harry L. Davis imported them from the deep south to work in steel mills during World War I. They came, stayed, procreated and wrote to their relatives and friends who came and stayed. It is doubtful that Mayor Davis was personally responsible for the influx of the blacks at that time and, certainly, the steel mills must have had something to do with it, but that's what the talk was at the time.

Harry Davis lived on Miles Avenue, one time it was Newburgh. The area around Miles had fine homes and was populated by a good class of Irish who considered themselves "Lace Curtain." The Newburgh "Lace Curtain" Irish looked down on the west side Angle Irish as "Shanty Irish" any day in the week and twice on Sunday. I am of the opinion they could.

Many of the colored in the 3rd Precinct at that time, being from the deep South, inherited the superstitions of their parents and grandparents. Some still believed in Plat-Eye and wouldn't talk to themselves around a Jaybird because he went to hell and reported to the devil on Friday. This has long since changed and education has overcome superstition.

Among these good, black, citizens of the 3rd was some laxity in availing themselves of the marriage ceremony, some couples living without benefit of the preacher. It wouldn't surprise me if the old time colored persons, at that time, still considered a "broomstick marriage" legal. Just living together seemed to be accepted and nothing thought of it. When we questioned them as to their marital status we used an expression which was understood by them. If the answer to our question, as to whether married or not, was "Yes" we'd ask them if they were married "on paper." If the answer was "Yes" we knew they had a license and were officially married. If the answer was "no" we knew they were not married and just living as common-law man and wife without benefit of clergy. (Now we call it shacking up).

There was no offense meant and none taken. When I was taking statements in the Criminal Investigation Bureau for those not "married on paper," we'd type "common-law." Most of the old time colored people were quiet, respected the law and were good Christians in their own way. Third Precinct veterans would tell of occasionally couples not "married on paper" coming to the station after a quarrel and asked to be divorced. Sometimes when this happened, an officer, knowing that they were not married anyway, would have the couple stand before the booking window while he placed his hand on the large police blotter, which is a book with the daily arrest record, recite some law phraseology and wind up with saying, "By the power of the Constitution invested in me you is now divorced." They'd leave the station satisfied and no harm done.

I've told, here and there, of an amusing incident which occurred when I was in the detective bureau. I investigated a report made by the 5th District Police of property stolen from a fine, gentle, old colored lady. The amount of the theft was in the felony range so it was necessary that I interview her in the hope she could shed some light on the thief's identity; which she couldn't. The complaint had first been answered by a colored police sergeant, a man I knew and a very good officer. Apparently the lady didn't have a high opinion of colored officers in general because she wasn't satisfied with having reported it to a colored man. She said, "Dat man come and talk to me yestidy but Huh! What he know? I tol' him I wants to talk to a High

256

White Sheriff." In her eyes I was the "High White Sheriff" and she was satisfied. I've wandered a little afield here so let's get back to more mundane things.

It's a good thing we don't know what goes on behind the scene in restaurants. One of our lieutenants, while prowling around in the back alleys of W.25th one early morning, observed a Greek cook frying a hamburger in the kitchen of a restaurant. The lieutenant was in the dark so the cook wasn't aware that he was observed spitting on the frying hamburger. The lieutenant entered the front and told the sole customer, a cab driver, not to eat it when it was served. He closed the restaurant that night and took appropriate legal action against Mr. Cook.

One early morning when I was on the beat on Euclid near the Public Square I tried the door of a well-known restaurant. I believe it to have been the same location where I saw a holdup man shoot and kill the cashier when I was in my teens. The restaurant usually had a tray of beautifully decorated cakes on a side shelf near the window. I found the door secure so I looked through the front window to see if everything was normal. I noticed a slight movement among the cakes but couldn't see what it was. My flashlight showed the foot marks of a small animal on the frosting with the drag marks of a long tail. It could only have been that of a rat. Public buildings downtown were infested with them. On my day beat I mentioned it to one of the waitresses and she said, "Oh sure. We just smooth the frosting over with a knife."

If I had been in my regular civilian clothes, I'm sure she wouldn't have been quite so frank but they tell a policeman anything, something like being a father confessor. It brings to mind the night I was working as desk sergeant at Central Station. It was in the wee hours of the morning and the charwomen were mopping the floor when a woman, about 35, came in and complained of having had a quarrel with her husband which he climaxed by kicking her in the behind. To back up her statement she turned her back to me, lifted up her dress and there was the red imprint of a shoe on her bare butt. No pants. The charwomen cackled and cackled. It was one of the hilarious things that happens in the life of a policeman.

Since I spent many years on the outside I believe I'm somewhat qualified to talk about beats. I can't say I had a preference for walking any particular beat since, as I mentioned before about shifts, each one had its good and bad side. A day beat was okay except one was many times used to clear up a traffic situation on a corner and stuck there all day. Also, we'd fill in for the regular traffic man on his day off. There were no electric traffic lights then but hand-operated

Edward Stein--Walking the Beat

semaphore with stop and go signs which we rolled to the middle of the intersection. We'd stay there our full eight hours, blowing our whistle twice for north and southbound traffic before we swung the semaphore to the "GO" side and one whistle for east and west traffic before swinging the semaphore to the "STOP" side. Later we had electric stop and go signals hanging from the middle of the intersection as many of them still are. These were operated by hand from an electric switch attached to a pole on the corner of the intersection. The annoying thing about traffic then was that occasionally a wagon and team of horses pulled through and one of the horses decided to stop and relieve itself in the middle of the intersection to the amusement of the pedestrians. It couldn't be moved until done.

We also answered minor complaints more often during the day, such as the frequent complaint of dogs barking or neighbors quarreling. Besides looking for snakes under a bed, the most nonsensical complaint I ever received was from a person about his neighbor stealing worms from his lawn. Often we'd be required to be judge, jury, psychiatrist and, at times, a seeming "so-and-so" to keep the peace. A policeman is in the middle, you see. When there is a quarrel one is usually right and the other wrong. Therefore, you are a friend of the one in whose favor you decide and an enemy to the one in the wrong. We were ridiculed many times and the department condemned in general. We got used to it--we ignored it. If we stayed to bat insults back and forth it would be endless plus being reported for being discourteous. Out of kindness I will not name the lady principal of Buhrer Avenue School, but she was a bitter old spinster, a harridan or shrew par excellence. Her family roots started in Cuyahoga County somewhere in the early 1800's and a road was named after her ancestors. She informed you of it.

She was a frequent complainer about rowdies in the school yard and someone from the first shift, each month, was called to her office and complained to. It seems that everyone sent to her, in her mind, was drunk. I can only surmise that somewhere along the line one of the boys answering her call one time had liquor on his breath. One time, on the morning shift, Frank Svatek and I were sent there and were recipients of her bilious attack. The laziness of the police department was unbelievable, the drunken policemen sent to her office was an insult, in general we were the lowest on earth, she told us. We listened while she raved on and I could see she was doing this to impress the poor timid little girl in the office sitting behind the typewriter, who was quiet as a mouse and hardly glanced in our direction. I believe her sympathy was on our side. We listened, said nothing and at the first break, quietly left the office. I think this really infuriated her not being able to get a rise out of us. I wonder if she complained to the next one about us being drunk.

A beat on the afternoon shift was alright in the sense that complaints were of a different variety. A lady called in the evening one time to get her cat which had climbed high up into a tree. It was in the fall of the year, chilly, and she didn't want the cat to freeze. I wasn't about to climb a tree for a cat, especially in uniform, so I called the Fire Department because they're equipped with ladders but they politely and sarcastically refused. The Humane Society was closed by that time so I told her the cat had a fur coat and wouldn't freeze. Cats have a way of getting down and I never heard what became of it.

In the evening, restaurants and beer parlors were doing a good business and trouble of the personal fisticuff variety was on the upswing. The working man came home for super and went out for a night's pleasure with the result that we had more accidents, more beer parlor trouble, and more things we had to settle. We had corner gangs then, especially in summer, who were young fellows with nothing better to do than meet on a corner, create noise, spit on the sidewalk, litter it with cigarette butts, make insulting remarks to girls, and block the sidewalk for pedestrians. They were a nuisance and a cause of many complaints but a corner gang was a little difficult to break up permanently. They'd run when they saw a policeman approaching and be right back when he was gone. Warnings didn't mean much to them. If the nuisance persisted, one fine evening two or three of us would be told to report to the station and change to civilian clothes. With a sergeant in charge we'd watch the corner and observe their conduct and the length of time they were there. At a prearranged signal we'd stroll down the street, each from a different direction, and round them up. Being in civilian clothes they hadn't noticed us so we'd usually get the most of them. They'd be charged with Sidewalk Ordinance Violation and be taken to court the next day. That usually stopped it for a while. Young folks then did not have automobiles as they do now so the place to meet was a poolroom or corner. I don't believe they are bothered too much with this type of complaint now.

The beat on the night shift was something else again, especially if it was a rough neighborhood. I liked walking a beat at any time except when it rained. Walking in bitter cold weather on the night shift wasn't any pleasure either. The coldest beat I ever walked in winter was in the wholesale district from W. 3rd west to the river and from Superior north to the lake. There was nothing open except Hutter's restaurant on W. 9th. Hutter sold no beer or liquor, officially that is.

You see he had no license--they cost money. However, go in there any night and there'd be railroad men from the Pennsy Railroad down the hill sitting at the lunch counter. Frequently one of the waitresses would go into the kitchen and come out with a brown paper bag, about the size which could hold a pint, and give it to the railroader. He'd pay for his coffee at the front cash register and, I'll bet, the cup of coffee cost him about two bucks. Perhaps the bag contained cough medicine. Nobody seemed to be concerned and I hadn't seen any liquor or money change hands so I kept my snoot where it belonged. However, Hutter did have good thick sandwiches and a thick bowl of soup.

The wholesale district streets were deserted, especially in winter and no self-respecting bum could be seen. The buildings would all be locked tight and night watchmen were inside. The alleys were deep and dark and one walked, stood on corners with earlaps down, or in doorways out of the wind. They were long, long nights. Except for these beats all of us usually had a spot to get in out of the weather. We called them "cooping places" where we could get in out of the inclement weather. It might be a hallway with a chair; it might be a bakery where the baker was baking for the next day's trade and it might be someone's warm basement. These were places known only to the beat man himself and rarely did he divulge it to anyone else. They were arranged for by the beat man through permission of the owners who were friendly to him so you can see why he didn't want to divulge it since he didn't want to spoil it for himself. This was always quietly done by the beat man, no noise to disturb anyone and absolutely no litter such as wrappers, or cigarette butts. Actually, the people appreciated it since it gave them a comfortable feeling with the added protection.

There was a doctor on the second floor of the building which housed the Honecker Drug store on the northeast corner of W. 25th and Clark who gave the beat man, a friend of his, keys to his office. The window overlooked the corner and when he saw the beat sergeant or lieutenant come around he'd leave by the back stairs and out of the door as though he had been trying back doors. In actuality these little tricks were, you might say, almost necessary to keep the beat man comfortable in inclement weather on the night shift as long as it wasn't overdone. You can be sure it was overdone by some. I had my own cooping places too and I preferred the rear of a bakery in rainy and bitter cold weather. I never stayed in them long since I had to make my box ring to the station and, also, I didn't want to wear out my welcome.

I had one at the Acme Bakers on Scranton where they made pies wholesale for the restaurant trade, but I didn't go there often since the kitchen was filthy. They filled the pie shells from wooden tubs set on the floor. Each tub had a woman, bless their Polish hearts, sitting on a chair in back of it, in their encrusted dirty clothing filling the pie shells with canned fruit from the tubs with dirty ladles and, I suspect, even with their cupped hands. The tubs and women were in a circle, like a sewing bee, and they'd have a good time jabbering in Polish. When I walked in I'd greet them with a, "Yaka eedja Panyees," (correct my Polish spelling) and they'd reply with the Polish, "Yaka eedje, Yaka eedja." It was a greeting similar to, "How do you do, Ladies" and the answer would be, "How do you do. How do you do." They'd all smile and make some side remark in Polish and laugh. I suspect it was some snide remark about my sexual ability since they knew I couldn't understand them. I didn't mind, everyone was happy and I knew I had them on my side. Ever after when I

263

ordered pie in a restaurant I'd first inquire if it was baked by the Acme Pie and if it was, I'd do without my dessert.

An occurrence comes to mind when I was walking a beat on W. 25th after midnight which points up what the beat man can run into. The telling takes longer than the occurrence. We had been having quite a few burglaries committed by means of breaking the front plate-glass window in stores, jewelry stores, and shoe stores in particular, where all the culprit had to do was lean forward and take what he could reach and be on his way. I was trying the door of a shoe store south of Bridge Avenue when I heard a plate glass window shatter. When I started north on W. 25th to see what it was all about, a passing man told me two fellows had just broken the window in the florist shop. The shop was about two or three doors north of Bridge and I could see two men shuffling around in front of it. I reasoned that I may have the ones responsible for breaking windows and committing burglaries along the street.

I removed my right glove and put my hand on the butt of my revolver under my overcoat. Overcoats had slash pockets permitting easy withdrawal of a gun. With my night stick tucked under my left arm and glove in hand I walked toward them. When I drew near them they saw me and started to walk north. Both had their hands in their pockets of their overcoats. I told them to stop and since I didn't know if they were armed, I told them to get their hands out of their pockets too. They turned around and I saw both were in their early twenties with one being taller than the other. Big Boy said "To hell with you. You ain't going to search me." This indicated to me that he was hiding something. The shorter man started around my right side and I was sure he was going to try to get me from behind. I knew Big Boy's hands had to come out of his pockets, armed or not.

My readers can pause for a moment, like it "sez" in the Detective stories, and think what they would have done in the same circumstances--remember they were burglary suspects, could very well be armed and one refused to be searched while the other was going to get me from behind. Anyway, it was perhaps due to experience, an instinctive reaction on my part. I removed my hand from the butt of my gun and hit Big Boy on the point of the chin, knocking him to the sidewalk. His hands came out alright--empty. I then made a quick turn and put my gun on the other fellow. (Gee! Just like on TV). After a stunned moment or so, Big Boy crawled up on his hoofs and I lined them both up against the building and searched them--no weapons. Luckily about this time the cruiser came by and the emergency was called and they were taken away. I held them for investigation to find out what it was all about, still having in mind that they were good burglary suspects.

I separated them while in custody and questioned them separately but could never get them to admit to any intent to break the window. Their records were clean. They both worked and were out on the town for the evening and had imbibed a little beer in a beer parlor on W. 25th, were feeling frisky, were on their way home and waiting for a streetcar. In front of the florist shop they had engaged in a little horseplay, pushed each other around and one went through the window. I had obtained the name of a woman at the time who had been waiting for the streetcar and she substantiated their story of horsing around. I believed them. The florist did not want to prosecute since he had insurance and didn't want to bother going to court. I might have let them go on a Disorderly Conduct waiver but I had draped one of them on the sidewalk and thought it wiser to send them to court to get a conviction for my own protection. I charged them with Disorderly Conduct and they received a fine. They were satisfied since they weren't charged with a more serious offense and that ended it.

Now, Sob Sisters and the Righteous can cry police brutality and say I should have used persuasion. Also, if the reporters had gotten wind of it, most likely they would have written it up as a good story with headline, "Policeman Slugs Innocent Man," but let's look at the other side of the coin for a moment. If Big Boy had been armed and I had tried gentle persuasion, I could very well have been shot dead. Leona would have been a widow. Or the shorter fellow could have climbed my frame from the back--or slugged me instead. Various possibilities, you see. This side of the coin is not quite so shiny. Under the circumstances I believe I used the right "Persuasion" and I'd do it again.

Another instance comes to mind when I was patrolling W. 25th one night. The street was called "Rowdy Row" by the newspapers because there was always something brewing there at night. Clark's Restaurant was a chain outfit and had a restaurant on W. 25th. It was a clean place and served good food and this particular spot was open all night. It had a "U" counter with a pay phone attached to the rear wall, close to the kitchen entrance.

In passing it about 2:00 a.m. I saw a commotion--dishes were flying across the restaurant at a man who was trying to use the phone. He was dodging the dishes and sugar bowls while trying to put his nickel into the slot and at the same time trying to ward off other hooligans. The man was in a spot. The restaurant manager and help were in the kitchen looking out at the commotion with white faces but no offer of help. The place was full of customers and in an uproar. I thought, "What the hell's going on here." I entered the place and when the

266

man turned around I recognized him as an officer in civilian dress whom I knew and had worked with on an occasional detail. "Packy" was his nickname--his last name doesn't matter. Packy was doing the best he could but right then it wasn't enough--he was outnumbered. In order to help him I had to take quick action. The space between the counter stools and the wall was narrow, filled with men and Packy was at the end against the wall. In order to get to a phone I would have had to run down the street and to the corner call box which would take time and Packy could very well take a beating. There was only one thing to do. I propped open the street door, grabbed the first man in the row by the collar and dragged him to the street. I pulled or threw about eight of them out onto the sidewalk until I reached Packy. This quelled the whole disturbance. As I recall Packy arrested several but I don't remember on what charge. He was a relieved man, naturally, and thanked me afterward.

The story was that Pack had been to a show downtown and on his way home had decided to have a bite of lunch in Clark's Restaurant because he knew the food was good. While there, several young men apparently liquored up, started a quarrel either among themselves or with the manager and when Packy tried to calm them down and use the phone to call for assistance the fun began. I'm sure Packy displayed his badge or declared himself a policeman but being in civilian clothes it had no effect. He could have walked out of the place but he was not that kind of a man and, besides, the manager knew him.

At night we were expected to try back doors of business places and check for open doors, burglars, and such. In the days, perhaps around the turn of the century, when the town was not as big, they may have had one officer for one or two beats. When I entered the department this was impossible because they had too many beats and not enough officers. Therefore, the beat man had, perhaps, four or five beats to patrol. To get around, all the beats would take miles of walking and, actually, not much would be thoroughly covered. For burglaries and general trouble we'd concentrate on the main business streets or group of stores in order to, at least, prevent as much crime as possible. When everything was quiet at night, the beer parlors closed, the noisemakers gone and nothing open but a restaurant at some main corner, we'd start shaking doors.

I didn't mind the front doors since they were more or less in the open; however, I wasn't quite enamored with back doors and, I believe, all officers felt the same way. My reasoning was that the rats, cats, occasional vicious dogs, and overflowing garbage cans with rustling noises inside weren't exactly conducive to health and peace of mind. A squealing rat or a frightened cat isn't something I'd like to have clinging to my legs. The shufflings and rustlings in garbage cans, plus avoiding objects lying on the ground take one's mind off of trying doors and looking for jimmy marks. Flashlights can only be shined on one thing at a time. I recall one time, on the shabbier end of Woodland, while trying a back door I heard squeaking and pointed my flashlight in the direction of the back fence from where it was coming. There I saw a line of rats on the fence rail, one large one and a row of smaller ones following. Mama rat was teaching her young how to forage at night.

A burglar does not care to enter through the front door if the back door is easier. He'd rather work in the dark, jimmying a door or window. Therefore, I wasn't too concerned about the front of the building, although I'd shake the front doors, but I'd work the back alleys.

Chapter 22

One early summer morning we were cruising east on Detroit just west of W. 25th when I saw a colored man leaning against the door of a barber shop. His leaning position was a little out of the ordinary since he had his one arm extended over his head with his hand near the top of the door window. It struck me as peculiar for two reasons--the first was that he was out of place in the neighborhood, especially at that time of the morning; the second was the peculiar position of his leaning. I told the driver to keep going and we'd round the block and go by him again since I didn't like the looks of it. When we came by a second time he was approximately in the same position but his leaning had shifted a little. We stopped the car and I walked over to him. He had a shifty look. He was very wary and didn't look at me when I questioned him. He said he was the porter in the barber shop and was waiting for a friend to give him a ride home. I knew by his actions that there was something decidedly not kosher. I examined the door and found out why. The wood beading holding the glass in the door was in partial splinters. I was satisfied that he was attempting to remove the glass by first removing the wood beading with his fingernails while leaning nonchalantly against the door and hadn't we come by he may have completed the job.

Naturally, we took him into custody, although if I couldn't get him to talk we had a very poor case since we didn't actually see him work on the beading. He wouldn't admit to a thing so I held him in custody until I did some further investigating. I talked with the barber shop owner the next day and was told that the man had worked for him for a while but did not at that time. He wasn't interested and said if he had gotten in all he would have been able to steal were a few barber tools and he intimated he wouldn't prosecute anyway. I checked his record but found he wasn't wanted and on consulting the police prosecutor I was told, as I knew I would, that there was not enough evidence. I released him and there went an Attempt Burglary case down the drain as it many times does. This fellow must have been through the mill somewhere. It just points up the fact that many times the culprit digs his own way into the jailhouse by talking, whereas, if he had kept his mouth shut the police had no evidence. I've seen this happen many times when I worked in the detective bureau. The experienced culprit will deny, deny, deny, even if caught in the act, knowing full well that if the police have the evidence, he will be charged anyway, but on the other hand, if they didn't and he kept his mouth shut, he'd be released since there could be no charge without evidence. Take heed, you future culprits.

To get back to shaking back doors in alleys, I'd examine a door first for marks of forcible entry. If there were windows, I'd flash my light for marks or breaks. If everything looked in order, I always made a practice of standing to the side of the door and turning the knob quietly. If it was a locked door, I'd give it a good shake to make sure it was secure. If, on the other hand, there were entry marks on the door it would be an entirely different ball game. The telling takes longer than the doing.

A policeman going through an open door at night makes a good target. I believe each one of us worked out his own system. If some preferred to enter the door like strolling for a walk, that's their business. I preferred to move fast, open the door and jump aside if possible, crouch down a little and extend my flashlight away from me at arms length, and flash the light around the room. I also always made it a habit when entering a door to open it all the way till it stopped. I learned this from an old timer--it was a protective measure--someone might be hiding behind it and waiting for you. If it was a large establishment, I'd make my way to the office phone and call for assistance to search. One man cannot thoroughly search a large establishment, especially a furniture or clothing store. There are too many places to hide. Do we keep cool in situations such as this? Sure! However, if anyone says they are not a little apprehensive there's something wrong in their head. I could, of course, walk away from an open door and forget about it but, in my book, "tweren't the right thing."

I recall one time on W. 25th between Detroit and Lorain when I found a back door unlocked. I followed the same procedure and was met with screams. I was taken by surprise and flashed my light in its direction and saw a Chinaman and his wife sitting up in bed screaming. It was the back door to their laundry and they had forgotten to lock it.

Another night on W. 25th I was hung with horseshoes when the burglar alarm to Solomon's three-ball pawn shop went off. The alarm had a habit of going off at the slightest jar. The store was in a two-story frame building with an outside side door leading to the tenant's apartment upstairs. I tried the side door to see that it was secure and the tenant stood on the inside landing firing shots at me through the door just as I was shaking it. Luckily, as was my practice, I had stood aside while trying the door so I was not hit. The tenant had heard the alarm and thought I was trying to break in. I took no action against him since it was a mistake with no harm done. Of course, there was an ordinance against firing a gun within the city limits but it would have been a chintzy thing to do to make an arrest under the circumstances. The stories are endless. There was humor and there was tragedy.

One of the humorous things I recall is the time, about 10:00 a.m. on a summer day, we were notified to go to an address to remove snakes from under a bed. It seemed strange and as we pulled in front of the address a man with a foolish grin was leaning on the gate. He said to forget about it since he had been the one who had called; that he had been drinking and had been seeing things. We reasoned that if he was smart enough to know that he was snaky he wouldn't harm himself; however, as with all complaints, they must be checked out to make sure everything is okay so I went into the house and looked around but found no snakes. We left and never heard from him again.

To get back around the bootleg days there is no doubt that some police were paid off. We all heard of it. Rumors were floating around all the time but to actually pinpoint anything was impossible. Officers like myself never really got into the enforcement of liquor laws. It was left to the Liquor Detail who knew all the tricks and suspected places. Some of the Polish area was on lower ground and I was told by one of the men of the Liquor Detail that in winter they could tell which attic had a still since the snow on the roof would be melted while the other roofs would be covered.

The law was very unpopular with the general public and when a law is unpopular, the citizens soon find a way to disregard it. To many it was a lark to beat the law. Speakeasies were plentiful and some were posh affairs, well furnished and very decorous. There was usually one man to inspect the customers through a peek hole or two-way mirror in the door. If the supposed customer looked like the law, he'd signal the bartender by means of a buzzer to give him and customers time to dispose of the booze. While this was going on, the doorman had one hard time opening the door--real hard. It was an art. You see, the lock would suddenly become stuck and took time to open which, unintentionally of course, gave the bartender and customers that vital time they needed.

It was surprising how well-oiled and working locks one minute suddenly became stuck the next minute. In some cases the police had obtained search warrants for those with whom they had difficulties. Then it was handled differently--the door was smashed down with a sledge hammer. Downtown we had some well-appointed speakeasies and night clubs, especially on Short Vincent. It was the nightclub area of the downtown section--hot stuff, good food, and service. Around E. 105th and Euclid was another area. There were others also. The man on the beat, if there was one, or man on the scout car "kept his nose clean" as we said in the department. He wouldn't go in unless called in because of trouble. They knew that these "joints" as we called them, were under someone's protective wing. It could be a politician, police in the higher echelon, who knows? Don't ask. None of your business--"Keep your nose clean"--go home and sleep in peace.

There was a nightclub on Vincent Avenue on the 2nd floor of a building, well-appointed and had excellent food. To get upstairs one had to be recognized by the doorman before one passed through two doors on the ground floor, both controlled by buzzers. Evidently the owner hadn't been paying his dues on time because a uniformed officer was stationed in the restaurant to watch for liquor sales and discourage customers. The place still had trade in the wee hours of the morning but not much. The officer detailed there told me that he noticed a curious thing--the coffee served to the guests at the tables was hot because it steamed; however, occasionally the waitress would go to the kitchen and bring out coffee in a cup--no steam. Could it be that liquor was being served in coffee cups? You bet!

I assisted in my share of raids but the actual gathering of evidence and going to court was the job of the Liquor or Vice Detail. There was many a slip between the time of taking evidence and the time of going to court. Sometimes, surprisingly, the evidence didn't test enough alcohol so there would be no case. Also, it was known that evidence could mysteriously become lost. There was conjecture and rumors but no proof.

I recall one time working the night shift when all the beat men were stationed at certain corners of their beats until 2:00 a.m. This was unusual but we went and stood. The grapevine had it, true or false, that certain bootleggers didn't want to be interfered with in making their deliveries.

On February 14, 1929, gangster extraordinary, "Scarface" Al Capone, settled a quarrel with gangster George "Bugs" Moran. No one dared call Moran "Bugs" to his face perhaps because he actually was a bit bugs or crazy. According to what I read in the papers it climaxed a 10 year feud between Al Capone, the southside Beer Baron and "Bugs" Moran, the northside booze king. Seventeen men associated with "Bugs" Moran were lined up against a brick wall inside a Chicago northside garage and rubbed out.

I remember the news headlines and pictures well. According to accounts, the garage served as Moran's booze depot and "Bugsy" missed his demise by chance. Apparently the Capone mob had lookouts posted somewhere and when they saw some of the Moran boys enter the garage they mistook one of them for "Bugsy." The lookouts phoned the Capone henchmen, who were ready and waiting, two of whom were dressed in police uniforms and the others in civilian clothes. They had an automobile resembling a police detective's car and went to the garage and lined up Bugsy's men and polished them off. The police suspected Al's mob but didn't have the goods on them so no one ever went to trial. According to an article in a paper, Frank Gusenberg, one of Moran's tough musclemen, crawled out from among the bodies with a couple of dozen slugs in him and when asked who shot him, he said "Nobody."

There were, and perhaps still are, according to a news item, 417 bricks in that wall which were bought by a man named Patey, a promotion man from Vancouver, British Columbia. He is said to have turned down as much as $1,000 for one of the bricks. Al Capone was much in the headlines then and it took Elliott Ness to put him out of business. He went to Alcatraz, not for murder, not for bootlegging, but for evasion of taxes. It seems they couldn't put anything on good old Al, bless his pure heart.

In thinking back to the buzzers on speakeasies reminds me of the time I was detailed to the Vice Detail at the 1st Precinct (now the 3rd District). On prospect between E. 9th and the Colonial Hotel was the Cuyahoga Hotel. It was small and on the corner of an alley. A first-class hotel it was not. It had about three floors and catered, although, not entirely, to whores. Its trade was so select that with a little imagination it could be called a whore house. The first floor of the building was occupied by stores and the upper floors by the hotel. Entrance to the hotel was reached by pressing a button at a door on the first-floor level and then climbing a stair to a small so-called lobby which was equipped with a counter behind which sat the room clerk. Complaints must have been received about the nefarious activities and goings-on at the place. It was strange. With any other hotel, faintly worthy of the name, one walked right in and registered with a room clerk. The Cuyahoga Hotel was different--it had a buzzer arrangement. They were careful about who was let into its domicile--especially the cops.

We had gone there to raid it and after pressing the button, the latch finally clicked and we mounted the stairs. I presume we had somehow been observed before being let in. The clerk, a middle-aged man, was flustered and his face was a bit drained of color. Our captain told him to call the girls down and he denied having any. We searched the rooms and found none. We knew the dear man was lying but where were the girls? It was a chilly night out and the window on the alley side of the lobby was closed. One of us had a hunch and opened the window and there, lined up on the iron fire escape clinging to the skimpy rail, were five or six frightened and dismayed ladies in various stages of dress--or undress--take your choice. So, what were six young ladies of supposed gentle breeding doing on a fire escape in the dark of a chilly night? We ordered them in and they were glad to comply because staring at the alley pavement one floor below wasn't exactly exciting. The clerk had used the warning buzzer button under the counter to warn them and therefore the delay in letting us in. Having no evidence, they were allowed to dress and we chased them out of the building and they were happy to go. I doubt if the hotel management changed its policy.

About October, 1929, we had the stock market crash and the beginning of the Great Depression. History gives the time as 1929 to 1933 but, actually, it lasted longer than four years. I remember it well, it was a rough time. I believe the big crash came because of speculation in stocks, a build-up since World War I of the attitude of "Boom times forever," and other economic factors. The Stock Exchange wasn't regulated as it is now nor were bank accounts protected by federal insurance such as they are at this time. If banks failed, your money went down the drain and could, given an unknown length of time, be returned at a great reduction on the dollar. The nitty-gritty of it can be looked up in the library. I do remember stocks had been purchased on margin and when the crash came, people lost their shirts when they couldn't produce the money to cover the cost of the shares and stockbrokers in New York jumped out of windows. I didn't play the stock market, only twice on a small scale, mainly because I didn't know enough about it and was too conservative to take a chance with the little money I had. I'll relate several occurrences I experienced which should indicate the "make money" miasma of the times.

276

It was in the twenties that I had several hundred dollars in the Pearl Street Savings Bank, W. 25th and Clark when one day I received an invitation to a preview of a new type of engine which was expected to be manufactured by someone. According to the invitation I was one of the selected few who were invited. I didn't feel at all honored but I was curious, as usual, as to what was going on. The place of the preview was in a large building on the east side, the location of which I have forgotten. There must have been quite a few "select" people since there were plenty there. To this day I don't remember what the engine was supposed to do but there it was, about 8 feet high, a large revolving wheel with a traveling belt and it was chomping away, ka-pam, ka-pam, ka-pam, ka-pam.

The Master of Ceremonies was windy in statistics explaining the workings of it and its advantage over something or other. The crowd was looking at it and it didn't take a Sherlock Holmes to detect that few knew anything about it. Indeed, we would have all had to be graduate engineers to understand it. The climax to the whole exhibition came when Mr. M.C. said they were forming a new company to manufacture and market it and we were invited to buy shares in the venture. That broke up the camp meeting. It was a good time to put your watch in your shoe and I led the crowd going out the door. It was a 1920's promotion deal and that's all it was. However, it may have been a good investment, but I never heard of it again. Someone had been furnished a list of the depositors in the Pearl Street bank.

It was also during those years that I was making a meager deposit in the same bank when the young teller engaged me in an extra-unofficial conversation about investing my money in the Cleveland Discount Company. The company had a large newly erected building on Superior near E. 9th, known as the Discount Building. I must have looked like a likely young sucker, with a few bucks. The company was prominently mentioned in the papers and, if I recall correctly, was known for its high investment return to its shareholders. I do not remember what the company was supposed to be investing in to give it such profitable return. I do recall there was so much publicity that even I, in my inexperience, was a little skeptical. I told him I didn't think the company would hold up. It was a good guess. He became slightly incensed at my statement and said, "My own grandmother invested in it. Do you think I would have sold it to my own grandmother if it wasn't any good?" Cleveland Discount folded up and the promoter was indicted and went to jail. It seems the shareholders were being paid the high returns from money received by the sale of shares to other would-be shareholders and it pyramided to the point of collapse. It was a sort of robbing Peter to pay Paul. The teller had hooked his own grandmother. I don't know when the head of Discount expected to get off of the merry-go-round. In retrospect, I think my mom's conservatism had rubbed off on me and I just didn't want to let go of that cold cash.

The man I worked for in the Mechanical Rubber played the stock market on margin. He was always broke and borrowing money to speculate, expecting to make a killing. He had a hot tip one time from his broker in New York--real hot, important telegrams back and forth almost daily. I don't know why he didn't have a Cleveland broker, maybe they were on to him. I don't recall what the stock was but it was so hot that he suggested I turn a little cash loose to make some quick money. I don't remember how much it was, I didn't have much so it must have been a nominal sum. I waited for this big deal to bear fruit but I heard no more for a while so I asked him about it and he said it hadn't paid off.

I was suspicious and what helped in that direction was that I knew his car had been replevied for non-payment. I had the broker's address from previous correspondence and wrote to find out about the stock which the boss and I had purchased. His reply was that he had never received a purchase order for the stock. I knew what happened, my dear boss had pocketed the money because he was broke. I kept the letter buried in my desk drawer and waited for a good opportunity to face him with it. It amounted to locking the barn after the horse was stolen. I had to use my head, he was my boss and I had a job. The amount wasn't much, but I was determined he wasn't going to get by with it--it would stick in my craw. One fine day I decided the time was right so I looked for the letter but it was gone. I'm sure Mr. Boss had searched my desk and swiped it--no proof, so shut up.

I recall the first time I decided to play the stock market on my own. It was in the air--make money in stocks--on margin. I didn't know a stock from Adams off-ox so I picked a cheap one to play with, something within my means. Mexico Oil. Yep! It was on the Curb Exchange and I figured when it went up I'd sell and make a few dollars--just for fun. I bought it on margin, the stock went down. I paid the balance to protect my investment and received a beautiful printed share certificate for 76 shares with the name MEXICO OIL across the face, in a curve yet. It never did recover and finally disappeared off the market. I kept the share paper as a souvenir and some years late I wrote to find out what had happened to MEXICO OIL stock and was told it had folded up. All-in-all these occurrences were a good investment--I stayed "learnt".

To continue with the Depression, people lost their jobs, their homes and the city was in dire straits because citizens couldn't pay their taxes. I saw men rooting around in garbage cans in back of restaurants for food for their families and others selling apples for 5¢ on street corners. I have a clear recollection of one man in his forties, well-dressed and clean-shaven, selling shoe strings on a corner. Railroad gondolas were filled with men who were going from city to city in the hopes of finding jobs.

Rules of the Welfare Department were stringent perhaps due to the great demand for help. In order to qualify for assistance, one first had to sell or dispose of all but the barest necessities, such as table, chairs, and bed. If you owned a piano or rugs, they would have to go. The Police Department received continuous calls for help and I answered many of them. We acted only when a family was without food or heat. It was a sort of emergency fill-in and unpublicized. Periodically a collection was taken up among the members and the money was placed in a fund under the supervision of an inspector of police. When we received a call we'd go to the home, make a cursory inspection to see that their claim was valid and then go to the nearest grocery store or meat market, explain the situation to the store owner, and pick up one or two baskets filled with groceries and meats to tied the family over until help could be arranged. The bill for the groceries and meat would be forthcoming and taken to the merchant. Invariably the grocer or butcher added his own contribution to the basket. In many cases it was a life saver and there were many times when we threw a 50¢ piece on the kitchen table before we left.

At Castle Avenue and Scranton Road was an old building, formerly owned by the Cuyahoga Telephone, which was used as a relief station where applicants registered for relief. These were working people who had to pocket their pride and ask for help and the feeling many times was bitter. Frequently, arguments began because the applicants asked for more than they could be given, consequently a policeman was stationed there at all times. I filled in on the assignment a few times and didn't like it. I felt too sorry for the people and there was nothing I could do but sympathize. I recall a large, shiny sedan driving in front of the building and two well-dressed women got out. One could see at once that they were used to the good things in life and looked out of place in their fur coats and earrings among the working class dressed in sweaters and jackets. Hard times had struck them and they stood in line with the rest. I heard the oldest say, "My heavens, do we have to stand in line in this place?"

Whiskey Island, which I have spoken of previously, was then owned, and perhaps still is, by the Pennsylvania Railroad. It still had the ore docks on the lake side but ships were unloaded in a modern way and the island was used by the railroad for keeping empty and loaded freight cars until they were sent to their destination. A village of unemployed homeless sprung up consisting of one or two room shacks built of flattened tin cans, scrap lumber, tar paper and anything which would keep out the weather. There were from one to three men living in each shack and I conversed with quite a few of them when assigned to the scout car at the 8th Precinct. It was a pity. Most of them were family men who had left some other city to look for employment and were stranded with no place to go. Others were from Cleveland who had to leave home to shift for themselves while the wife and children lived with the grandparents. A few were just plain bums. However, they had erected the shacks from whatever they could find, fixed up the interior as best they could and furnished it with makeshift stoves, old chairs and bunks. It was temporary home to them. At night they'd forage garbage cans in back of hotels and restaurants while some begged from grocery stores or from people during the day. The food was brought back and shared with the occupants of the shack they lived in.

I recall one man sitting on a stool eating the waxed and tough rind of cheese which, apparently, he had found in a garbage can. I suppose it was just as nourishing as anything else and kept him from starvation. Another one I remember was tending a small, black pot bubbling over a small outdoor fire which held a piece of meat, no doubt from the same source. Some of the shacks were fairly comfortable and a few even had a small garden. It was a lot better than sleeping under a bridge or in a packing case on a loading platform which some of them did. I recall one cold winter night I was prowling the alleys off of E. 9th between Euclid and Prospect when I passed the loading platform of a large store. There was a rustling and shuffling in the large packing box standing in a corner. It was unusual since the noise was made by something much larger than a cat or rat. I investigated and found it to be a middle-aged woman, no home. We did have problems with some wayfarers who'd build large fires between buildings or under a bridge which would be a hazard, however, this woman was harmless.

It wasn't too bad in summer on Whiskey Island but pitiful in winter. We didn't bother them except for checking with them occasionally to see how things were going. However, one fine day we were ordered to warn all the tenants to move, give them two or three days and then destroy the shanties. The Pennsylvania Railroad had complained that their box cars were being broken into and property stolen and wanted the wayfarers moved. I was on the cruiser the morning we warned them. They were disappointed and said it was none of them who were breaking into the cars since they were making out one way or another and that it must be someone else. I was inclined to believe them, knowing that most of them were mechanics, family men and people down on their luck. In a few days we returned and they were gone so we demolished the shacks.

Chapter 23

*I*t was during the thirties when the Depression was at its peak and Hitler was ranting and raving in Germany that I saw, while walking my beat, an old man, clean, fairly dressed in clean clothes, on E. 6th at Euclid holding his hat in his hand and waiting for people to drop coins in it. He wasn't saying anything but just standing there. It could be classed as begging. I questioned him and found him to be a fine gentleman down on his luck. I noticed his German accent and he gave me his history. He was born in Germany, came to this country as a young man, married, and had two sons. Both sons passed away years ago, one having been killed in World War I while in the U.S. Army. He had owned his own home, saved his money for his old age but his wife became ill and due to age he couldn't work so had no income and, consequently, used up all the money he had saved. Doctor bills for his wife mounted and he had to sell his home to make ends meet. There was no Social Security at the time. After his wife died and money ran out, he had to take to the streets and make the best of it which he was trying to do by, to him, shameful begging. He tried to communicate with his close relatives in Germany by writing to Hitler for help in locating them since he knew no one else to whom to write. I never found out what Adolph Hitler answered since the last thing he said was, "and you know what that son-of-a-bitch said?" at this point we were interrupted by a woman who asked me for information and when I turned back he had left. I've often wondered what the answer from "that son-of-a-bitch" Hitler was. I was sorry my street friend had left since I was on the point of giving him my change.

It happened in the 1930's when the Communists, formerly called Bolsheviks, demanded that Patrolman Edward Stein, identified by badge number, be fired from the Police for, as the <u>Cleveland Plain Dealer</u> newspaper had it, "kicked a non-resisting prisoner in the back." It's been a puzzle to me why the paper suddenly became sanctimonious in its choice of words. A more accurate description would have been "kicked in the pants" or, to make it precise, "kicked in the behind." I would not have felt so disgruntled about it if it had been true but it wasn't. You see, I tried but missed. Let me tell you what happened.

During the Great Depression, Communist agitators and their trouble-making cohorts took every opportunity to arouse ill feeling against authority. The Police Department was the recipient of much of their abuse, as was any governing body, be it city, county, state or national. Yetta Land, a short, stocky, bob-haired woman with a loud mouth and a rabble-rouser par excellence in the Communist party in our area, took great pleasure in stirring up trouble at public meetings, anywhere, chastising and ridiculing the governing body on the basis of help for the unemployed and the "struggling downtrodden masses." Her favorite places of operation were the Public Square and the Council Chamber at city hall. At that time, with all the unemployed, taxes weren't being paid so the city was short of cash but doing its best to help the poor and unemployed. However, it was a good opportunity for Yetta to get her snoot in the paper, gain free publicity and recruits.

The city councilmen had council meetings almost every Monday night in the Council Chamber of city hall. The Communist party, with Yetta Land in the lead, had been giving them much trouble disrupting meetings with their demands and shouting. The mayor and councilmen finally became tired of the continuous abuse and disruption of meetings and decided to end it.

Came a Monday night I, with a large group of officers, were detailed to city hall where we were kept in a room out of sight of the council chamber. The plan was that we were not to show ourselves until notified; that if there was no trouble we would be on our way after the meeting but if trouble arose we were to remove only the troublemakers pointed out to us by the mayor. We all knew this would be a rough deal and a hassle because we knew how the troublemakers operated.

The council chamber had quite a seating capacity for citizens who wanted to hear the council deliberations on their meeting nights. The seats were similar to those in a theater but were in a semi-circle, the largest section being in the center of the chamber with one aisle on each side separating smaller sections. After the meeting was under way for a time, we heard shouting and yelling and the pounding with the gavel by the mayor to bring order. This went on for some time when finally we received the word to go into the chamber, which we did. When we lined up, the yelling, shouting, and insults became worse but the mayor and his gavel had no effect. Finally, the mayor pointed to the agitators and called, "Take them out." We all had our eyes on him and this was the cue we were waiting for. Remember, the seats were in a semi-circle with the troublemakers in the center of the large section, protected on each side, front and rear, by their cohorts who wouldn't move out of their seats which made it difficult to remove anyone. So, to get at them we had to squeeze our way past the seated Communists who wrapped their legs around ours in an attempt to immobilize us. They had it well planned. With the cursing and yelling "Commies," the pulling and tussling of police to remove the culprits and to extricate themselves from the legs of the communists, it was a holy mess. It's a wonder to me that some of the police restrained themselves from using their billies. I was in the middle of it with the rest of our men.

Orders had been given that when we removed a person we were to place him in a side room where he would be held under guard. The reporters were having a grand time buzzing around with their notebooks, interviewing this one and that one, getting in the way and were a nuisance. However, it was their job. I had my share of work too, especially with one belligerent man who pulled and punched at me and refused to come along. It was a task since my legs were pinned between the legs of a Communist, my pants were slowly being pulled to half-mast, I was disheveled and out of breath but finally made it. By this time my feathers were thoroughly ruffled, my temper a bit high and in my enthusiasm to facilitate his movement into line with the rest of the troublemakers, and more in a reflex action, I raised my foot to kick him in the pants but missed. Due to the action and uproar my reflexes were, perhaps, ahead of my thinking then. He happened to turn his head and saw my raised foot and yelled, "You kicked me." It was an assumption on his part. I wish I had. While all this was going on, the screaming and shouting was a thing to hear, something like a riot. A reporter heard my belligerent friend and took my badge number and wrote a juicy story about the melee, including my name and the happening. I do not recall whether we released the troublemakers after the meeting or charged them with disturbance. To my knowledge Yetta Land was not among them but, as in most of these affairs she may have, as the leaders usually did, stayed in the background and out of trouble.

286

After a workout such as this we like to read the reporter's version and lies so we watch the newspapers. It was in the morning <u>Plain Dealer</u> with the Communists' demand that I be fired; however, the mayor and councilmen had seen the whole thing and were in our corner. In fact, I seem to remember some of the Councilmen helping us. The mayor was interviewed and said it isn't the officer who should be fired but the agitators and commented on the trouble they had caused. That ended it.

I received my share of good-natured kidding from my fellow officers who knew the truth. I consider having gained the attention and aroused the wrath of the Communists to have been an honor and one of the better moments in my police career.

I'll sidetrack for a moment and get back to the Communists and strikes shortly. During the Depression we had crime as usual and recalling the times I was assigned to the cruiser brings to mind that for a time, business people were permitted to call for police protection when they were about to bank a supposedly large sum of money, since one or two employees had been robbed on their way to the bank. So, when a deposit was to be made they'd notify headquarters and our cruiser would be dispatched to convey the depositor to the bank. This turned out to be ridiculous since the cruisers were tied up many times just hauling employees to the bank to make deposits when they should have been engaged in more serious work.

Some of the companies were chiselers. Their employees received, what amounted to, a free taxi ride downtown to their shopping. We didn't know how much money they were banking nor, indeed, if any was being banked at all but we had our orders so we went; however, we talked about it and knew it was happening. One day I decided to stay in the background to see just what the supposed depositor did after entering the bank. There was one company who called for conveyance at least once a week. The depositor employee was a big, buxom Jewish woman who didn't engage in conversation on the way and was very reserved in manner as though bestowing a favor on us. We stopped in front of the Guardian Bank on Euclid and, with a short thank you, she unloaded. The bank had two entrances, one on Euclid and the other on Vincent Street lower level. I followed her as she walked straight through the bank, down the stairs to the Vincent level and stopped at the last window next to the exit. This cookie was no dummy. She had either noticed me or was playing safe since I don't recall seeing anyone behind that window. Perhaps she had the wrong bank. It wasn't long after this when the money transfer business was stopped.

I have been at many Communist rallies and strikes in my time and found that they were no dummies when it came to agitating, usually staying just within lawful boundaries. They must have been taught somewhere. They had their songs and slogans too and one I remember was an endless chant:

"We want bread not bullets
We want bread not bullets
We want bread not bullets."

One of their favorite songs at a rally or strike must have been taken from the melody of a church hymn. It was--

"We shall, we shall, we shall not be moved
We shall, we shall, we shall not be moved
Just like a tree standing by the water
We shall not be moved."

None of us ever liked to work at these rallies or strikes since we were sometimes the victims and targets of rock throwing and we didn't know what plans had been made for a disturbance; however, it was our job and we worked.

There were many bitter strikes for higher pay during that time and, personally, I feel most were justified. Business was poor and the workers, sometimes, were exploited. The police were in the same low pay bind too. We can't class all union organizers and agitators as Communists; however, I am convinced that there were some in the garment industry in Cleveland. On about the third floor of a building on W. 3rd near Lake Avenue was the L. N. Gross Company , a maker of ladies garments. Employees consisted of young ladies and men. I understand the reason for going on strike was the usual poor pay.

Picketers on a strike had to observe the city ordinance regarding blocking sidewalks, allowing people to enter buildings unmolested and not detaining a pedestrian to talk in the interest of the strike. In others words, the public is to have free use of the sidewalk without being bothered by anyone. The rule or ordinance is that a picketer must keep moving and not stand around; therefore, they usually walk in circles. There are good reasons for this since stationary pickets could block a drive or doorway to keep people from entering for legitimate reasons. However, it doesn't mean too much since, if the picketers so desire, they can gang up and block anything, momentarily anyway, but it's a help.

L.N. Gross had trouble with persons not being permitted to enter the building and a few shoving matches had occurred so they were given police protection. A 24-hour detail was established and, with others, I happened to be detailed on the day shift when trouble usually occurred. The young people on strike were nice youngsters and we joked back and forth to pass the time; however, they had to abide by the rules.

Across the street from the building I'd see a man with a camera taking pictures from various angles. I had been to plenty of strikes and knew how business owners operated. There was one young man who seemed to be a leader of the picketers. He was a nice fellow and I learned he had a wife and family and was just out there trying to get a raise in pay. I advised him to get in the background anytime the man with the camera was around, preferably back of the building or in the alley out of sight. He was there for only one purpose, to take pictures of the strikers who, when the strike was over, would be out of a job. I could see he was skeptical and didn't quite believe me. You see, strikers usually don't trust police and regard them as their enemy not realizing that a great many of us are in sympathy with them. After the strike was settled I was told that he and several others were without a job and I'm satisfied our cameraman had something to do with it.

The L.N. Gross Company strike turned out to be a bit violent in the end. The picketers walked in a circle, round and round, most of the day but leaving just enough room for the pedestrians to move along unmolested. Mr. Gross could be observed watching them from a window of this third floor establishment and to the tune of "The Old Gray Mare, she ain't what she used to be," the picketers would sing

"L. N. Gross is playing Peek-a-boo,
Playing Peek-a-boo, playing peek-a-boo,
L.N. Gross is playing Peek-a-boo..."

Occasionally they'd sing the, "We Shall Not Be Moved" song. The strike was dragging along with no settlement in sight so the union

290

used tactics I had seen before. Members of other unions assembled to walk the picket line and swell the crowd. They had nothing to lose when it came to the rising hell department because they couldn't be identified as Gross employees.

There was a big bull of a man, about 40 years of age, in a dirty felt hat and a seedy coat who looked like he was against the Bourgeoisie class and for the"struggling downtrodden masses." He had a definite foreign accent and it was said he was imported from the New York Garment Industry Union; however, he may have been from the local union. He had all the mannerisms and slogans of the Communists and a name which could fit a Russian. As someone said, "If it looks like a duck, if it walks like a duck and if it quacks like a duck, we can presume it's a duck." This man was much in evidence heckling with his loud voice and walking around and I noticed he was deferred to by the strikers. I did notice he was very careful not to overstep where he could be removed to the jailhouse for some violation or ordinance. The union organizers are not dumb by any means and have the angles figured out in advance.

Came the time Gross must have decided to get an injunction against the picketers to limit their picketing to a few persons. To do this one must have evidence, pictures--things like that. One of the ways to obtain an injunction is to have pictures showing that people were being blocked from entering the building. It was noon, the crowd of picketers was unusually large, in fact, some were out in the street and, I'm positive, were from other unions that came to help out. Several officers, and I had just finished our lunch and left White's Restaurant which was close by, but on the opposite side of the street, when we saw a tall man walking in the middle of W. 3rd towards the Gross building. Something like an old western movie where the sheriff is walking down the main street to a shoot-out with the bad guys. We recognized him as having tried to enter the building before but having been stopped by the picketers. The strikers said he was a Pinkerton man hired by Gross, true or not. They referred to him as "the Fink" and called him "Fink" to his face. The name-calling didn't seem to bother him since he never said a word. He had guts! As he came opposite the entrance of the building the picketers surrounded him, punched and kicked him and started to rip off his clothes. He didn't resist much nor did he say a word but continued to struggle.

The police from the LN Gross Company side closed in on the crowd to rescue him while I, and the several officers who had just left the restaurant, closed in on the other side. The crowd could only be described as a mob intent on giving him a thorough beating. We started to pull back the strikers who were mauling him when I heard my loud-mouthed garment union organizer directly in back of me shouting, "Kill-da-son-uff-a-bitch, Kill-da-son-uff-a-bitch", at the same time punching at him over my left shoulder, his fist passing my left ear. I'm sure he wasn't aiming at me but at the so-called "Fink." Suddenly I heard the organizer yell and I glanced around and saw a billy club lying in the groove of his felt hat on the back of his head. The billy belonged to my buddy Fred Fleischer who was behind Mr. Organizer and thought I was being assaulted by him. From the point where Fred was he couldn't see the fist passing my ear and he wasn't about to see me take a licking from behind. This whack on the noggin took the steam out of our organizer and quieted the mob somewhat, enabling us to rescue the victim. Fred had opened the organizer's scalp about an inch and he was running around in circles calling for the police. Keereist! He was acting true to form-- condemn the police but call for help when you need them. The police took him to Lutheran Hospital and, after some fancy needle work, he was released and returned to the scene a very much subdued troublemaker. We had no more difficulty with him. I believe LN Gross obtained his injunction and the strike was settled soon after.

One union local helps another. I recall when I was beat sergeant in the 3rd District, the Sterling & Welch Company, a large top-quality furniture store of excellent reputation, located on Euclid at E. 12th had a strike going. The strike was for the usual thing, more money. They weren't getting anyplace so other locals helped to swell the crowd of agitators. At noon, when the downtown lunch bunch was out, there'd be shoving matches, yelling, you name it. The mounted police were used to control the crowd and one of the horses was stabbed. Crowds would line the opposite curb and watch the men in blue get a workout. One noon, the plate glass window caved in, showering the police with glass. The strike was eventually settled and it was some time later that I met one of the agitators on Euclid and we discussed the strike. I asked him how he was getting along with his job at Sterling & Welch's since the strike and he said, "Hell, I don't work there. I'm a baker. I work nights and came there at noon to help swell the crowd. We had fun. I know who broke that window too."

Jobs were scarce during the 30's and some of the unions used dirty tricks to create jobs for their members. The Painter's Local was one of them, as was the Glazier's Local. A call of a stain or paint-sprayed house was common. A homeowner was afraid to paint his own home for fear of having it sprayed after it was finished. I recall one man who painted the interior of his grocery store on a side street. He and his wife were just about making a living and he was painting the store by himself to save money. While the painting was in progress he was visited by a stranger and asked if he had a union card, or some such. The store owner told him it was his own store and he was doing the job himself. The stranger looked around the store, at the walls, at the ceiling, said nothing and left. A few days after the job was finished the building was sprayed on the outside with red stain. That's the way it was done. Apparently someone reported him.

We had moved into our home on Greenway in 1936 and about 1940 decided the trim on the house needed painting. I knew that a spray job could happen so, before I started painting I went to the Painter's Local, in uniform, and handed the man behind the desk my address. With a direct eye balling and no smile I told him that I was going to paint my house, that I was doing it myself and I didn't want any trouble from them. I'm sure he knew what I meant. The man said, "Don't worry, you won't have any trouble." I don't know whether my visit had anything to do with it but, I had no trouble.

The Glazier's Local, I suspect, had much to do with the breaking of plate glass windows all over town. I talked with one of their organizers at the scene of a broken plate glass window one time and we spoke of union activities. He said, "You don't know what's going on." His meaning was that I didn't know what was going on in their union. He was right, up to a point. None of us knew who committed these vandalisms nor, to my knowledge, were any of them caught. We all suspected the locals were behind it but lacked the proof.

Stink bombs, as they were called, was another little item used. At one time I knew the formula for making the stink fluid but time has erased it from my memory. The fluid was usually put in a fruit jar and thrown through a window of a store at night or it was put in a Christmas tree ornament and dropped on the floor of a store. The odor is nauseating and permeates the clothing and merchandise. I know, I have responded to these complaints and I had a time getting rid of the odor in my clothing. Usually a couple of days airing outside in a good breeze would do the trick but sometimes it lingered on and even dry cleaning wouldn't dispel all of it.

The location of the LN Gross strike on W. 3rd recalls an amusing incident when I was detailed at the German Consul office in a building in that area. It was some time in the 30's when Hitler was on his way up but before General Paul Von Hindeburg, President of the German Government, stepped aside and Hitler came to power, that someone complained of the German flag being flown from the Consul's office window. The German representative was a tall, portly man with a military bearing who may have been trained in the German army. About that time anti-German sentiment was a bit strong around the country and the story goes that one of our police lieutenants, in patriotic zeal and perhaps not liking the Germans anyway, in answer to the complaint, removed the German flag. Our German Consul knew his rights and raised a bit of hell with the result that our worthy lieutenant had to put the flag back and apologize. I believe it to be mainly true since the officer who told me was around at the time and I have a faint recollection of an item being in the newspaper to that effect.

I was detailed at the consul's office only for a day or two, no more, when the amusing incident occurred and over which I have chuckled ever since. The German representative had received some screwball threats so an officer was temporarily detailed to his office. The office was not large, the front end being railed off for visitors. I was in uniform and when I reported I was greeted pompously by Herr Consul. Having long since been baptized in the fire of public criticism it was obvious to me that he was looking down his Teutonic nose at me with distaste and that, to him, I was some sort of microbe. This was okay. Who cared? I did not want to be too much in evidence so I stayed in the background, around the hall, to keep out of his German hair. Later in the morning a buxom, hausfrau type, woman entered the office, with authority, and it was apparent that she was his wife because of the riot act she read to him--in German, yet. Neither knew that I could speak and understand their language or, I'm sure, they would have been more cautious. The incident was short but to the point. The dust of her entrance had barely settled when she lit into him about his sloppy appearance. In my opinion he was neatly dressed. She asked him if his mother had ever taught him anything; that he was a pig and a slob; that he ate like a pig, dressed like a pig and snored like a pig; that he had food stains on his vest and his shoes weren't shined, and on and on. It was a complete army sergeant's dressing down and he had very little to say. I made myself very scarce down the hall until the storm was over but it made my day. I've often thought that I should have stepped into the office and politely told them, in their own language, to be quiet to see what their reaction would have been.

Chapter 24

*I*t was in the afternoon of a day during those years when I worked at the 8th Precinct that I was assigned to the cruiser. Sergeant Angie Krust was in charge and Joe Hasek was the driver. We received a call of a policeman shot at an apartment house on W. 25th just south of Franklin. It was a large brick, two or three-story building with stores on the ground level and apartments upstairs which were reached by a stairway from the W. 25th street level. The building has since given way to a parking lot. We found Officer Ryan lying in a store doorway--shot. In a weak voice, he said "Get Cleary upstairs. Get Cleary." Officers Cleary and Ryan had been assigned to citizen dress and had received a tip that a John Glasscock, wanted for a holdup on Franklin hill, was hiding in his sister's apartment. On the second floor in the hallway, Krust and I found John Cleary lying on the floor, shot and unable to move. Glasscock's sister had an apartment on that floor which had the living room facing W. 25th with the bedroom and kitchen strung out in line in back and to the side. The apartment had two entrances, one to the living room and one to the kitchen. From my recollection it was Cleary who knocked on the kitchen door while Ryan guarded (covered, as we called it) the front entrance. Cleary was let into the kitchen by Glasscock's sister and he proceeded to walk through the bedroom and through the living room on the lookout for Glasscock. He had just about reached the front entrance where Ryan was stationed when Glasscock stepped out from behind a door and shot him. Cleary staggered or crawled out into the hall where we found him. Glasscock burst out of the front entrance and he and Ryan had a shoot-out. It may be that Cleary also had fired several shots. The rest was never quite clear. Some said Ryan followed Glasscock down the stairs, exchanging shots and some said Glasscock escaped through an open upstairs window and onto a garage roof. Ryan couldn't talk because of weakness and died that night and Cleary was down on the floor and hadn't seen the windup. None of us knew the name of the culprit at that time.

Krust told me to cover the back which meant to go outside, in back and prevent the culprit from escaping--or capture him. When I, with the shotgun, reached the rear of the building I noticed blood spots leading from the rear of the building to a back fence. I assumed the culprit had been shot so I followed the spots over the fence, between houses, expecting any moment I'd be shot at. The blood drops lead to Fulton, crossed the street and into an alley. Just then the detective drove up with Lieutenant Jones in charge and I explained to them how far I had traced the blood spots and they took over from there while I returned to the building. I learned later that as Lieutenant Jones and his men were following the blood marks down the alley, they stopped a young man coming toward them. On questioning him he told them that Glasscock, whom he knew slightly, came to his front door and asked him to call a doctor. The young man let him into the house and then Glasscock told him he had been shot. While Glasscock lay down he went out to look for a policeman. Lieutenant Jones decided to accompany the young fellow back to his home and pass himself off as a doctor, which he did. When Jones entered the room Glasscock must have been suspicious because he was just raising his pistol to shoot him when Jones beat him to it and took the gun away from him. I was glad I had a remote part in Glasscock's apprehension although he would have been caught anyway but, perhaps, not so soon. Glasscock was tried and eventually electrocuted. Cleary had been shot in the spine and never walked again, passing away some years later.

Doctor O'Malley, police surgeon, was at Lutheran Hospital attending to Ryan and asked for blood donor volunteers. I was among them and about 8:00 that evening was notified to go to Lutheran Hospital for the transfusion. Perhaps it was the way it was done then or perhaps it was necessary for that occasion but I thought it an odd way to give a transfusion since they put me on a cot next to Ryan, cut a vein in the crook of my right elbow, hooked a tube between my vein and Ryan's and made the transfusion. I have the scar to this day. Ryan had been shot three times, all in the torso. Safety Director Barry was at the hospital and told me not to go back to work until I felt okay. I stayed home for a day or two and by the time of the funeral I went to St. Ignatius Church as one of the pallbearers.

It was on the Christmas Eve in the year before Ryan and Cleary were shot that I was assigned to the cruiser at the 8th Precinct when we received a call of a man shot at about W. 32nd and Bridge. When we arrived at the corner there was a man lying beside an iron picket fence on Bridge. He was on his way home to his wife and two small children for whom he had toys in his pockets, purchased for Christmas, when he was held up and shot by a man. He was weak by this time so we lifted him onto the back seat of the cruiser in a lying position and headed for Lutheran Hospital. On arrival he was taken to the emergency room. I was beside him when he made a half roll and died. Out of the back of his coat rolled the lead from the bullet which had killed him. It was some time later, after the shooting and the capture of Glasscock, that I was discussing Ryan and Cleary's shooting with a shoeshine boy who remembered the incident, particularly since he knew Glasscock who had had his shoes shined by him the day after that Christmas. He said Glasscock was highly nervous and shaken for some reason at the time. I often wondered whether Glasscock was the man who shot the father of the children on Christmas Eve.

Some time in the thirties I was transferred from the 8th to the 1st Precinct, our Central Station Headquarters at E. 21st and Payne. I didn't know why since I felt I was doing a good job and no complaints from the bosses. However, transfers were made all the time and one just accepted them.

Central Police Station--Courtesy of Western Reserve Historical Society Cleveland, OH

Some time afterward I met John "Pig Iron" Miller, a veteran patrolman who had been assigned to desk duty in the lieutenant's office at the 8th. "Pig Iron" had received his nickname from the time he fought two men to a standstill on a street corner. He was a tough German and outspoken. I asked him if he knew the reason for my transfer and he said, "Hell, I know how you were transferred. I was at the desk the morning the chief called the lieutenant and told him he wanted a good man for Central Station and he wanted his name immediately." The lieutenant, whom I had never worked for, opened the roll call book, chose a shift other than his own (heaven forbid), ran his finger down the list and when it stopped there was my name. At least he gave me a chance. It was a good move for me and added to my experience. After I settled in, I enjoyed it, spent most of my years there, it became like home and I made many friends.

While assigned to the 1st I was detailed to the Erie Street Cemetery one Decoration Day. All Clevelanders know that the early settlers are buried there, some having served in the Revolution before Moses Cleaveland came. Erie (now E. 9th) and the cemetery were then on the outskirts of Cleveland but now is downtown, opposite Eagle. If you're history-minded, it's an interesting place to visit and interesting to read the old headstones, many of them being weathered so the names are difficult or impossible to read. On this particular Decoration Day, Chief Thunderwater was going to have his annual Decoration Day ceremony at the grave of an Indian named Chief Jok-o-sot. Chief Thunderwater, if I recall correctly, was of the Delaware tribe. Around Cleveland there always have been a few Indians although, it is not generally known. At one time they had, and perhaps still have, a small organization of their own. They are quiet and good-working people like anyone else.

He came in full Indian chief regalia accompanied by a woman I judge to have been on the sundown side of 70. She, too, was dressed in Indian gear and said to be an Indian princess. Anyway, that's what the chief called her. They were accompanied by six young men of Indian descent. Chief Thunderwater was a man about 5'8" about 75 years of age, had true Indian features and carried himself with dignity. He had personality, he had "presence." Chief Jok-o-Sot's gravestone was a marble, or granite, slab lying flat on the ground. It was cracked in four or five pieces, the cracks radiating from the center of the slab. The ceremony was very interesting. He placed a quart-sized strawberry basket at each corner of the slab. The baskets were filled with wood chips and a bit of hay. The chief began the ceremony with a talk of how the white man stole the land from the Indians and continued with how Chief Jok-o-Sot's gravestone had been cracked. His oratory and emphasis with his hands was impressive. It was this way:

When Thunderwater was a young man there were plans made by the then Mayor Tom L. Johnson to cut a thoroughfare through the cemetery. Johnson's sitting-in-a-chair statue is still on the northwest corner of the Public Square. He was a good mayor and started a 3¢ car line by outfoxing the opposition privately owned car line companies by building a city-owned streetcar line one night, with the help of citizens west on Superior from the Square to the old viaduct. There was some legal hocus-pocus so it had to be built in one night. I have recollection of Dad talking about it and it was the topic of conversation. I seem to recall that the line was built on the sidewalk. The facts should make interesting reading for anyone who cares to look them up. Johnson didn't get along too well with the newspapers who needled him about the manner in which he drove his fire red automobile, known as the "Red Devil," and he was finally defeated in an election by a man whose name I believe was Burton.

To get back to the good Chief Jok-o-Sot's grave, the workers were assembled to start the new thoroughfare, with the mayor present. Apparently there was to be some sort of ceremony when Chief Thunderwater arrived with an injunction to stop the work just after the first sledgehammer blow had been struck in the middle of Jok-o-

Sot's gravestone, cracking it. The work was never carried out. After the talk, the chief lit the hay in each box and threw corn at them. Some struck the boxes and some scattered on the grave stone. From the position of the corn the chief foretold events for the coming year. They were of a general nature and I don't recall whether any of them came true.

About 1928, Alfred E. Smith was nominated to run for President of the United States. He was born and raised in New York City, educated in Catholic schools and became governor of New York State. He was a politician all his life and was known for wearing a brown derby hat and smoking cigars. He was called the "Happy Warrior" and when asked about his educational background he said he had graduated from F.F.M. When questioned about what college or university F.F.M. stood for he said, "Fulton Fish Market." The fish market was in the area where he was raised and, perhaps, worked in his youth. He ran against Hoover but was defeated largely, it was said, because he was against prohibition and because he was a Catholic. I was working in the detective bureau, Auto Theft Unit, then and recall some of the boys being against him because they "didn't want the Pope to run the White House." What nonsense! I recall the same being said when John F. Kennedy was running for President.

Franklin Delano Roosevelt defeated President Herbert Hoover in the election of 1932. He became our 32nd President, remaining in office until he died in 1945. Starting with President George Washington, former presidents only ran for office for two terms until the tradition was broken by President Roosevelt. Hoover is to have said that people followed Roosevelt's golden voice like the Pied Piper and that Roosevelt would take credit for the things which he (Hoover) had planned to do to lift the nation back on its feet. It could be so. Hoover was an engineer and it would be in his nature to make plans.

303

Personally, I could never quite swallow Franklin Delano Roosevelt. I can't pinpoint why, it's just a feeling I had that he was a showman, a slick politician, and a good talker. He was ruthless too. It could be that my memory of Roosevelt's statement before the war that, "Our boys shall not fight on foreign soil," left a bad taste since some months later we were in it up to our ears. Also, perhaps I have an uncalled-for aversion to slick talkers since it has been my observation that the talkers get further ahead and do less than the doers must do to keep even. (A bit of windy philosophy there, don't you think?)

When it came time for nomination, Roosevelt didn't make the mistake of "Silent" Cal Cooledge who, prior to the political convention at the end of his term, made the statement, "I do not choose to run." Accounts have it that he didn't mean he didn't want the job but what he actually meant to imply was that he wouldn't push for the nomination but if it came his way it would be okay. This would seem to go along with his cautious "Down east Yank" character; however, he had cooked his own goose. The papers immediately snatched it up, headlined it, and he was sunk for renomination. I read that Cal lay down in bed and kicked his heels in frustration. I don't believe it.

Roosevelt, you know, had a lady friend on the side. Since he was the victim of polio and moved in a wheelchair, it must have only been platonic. His wife Eleanor surmised it and there was some hoo-haw in the family about it at the time of Franklin Delano's death. Vicious rumors spring up like poison mushrooms. Eleanor was a real nice person, very kind hearted and tried to do what she could for the boys in service and for minority groups although it was spread around that she "liked niggers" (not my words). I have been a member of the Elks organization for a few years and I recall that in years past an

Elk's tooth as an ornament on the end of a watch chain was a thing to have. Eleanor had a wide smile and large teeth, so among brother Elks there was a joke circulating that the Elks organization was miffed because she had not willed them one of her front teeth. Republican Elks I suppose.

Anyway, Roosevelt was not the only president who had a lady friend on the side, if he did. Warren Gamaliel Harding had two, one of whom lived on K street in Washington, D.C. He is said to have fathered a child with one of them.

It was rumored that our revered President John F. Kennedy, whom I glimpsed in a passing motorcade in Cleveland, was quite a favorite with the ladies before he stepped into the White House and is reported to have had a girlfriend on the side while there too. This is gossip, true or not. If all this gossip column information is true, and I believe some of it is, it doesn't make a bit of difference to me and I have not lost my respect for the office of President and whoever may be holding it at the time. To me it proves that they were only human, just like the rest of us.

Adolph Hitler, corporal in the German Army during World War I, paperhanger by trade whose name formerly was said to be Shikelgruber and Chancellor of the German Reich during World War II (Sieg Heil! Sieg Heil!), had a "thing" about Jews. His underlings persecuted and passed hundreds of thousands in Auschwitz and Buchenwald prison camps. During the war, Adolph maintained that Roosevelt was Jewish and that his true name was Rosenfeld (literal translation of the name being field of roses) a name which, among others, is favored by the Jewish. It was not true since Roosevelt was of old New York Dutch ancestry.

305

Whether Franklin Delano Roosevelt was a slick politician and a smooth talker matters not. He was just what this country needed to give the people hope and confidence in time of distress and he pulled us out of the morass of Depression. This alone, besides being a great leader in time of war, makes him a great President.

Shortly after Roosevelt became President he declared a bank holiday. All banks were closed. Due to loss of jobs, people couldn't meet their mortgage payments consequently the banks, especially the savings and loan companies, were hit hard and when depositors became panicky and started a run on banks to withdraw their savings, many of them folded for lack of cash. It was a mess and a time of worry for many people. I think it was Will Rogers who said, "America hasn't been so happy in three years as they are today, no banks, no work, no nothing." I recall seeing Will Rogers on the stage many years ago. He wasn't well known then but his dry humor was evident.

Leona was secretary to the president and to the vice president of the Bailey Company, one of the oldest and largest department stores downtown at that time, and the president told her that if she had any money in banks to take it out that day, since they were to be closed the following day. He was on the board of one of the large banks and had a meeting that day so he knew what was coming. We had about $600 in the Central National Bank branch at W. 117th and Lorain so Leona called me first and then took a cab home and withdrew the money. The next day it closed.

I was detailed at the County Treasurer's office when Leona called me so I told Sammy Wolf, a fellow officer who was detailed there with me that day, that if he had any money in banks to withdraw it since the banks would be closed the next day. I didn't tell him how I got the information, or what source, but he knew I was telling the truth. Sammy was a good officer of Jewish extraction and sharp in finances and investments in his own way. He became a bit excited and said, "Is the Cleveland Trust Co. going under too?" He couldn't get away from the job but did make a phone call or two and I never did know whether he had someone get to the bank in time. Cleveland Trust was hanging on the ropes too but the bank president was a friend of a politician who had Roosevelt's ear so it was saved by some bank arrangement through the government. It was one of the major banks in Cleveland, and had it collapsed, it would have had a crippling effect on the City of Cleveland which had a large amount of operating funds on deposit with them. One of the oldest and strongest banks was the Society for Savings Bank on the Square, which released only a percentage of your deposit at one time. The bank was solid and always had been but was playing it close to the vest.

Roosevelt, or his administration, started the alphabet business in designating departments or projects which has remained ever since. In the three months after the inauguration, Congress was subjected to 15 ideas and programs. It was called the Hundred Days. If I recall correctly, among the first programs was the N.R.A. with its Blue Eagle symbol "We do our part" (National Recovery Act). The big industries such as oil and iron and steel did not go along with the idea and objected but in order to make N.R.A. work, there should be cooperation. The N.R.A. had to do with a minimum wage of $12, to $13 per week for a forty-hour week. Sweatshops in the garment industry had been paying as low as 15¢ an hour for a 60-hour week.

According to the book by Arthur J. Schlessinger Jr. "The Coming of the New Deal," Roosevelt called Myron C. Taylor of the United States Steel and Charles M. Schwab of Bethlehem Steel to the White House. When Schwab said he could not accept the code because of his obligations to the Bethlehem stockholders, Roosevelt asked whether he had been looking after his stockholders when he paid the million dollars in bonus to Eugene Grace, president of the Bethlehem Steel Co. And allowed his miners to live in coke ovens. The President told another visitor that day that he scared them the way they never had been frightened before when he told Schwab he better not pay anymore million dollar bonuses.

Then we had the W.P.A. (Work Project Administration) which had to do with helping people to work by means of public projects, such as repairing and building roads and many other things. I think the pay was about $2.50 or $3 per day, sufficient to keep the wolf from the door and keep one's pride. There were a lot of fakers on the job and it was said that all one had to do to hold a job was to lean on your shovel. I know some who quit because they actually wanted to work for their money rather than lean on a shovel but were ridiculed by the fakers who wanted to make the job last longer.

Many people were so far behind in their mortgage loan payments that they simply moved out of their homes and let the bank have it. The Representative Realty Company in Cleveland was building rows of homes in newly opened allotments when the rash came and stopped building because of lack of buyers. Most of the homes were left incomplete and were in all stages of construction. For years they remained that way with joists and studding exposed to all weather and no roofs to protect them. Some persons elected to leave the house incomplete, covered the first-floor flooring with tar paper or other weatherproof material and lived in the basement until they could accumulate enough money to complete the house. I've seen quite a few with smokestacks sticking up through the floor. Parma was a place of empty-paved streets where the developer had abandoned construction because of lack of money and customers. Incomplete houses were common and I recall thinking that Parma would never be built up. However, it survived and with government F.H.A. loans at a small interest rate--things finally began to move along.

It was a time for people to make money, if they had any and wanted to take a chance. There were some companies that bought bank passbooks, perhaps for 50¢ or less on the dollar and waited for the bank to get back on its feet. Mom had a few thousand dollars in the German Bau Verein on the west side. It had always been a solid, well-managed bank whose officers were very conservative. They, too, were hit and, for a time, had to skim along and halted withdrawals until things improved. We were living upstairs at Mom and Dad's home on Bernard, rent $35.00 per month, on which they survived. Mom was visited by a representative of one of the companies buying up passbooks but this was a little different. The passbook would be turned over to them, what money could be drawn from the bank would be used to complete homes and sell them, thereby making enough to pay Mom and Dad a monthly guaranteed sum with interest and, also, make enough profit for the company. People were going for it since there was no assurance that the bank in which they had their money would open its doors again. At least this gave one a chance to realize something.

We think Mom had about $3,000 in the account at the time which was a great deal for that time and, perhaps, represented all of Mom and Dad's savings. Mom discussed it with Leona who was very suspicious and didn't like the sound of it. After all, Leona was in the business world daily and had a different slant on things then Mom. Leona knew an official at the Morris Plan Bank downtown and explained the proposition to him and his advice was for Mom to forget the whole deal since the company would be unable to produce and she'd lose out. Mom signed an agreement and the company made a few monthly payments and then folded. We are of the opinion that the reason Mom didn't take Leona's advice is because she thought Leona was too young to know.

Mrs. Bergman, who was a close friend of Mom's, also did the same thing. Her husband had been a building contractor and had retired before the bust so she was fairly loaded at the time of his demise. She got hooked too, for plenty. I can't say I blamed anyone for taking a chance, things were in bad shape and it represented the only way to regain your money.

Chapter 25

*L*eona and I lived comfortably in Mom and Dad's home but with Leona leaving for work about 6:30 a.m. and my working the afternoon shift we did not see much of each other for two out of four months, since the second shift was worked two months in a row at that time. When she was home in the evening after a strenuous day at the office she took care of the housework, washed clothes, and prepared the next day's meal. Sometimes she'd stay awake until I came home at midnight and, if not, a snack had been set out for me. We were saving what we could to buy a home, which we eventually did on Woodbury Avenue; however, we didn't stay too many months because it was unsuitable. You see, we found drawbacks such as a corner lot, cinder roads, rather isolated location at that time so we moved to W. 129th north of Lorain, first floor of a two-family.

I forget what Leona's salary at Bailey was but it, too, had been cut. Police and fire wages had been cut 33% and the city issued script in lieu of cash or check in payment of wages. Script was a piece of paper issued by the city on which was printed a promise by the city to pay the amount designated on the paper at some future date. It was about the shape of a U.S. paper dollar. It was used as regular cash by us but some stores did not accept it at face value and deducted 10% while others refused it entirely. The chain stores Fisher Bros., A&P Tea Co., and Krogers accepted the script at face value and received the business of members of the two departments almost exclusively. I distinctly recall that during the hard times Cleveland's operating budget for the entire year was cut to $6,000,000.

Mom and Dad loved Leona because of her sunny ways. I guess she gave a lift to their declining years. Pop remarked that Leona pecked at me like a hen at a rooster. Good years stretched ahead of us, especially when our boys were growing up. Leona would ask Mom's advice on cooking and learned much from her. With what she had learned from Ma Touchner and what Mom told her, she was one of the best cooks around. I loved her pies, especially the fresh peach pies with the lattice of pie crust on top. I learned to cook a bit too and on the morning shift when I came home about 3:00 p.m. I'd put the fixings for a meat casserole together and we'd have a hot dinner when Leona came home from work. I was called to a man's home one day, on some minor police matter, where he lived upstairs with his working son. He was retired, a widower and kept house. Everything was neat and in order and from the oven came an aroma of something tantalizing. I asked him what it was and he pulled out, what he called a six-layer dinner. I still have the recipe and we use it occasionally. I became a fairly good cake baker, but pies were not in my line. The last one I baked was a custard pie which could have been rolled down a stairs without breaking the shell.

It was in the spring of 1934 that Dad had not been feeling well and, one day while in the garage, broke his collarbone while hammering or chopping a piece of wood. Dad was not one to run to doctors and treated himself by putting his arm in a sling. There was nothing we could do with Dad since he had a mind of his own. About that time Mom was planning a trip to Rochester to visit Uncle Bernard and Aunt Mary and she hesitated to leave Dad. However, he seemed to be doing okay and, since he had his arm out of the sling, told her to go and enjoy herself. Pop was never one to deny Mom a trip, especially to Rochester to see her brother, so she went, intending to stay perhaps two or three weeks. I believe it was prior to this that someone recommended a doctor to him whose office was on Clark or Lorain.

Dad must have been feeling low and his arm must have been troubling him so he asked me to take him to the doctor. I was in the examining room when Doc had him strip off his shirt and I saw he had a large black and blue swelling on his shoulder about at the point of the break. Doc didn't fuss around with his shoulder but gave him some ointment to rub on and told him that if it had not cleared up in a few days we were to go to a doctor who was equipped to take x-rays. Something about his look and manner didn't strike me right. Leona would say it was my police training showing up again but in a few days we went to see Dr. Cortner at W. 98th and Lorain who had a fluoroscope in his office. I noticed Doc Cortner seemed to be reticent too about what he saw. I knew it was something, but what it was I wasn't about to question in front of Dad. Indeed, Pop was very cranky at this time and wanted to be left alone, above all, no questions.

On the way down stairs from the doctor's office Dad became tired and sat on a step to rest, which was very unusual. Mom was still in Rochester and she kept writing to me and I'd keep her posted. When I noticed Dad was getting jaundiced and looking thin and haggard I decided it was time to alert Mom to return. She came home in a hurry and was very worried since she could see quite a change in Pop. I was in the dining room one forenoon when Doc Cortner came to examine Dad and I saw him motion to Mom, behind Dad's back, that Dad was going downhill fast.

Pop said to Doc, "You don't have to tell me. I know what I got." During these days I'd be with Dad as much as possible and one time he was lying on the porch swing and I'm sure he realized that he had not long to live for he said, "You've always been a good son but I've tried to be a good father to you." What appropriate answer could I give him? I said nothing. Now I know I should have told him about all the good things he did for me.

Near the end, Mom alerted Uncle Bernard and he came to Cleveland. We had taken turns sitting at his bedside at night and it was about August 3, 1934, the night before his death, that I was with him at his bedside when he said, "Mein sohn, stehe mir bei." (My son, stay with me.) I believe the next day to have been Wednesday, since it was my day off and Leona had a half day off. I met her downtown and we ate lunch and, on arriving home, Dad was dying. Surrounding his bed were Lucy, Mother, Uncle Bernard, Leona and myself, and I believe, brother Al. Dad's eyes were directed to his statue of the Blessed Virgin which had been with him all through the years and had been a wedding present to him in Germany. Lucy said to him, "Dad, pray for me" and the last word he spoke was, "Lucy." He was lucid to the end. I believe this is the way he wanted to go, surrounded by his praying family. I learned from Dr. Cortner that he had had cancer of the liver. He was buried in St. Mary's cemetery, age 73, near the grave of my two brothers who had died in infancy about the turn of the century.

I was working in the 8th Precinct in 1935 and Leona had quit Bailey to stay home and to await her time to go to St. Ann's Maternity Hospital. I was working the afternoon shift and towards morning I was notified that she had been taken there by her brother George who was at our house. I left immediately for St. Ann's, paced the floor all evening, all night and was still there until noon of October 8, 1935, when I was notified I had a fine son. I was not allowed to see her during my period of waiting and, of course, my first question was after their welfare. When I was assured that everything was going along fine and that mother and son were doing well I asked to see them and one of the sisters took me to the nursery where I saw our firstborn. I was now a father--an elated father. After seeing Leona for a short time I left, ate lunch and reported for work.

That evening I took time off for a visit to Leona, who was awake by that time. We were residing in St. Vincent de Paul parish and about 10 days later had the Christening by Father Vanner. He was baptized Martin after my dad and Francis after Leona's father. So there we now had Martin Francis Stein, future President of the United States-- who knows?

Father Vanner didn't know it but I recall him when he was toddling around in diapers and I'd see him from St. Michael's school window. Mrs. Vanner was a very devout person and attended mass every morning. After mass, she and two of her friends would stand in front of the church and visit. This was a daily occurrence so, the story goes, Father Kodelka, later Bishop of Superior, Wisconsin, sent a boy out with chairs one fine day and suggested they sit down while visiting. Good sense of humor there.

Sometime in the 30's we had the Great Lakes Exposition on the lakefront. It was a year or two in construction and was a great show, something never before seen in Cleveland and touted as something which would help our economy. That's where I saw President Franklin Delano Roosevelt. I had been detailed in the vicinity when his train pulled onto the siding in the rear of city hall. He was led out of the door to the observation platform and stood waving his hat at the spectators. Due to his affliction he could not stand upright long and was led back into the car. When he emerged again it was to be wheeled down a ramp built for the purpose. His coming was for the purpose of opening the Exposition and it was good for the morale of the people.

I don't recall what building it was where the banquet was set up for the President but it was near the siding. I believe it to have been one of the buildings built for the Exposition, later torn down. I was near enough to the loud speakers connected to the banquet area to hear the

President's voice and someone answering, "Mr. President, all this has been built..." the rest of it being drowned out by background noises. After the dinner was over and he had made his speech I saw him wheeled back to his car where he again stood on the back platform and waved to the people. There happened to be a slight grade where the presidential cars were standing so when it came time to move, the engine hooked to the cars couldn't pull them up. There was an old locomotive on display at the Exposition which had some history connected with it. Someone must have had foresight because they had the steam up and it was coupled to the other engine and the power of both pulled the cars up the grade.

Two detectives were detailed on the grounds during the exhibition to be on the lookout for pickpockets, boosters, shell game artists, con merchants, and the rest. They were enterprising detectives and wanted to play their part. I knew one of them and he was that type. On their own initiative, without obtaining permission from their superior officer, they deviated from their normal dress; they wore sailor straw hats with bright striped bands, blue jackets with gilded buttons, ice-cream pants, black-and-white shoes, dark glasses and a cane each. Hotsy-totsy! They looked like big-time Board Walk sports. When they appeared for roll call in their finery they created quite a stir. I was told it so happened that the inspector of detectives, head of the whole gumshoe bureau, attended roll call. They were dumped back in uniform; he didn't go for all the foofraw; he wanted his boys to look like detectives.

It's hard to sort out my memories in sequence of the years I spent at the 1st Precinct, later called the 3rd District, so I'll ramble here and there.

Walking a beat downtown was different than walking a beat in a west side precinct neighborhood. We came in contact with more

316

business people and people from all walks of life. This was evident when people were going to or coming from work, the noon lunch hour or just plain shoppers during the day from other parts of the city. Some of the people we encountered during the evening and night hours were a bit shadowy. Ladies of the evening (Soiled Doves, as they were referred to) prowled the theater district and hotel entrances. We had various gambling places, Chinese gambling, Greek coffee houses with card games, flop houses and flea-bag hotels. The red light district along Hamilton had been phased out in Mayor Newton D. Baker's time (later Secretary of War under Wilson). It was said that Mayor Baker's wife was a "do-gooder" and is supposed to have persuaded Newton to abolish the red light district and chase out all the ladies of the evening. They were chased out alright, but they scattered all over the east side, especially along Hough which was referred to as Little Hollywood.

Speaking of Chinese gambling places brings to mind China Town along Ontario Street between St. Clair and Lake Avenues. It consisted of old two or three-story brick buildings which had been there long before the turn of the century. They were occupied by Chinese merchants selling tea and other items imported from China. Buried somewhere in the complex of the old buildings was a Chinese temple, gambling rooms, and headquarters for their Tongs. They were good citizens and settled their own difficulties. Across one of the old buildings was a sign with Chinese letters which no one paid attention to. The department had no one on the force who could speak or read Chinese so the sign was there a long time until an enterprising reporter had it translated--it read "Gambling--Protected by Police." That cooked their sign and gambling--for a time anyway.

This reminds me of the time when I worked in the 3rd District. One of the policeman had the beat around E. 17th and Chester, where there was a small settlement of Chinese. He had observed, in one of the storefronts, a gathering of Chinese around a round table playing a game with black objects. He was no dummy and knew, in his own mind, that there was gambling going on. He called the lieutenant who met him there and he reported there was gambling going on in the store front. The lieutenant asked what sort of gambling there was going on and he replied, "I don't know." The lieutenant, who had been around, told him that if he didn't know what was being played how does he knows they were gambling? Further, if he had to testify in court he would be unable to state what type of gambling was going on and how it was played so, his case would go out of the window. He was told to forget it. I think it was good advice since they weren't hurting anyone and no one on the force knew what the game was all about. I had seen this game played many times but never saw money on the table or money change hands. I ignored them and was wise enough to know that I hadn't a chance of a conviction.

When I worked in the 9th Precinct they had a tongwar among themselves between the Hip Sing Tong and the On Long Tong. Chinese hatchet men were imported to chop down leaders in the tongs. China men with heads chopped off were found here and there. Ed Barry was safety director then and made an attempt to stop this nonsense. However, not much progress was made so Ed Barry, being hot-tempered, and noted for it, issued an order to Police Chief Jakey Graul to close down all Chinese establishments and put the owners and any China man found on the street in jail.

I guess Ed Barry hadn't realized that he was dealing with an old-time German policeman who believed in obeying orders down to the letter. We received our orders to close down all the establishments, chop suey restaurants, laundries and all the rest of it and the fun began. Habeas corpus went out of the window. Restaurants full of diners were summarily closed, the diners told to leave, and they did. The owners and help were locked up and laundries were treated the same. Very soon there were no more China men on the streets because they were all in jail. I recall one waiting for a streetcar in front of the 9th Precinct who was brought in and locked up. Those China men going to headquarters to arrange bail for their fellow countrymen were locked up too. In retrospect it was a good example of what could happen in a police state. The downtown jail was full of China men many of whom didn't know which side was up. I don't thing Ed Barry realized to what extent his order would be obeyed and, I believe, the order may have been only written for the benefit of the newspapers. However, it brought action from the tongs and a meeting was agreed to and the China men released. Peace was declared between the tongs and cemented by rolling a chicken or two over a China man's grave in the Chinese cemetery on W. 73rd. The On Long Tong, the last I recall, has its headquarters on Rockwell and the Hip Sings around E. 17th and Chester. Peace has reigned since.

Elliott Ness, the nemes's of Scarface Al Capone was persuaded to become our safety director to clean the police department of corruption. He got busy and in one way or another induced former bootleggers to tell of payments to police officials. Captains and lieutenants on whom he had the evidence were given a choice of resigning or standing trial. Some chose to face the issue and went to trial, invariably being found guilty and going to the penitentiary. With all the publicity I do not think an unbiased jury could have been found. At a time like that , one appreciates having been aboveboard and having tended to one's knitting. Almost daily there were pictures and headlines in the papers of police being investigated by Ness.

The papers had a field day. The Civil Service Commission was receiving adverse publicity too and, as time went on, some of the flim-flam of examinations were corrected. I had taken the sergeant's examination and the list ran out before reaching my name.

We changed safety directors every time there was a change of administration. I don't recall a safety director that didn't "Shake up the department," as it was called, shortly after being appointed. It was considered a shake-up when a large group of policemen were shuffled from one precinct, or district, to another. Nothing was accomplished but it made good newspaper headlines and good reading. Also it was good politics. The public liked to think that now good things were being done; that the police were not good anyhow and a kick in the pants would be beneficial.

When Adams became safety director he, too, had an idea from outer space. The traffic men who had been assigned to street corners for years were to be dumped back into regular duty in precincts and replaced with bright, young, slim, well-dressed officers who would lend a new aura of nobility to the police department as a whole. I was attending morning roll call at Central Station one summer morning when Captain John Savage came down, looked us over, took a few badge numbers, mine among them, and left. I didn't know what it was all about. Later in the morning when I made my hourly call to the station, the desk man, Patrolman Paul "Kraut Head" Schroeder, sometimes called "Cabbage Head," asked for my cap size. I asked him what it was all about and he said I was going to be transferred to the traffic division. Je-e-e-e-rusalem! Within a week I was.

As traffic corners go I had a good spot--W. 9th and Superior where all the rush hour traffic came to town. My hours were strictly days with Sundays off. For most of us, being shanghaied from a job we were satisfied with it didn't set well. Many of us put in our request to be returned to regular duty and, in some months, a few of us were, I among them. My time in the traffic division is a short story in itself.

320

I noticed that old timers in traffic, whatever unit they were assigned to, in time knew nothing but traffic. They were used for traffic only; they never worked nights and were away from the change of three shifts. Absent was the hurly-burly of regular duty and, consequently, all they seemed to know was how to wave their arms and direct traffic. Few knew how to make out a decent report and when, accidentally, they had to make a crime report most of them had to have help from a regular officer.

They loved the week before Christmas; the motorists handed out gifts and they did alright in the money gift department too. This was okay and more power to them. The day before Christmas they'd hardly leave their post for fear of missing a gift and, indeed, some gladly missed their lunch hour. I recall one at the corner of W. 25th and Detroit who put a barrel next to his semaphore for the people to deposit the gifts. The newspapers caught wind of it, wrote about it in the papers and that ended the barrel business.

We had a good mounted unit in Cleveland, the pride of the city, which had won quite a few national awards for best mounted police in competition with other big cities. They were really good. They were excellent for handling crowds at parades, mobs at strikes, park duty, and the rest. But, there again, take a mounted man away from his horse and he'd miss it like a wife. In connection with this, Chief George Matowitz, our Chief for 25 years, had a brother Jim who was in the mounted unit and had been there for years. I forget the title he was given but his job was to see that the horses were taken care of, doctored, enough grain and hay kept on stock and the horses generally kept in good health. Also, on occasion, when it was necessary to go to Kentucky to purchase a new mount he'd take another man from the unit along who was knowledgeable about horses. Jim knew horses alright and owned a couple himself which he kept on a small farm of his in the boondocks. I'm sure if a test had been made of his blood it would have been found to contain horse manure.

One of the officers whom I knew well told me that he had been in the mounted unit for some years when, suddenly, he was transferred. He never did know why but I surmise it was because someone else wanted to get in and they had to make room. It happens. He put a request in several times to be transferred back but to no avail. One day the opportunity arose when he saw the chief personally and spoke of his wish to return to the mounted unit. Chief Matowitz said "You're just like my brother, give you a pocket full of horse manure and you're happy." President Harry Truman had a habit of using the expression "horse manure" when he read or heard something he didn't believe. His wife, Bess Truman, was approached by a lady friend of long standing who thought she should persuade Harry to stop using the words horse manure. Bess said, "It took me twenty years to get him to use the word manure."

Chapter 26

*W*e'll digress for a moment from traffic and Director Adams and talk about gifts to police. It always amused me to recall the silent movies when the Keystone Cops were depicted as taking fruit from a fruit stand without paying for it. Perhaps they did in days of yore; however, if a policeman dared to take a piece of fruit from a fruit stand without paying for it when I came up in the department, they'd be reported in a hurry and put on charges. Did I ever get gifts? Sure! At Christmas time I'd usually be the recipient of a few bottles of liquor from a few merchants who were friends of mine. I never asked for a thing; however, if a discount was voluntarily given for merchandise purchased during the year I'd accept. Things of this sort were done out of friendship by merchants without favors asked or given.

There were some members, of course, who stepped out of line but persons of that sort are found in all walks of life and, while I'm not a good candidate for sainthood, my regard for this type of person is not high. I guess Mom and Pop had taught us to carry our own load for cadging or sponging was not in our nature and we all paid for our own way. The same holds true for Ma and Pa Touchner and family. I was not a drinking man and the liquor I received at Christmas was stored on the top kitchen cupboard shelf and used for social visits or, actually, for medicinal purposes when I felt a cold coming on when a snort or two--or three--would be useful in warming my system, put me in a rosy haze and usually discouraged a cold. Try it!

I believe it was Director Adams who had the idea of buying new uniforms for the entire Police and Fire Departments, but no money to do it with. He conceived the idea of having a Police and Fire Athletic Meet at the Stadium, charging admission, and from the proceeds outfit the boys with new uniforms. He did. It was a tremendous job of organizing with the fire department, competing against the police in such things as wrestling, boxing, and so forth. I'm surprised they obtained enough volunteers from each department to participate. The whole scheme almost collapsed in Director Adams' lap when participants asked if the city intended to pay their bills and salary in case of injury during the enterprise since it was not in the line of duty. It could very well happen. This gave the city fathers food for thought and finally word was passed that if injuries were sustained it would be considered in the line of duty--or some such. I'm pleased to say that the police boys won almost all the events especially when it came to boxing, wresting and throwing them out of the ring in the free-for-all. The fire boys won the tug-of-war. They were fatter. I heard that the fire laddies were hesitant to engage in fisticuff, wrestling, and the free-for-all since they felt we had the know-how from our work. There was truth in the thought because our boys were more or less used to rough stuff and had no fear of it.

The uniforms were bought from an outfit in an eastern state and it was rumored they were rejects from another city. They were fancier than the ones we had. We now had Sam Brown belts with holsters and colored piping to designate the unit one belonged to. The patrolmen had blue piping, the Traffic Division white, the Mounted Unit yellow and I believe, the Motorcycle Unit had red piping. They weren't bad outfits and were soon named Monkey Suits by the boys. Our traffic boys, myself included, also received a white pith helmet of the African safari variety. I can't say they improved our looks, in fact, some of the short, stocky men looked dumpy.

To show off our new uniforms it was planned to have a parade downtown, so we all had to be coached in military marching;

Forward march!, About face! The drillmasters weren't hard to come by since we had men in the department who had served in World War I. What displeased us was that we had to do the forward marching on our own time so the marching to a military cadence of hay foot, straw foot, belly full of bean soup, about face, was not done willingly.

Director Adams also had an idea in his head that exercise would make the boys slim and healthy, so he had us do sitting-up exercises every day after roll call, on each shift. This was more or less left up to the lieutenants of each shift. It was a fizzle and soon died out. Most of the boys weren't geared to setting-up exercises anyway so to be effective, after the exercise, one should take a shower. Showers were not available and time would be lost on a busy day in answering complaints. Night shift was the worst since there was no time at night roll-call because of the work and to do it after one was through in the morning was a bit nonsensical because we were tired out and, perhaps, had a case in court. We had a fine lieutenant who was an old timer and, I know, thought the whole idea was for the birds, who would order us out in the parking lot after roll call, line us up, give us a right face, a left face and an about face and say "dismissed." This we didn't mind. There was a sergeant in charge of the Mounted Unit and the west side traffic men, who would have roll call about 10:00 a.m., have his men climb the ladder to the hay loft at the 8th Precinct and give them their exercise in summer heat-- the roof was slate.

Old Barney who was a school crossing guard and stood roll call from time to time, I was told, was unfortunate enough to attend one of these exercises. Barney was a stocky, rotund man well into middle life whose only exercise was walking to his school crossing. This particular day, the boys had to lay on their backs and do the bicycling routine. They told me that Barney tried his best and he may have been better than some but when it came time for him to get up he had to be lifted and set back on his feet.

Prior to the day of the parade Captain Savage decided to have a sort of dress rehearsal on the street, in the cold light of day as it were, wherever the public and passersby could see us. This was a good precaution since he knew his boys weren't up to snuff on the "march" business and he wanted us to put our best foot forward and save us, and himself, embarrassment on the fatal day. So, he formed us into a marching body and we strode down Superior. I'm sure it was in military fashion.. We marched west to the prescribed, hup-aa, hup-aa, hup-aaa with him in the lead. When we reached E. 9th the noon lunch bunch and miscellaneous citizens started to line the curb when Savage called, " ABOOOUUUT FACE. SWEET MOSES ON THE MOUNTAIN!" What a 14-karat shambles. To this day I can see the on-lookers laughing. To perform this maneuver takes practice and precision and such practice we hadn't had. Ours had been more or less desultory because our hearts weren't in it and we all felt it was a lot of window dressing and hogwash anyway. Those of us who about faced met the others coming forward with the result that there was a holy jumble. We finally sorted ourselves out and continued on our way. Came the day of the parade in our new uniforms, Sam Brown belts and white pith helmets, we marched down Euclid to bands playing and flags waving and since we had no About Face commands, we did alright. I have a picture somewhere in the family archives.

Some time in those years I was transferred to the Criminal Investigation Bureau of the Detective Bureau. This was an altogether new type of police work and I enjoyed it, but it did take a bit of time to get the hang of it because one had to be thoroughly familiar with evidence in criminal cases.

My studies in the past helped a great deal but now I took statements from the accused and had to make sure all the proper elements of a crime were present. Before a person is charged with a felony, statements must be taken from the victim, the witnesses, the police officer making the arrest and the accused so that all statements can be presented to the prosecutor for evaluation. If all elements are not contained in the statements, there would be no case and the accused would be released. If, in the prosecutor's opinion, sufficient evidence is shown, a warrant was issued and a preliminary hearing held in Municipal Court.

If the municipal judge deemed there was enough evidence for a hearing by the grand jury the accused would be bound over, which means being held over for the hearing of evidence by the grand jury. The hearing by the grand jury is held behind closed doors and everyone is called in to give testimony except the accused who is absent. With the grand jury is the county prosecutor acting in an advisory capacity. If the grand jury finds enough evidence for trial the accused is indicted for trial. On the other hand, if the grand jury decides there is not enough evidence or not clear enough evidence, a No Bill is returned and the accused released. These are all safeguards in favor of the accused. Without a doubt, cases could go down the drain in the office of the Criminal Investigation Bureau if all angles weren't covered by the officer taking the statement.

Of course, the detectives or officers working on a case also knew the evidence necessary and had it well in hand by the time the accused was brought in to make a statement. Sometimes the officer typing the statement could draw out evidence from witnesses, or the accused, which the arresting officer did not know about, thus strengthening the case. We took statements daily for all manner of crimes and eventually we knew the basic evidence needed for any crime in the law book, murder 1st degree, murder 2nd degree, manslaughter, robbery, larcenies, rape, I've had them all, as did others in the office.

When the accused was brought in for a statement they were told approximately these words: "John Smith, you are accused of the crime of _____. You are asked to make a statement which you may make or need not make as you see fit. Anything you say here may be used either for or against you at the time of your trial in court. Now that you know this, do you wish to make a statement?" The answer "Yes" or "No" is typed down; then, whatever statement the accused makes is typed word for word. Nothing is left out, swear words, foul language, if there is any, was also mentioned. Sometimes the accused refused to make a statement or just sat mute. We would put it down. Again some of them would ramble on about things having no connection with the case but eventually arrived at the meat of the situation. Everything was put down. After the accused had stopped talking we'd start with the questions, covering the vital points necessary to make a case which the accused had failed to mention.

Finally, with the statement completed, we would type at the bottom "Now that you have read the statement is it true?" The accused had been allowed to read the statement or we would read it to him since sometimes the accused would have difficulty reading it. If there were any changes or additions the accused wished to make, we would type it in. Finally, with a "Yes" or "No" to the truth of the statement, the accused would be asked to sign it which was then witnessed by the stenographer and the arresting officer. Sometimes the accused refused to say whether the statement was true or not and, sometimes would refuse to sign. This was also entered on the statement. I took a statement one time from a fellow officer who was charged with 2nd degree murder as a result of a shooting he was involved in while off duty. He received a life sentence and, presumably, has since passed away. His son later joined the police department and he was a fine officer. I never told him about it.

Making a statement has its advantages and disadvantages. If a person refuses to make a statement, the prosecuting attorney at the time of trial will call it to the attention of the judge and jury which could put the accused in a poor light. On the other hand, if a statement is made it may very well be used against the accused but it can also work for him. In recalling my work in the criminal investigation bureau I believe the best way for the accused who knows he is in the wrong is to say that he does not refuse to make a statement but he would prefer to have his attorney present. This way he hasn't refused and if an attorney is allowed, it's to his advantage. Admittedly there are unforseen "ifs" involved.

I recall one particular statement I took where the accused told me everything as truthfully as possible, signed the statement without hesitation, was charged with 1st degree murder and was found not guilty. I always believed it was a just verdict although the accused had planned the act, waited for the victim, and hammered in his skull until he was dead. All the elements of 1st degree murder were present. It happened in the colored neighborhood. The accused and victim were colored. It developed that the accused was a good family man with three or four children, was employed in the post office, handling mail and had been so employed for some years. His record was good.

However, he had a wife of easy virtue who became acquainted with the victim, possibly at some bar. The two started to keep company and going places and, no doubt, there was hanky-panky going on. The husband learned of it and objected but his wife paid

329

no attention. He voiced his objection to the victim on several occasions but was beaten up by him. The accused was a small man and, no doubt, no physical match for the victim. This went on for some time, so came the day the accused had his fill. He knew where the victim lived and that it was in the upstairs of a two-family home which was reached by a stairs from the 1st floor level. He hid beside the stairs until the victim came down on his way to work one early morning and played pinochle on his skull with a hammer, after which he went to the lake front and buried the hammer in the sand and then gave himself up to the police.

It can be surmised that this man was desperate; that he tried to stop the goings-on amicably and, in order to save his marriage and family, had killed. One might say that he had killed in defense of his family. At the trial his attorney attempted to downgrade the manner in which the statement was taken and claimed that the accused was forced to make it; that the arresting detectives each held a gun to his head while I typed the statement. I was called as a rebuttal witness to deny this, which I did. I did not blame the attorney, it was his job and I'm sure the jury was not fooled. Now, here was a statement which the accused made admitting everything and it worked in his favor. As I mentioned, there are unforseen "ifs" involved.

I was always a trifle suspicious of rape stories by young teenage girls. Their imaginations run rampant at times and why they make false accusations only a psychiatrist , I believe, can explain. I have had many rape cases, both as detective sergeant and while taking statements in the Bureau of Criminal Investigation and could usually spot an untruth or weakness in the accusation. There was usually a certain hesitancy or shiftiness about the accuser. I recall taking a statement from a man accused by a 15 year old girl of having been raped by him. He was well-dressed, intelligent and a man of about

330

40 who was accompanied by his wife. During the process of taking the statement he absolutely denied having had anything to do with the neighbor girl. I do not recall what the circumstances were but his wife was also very positive and backed him up. From his manner I was inclined to believe him, especially so when he and his wife told me that he was ill, was taking treatment, and physically unable to have done so. The statement by the girl had been previously taken so I hadn't come in contact with her. I later learned from the policewoman handling the case that the accused was right and that the teenage girl admitted having lied. A false accusation such as that can ruin a man's reputation for life. My advice to a person is to beware of the imagination of a teenage girl and keep your distance. Way back--don't touch. In the department we called them jail bait.

As for burglars, I've seen and caught my share and took statements from many. I recall one whom I talked with after having taken his statement. We discussed dogs as a deterrent to burglaries and he told me that there wasn't a dog he was afraid of during a burglary (this is hard to believe) and the only thing which really frightened him was a woman's scream--he'd take off every time.

About this time Lucy, having divorced her husband, was living with Mother upstairs at brother Al's. It was about January, 1939 that Mom stooped to pick up the evening German Waechter and Anzeiger newspaper from the front porch when a strong gust of wind swung the storm door and knocked Mom down the porch steps to the sidewalk. She lay there for a short time until she was able to crawl up the steps and ring brother Al's doorbell. Doctor Cortner was called and diagnosed it as several broken ribs. Mom didn't want to go to the hospital so she sat up in the arm chair, padded with pillows, and waited to get well. It was about a week later that Lucy got up during the night to see after Mom and found she had passed away.

I surmise it may have been a blood clot in the heart, maybe cardiac thrombosis?. I believe had she gone to the hospital and received proper care she may have lived many more years. She was 73 and buried with Dad. Now there were four in the same grave.

It was in February, 1939 that our daughter Nancy Lee was born at St. John's Hospital, lived about 10 days, and passed away as the result of an RH factor blood problem. The date of birth, date of death, and the date of Mom's death is not clear to me after this length of time and our records were lost. She was buried with Mom and Dad. Now there are five in the same grave--three generations.

By this time Civil Service examinations came into their own. I passed the sergeants' examination, standing second on the list and was transferred from the Criminal Investigation Bureau back into uniform and to a zone car. Elliot Ness, Safety Director, had cleaned up the police department, reorganized the department into districts instead of precincts and divided the district into zones. I was now in the 2nd District, my zone being south of Denison with our headquarters being at the old 9th where I had first started. On the map the zones comprising a police district were circular in form so zones overlapped, supposedly providing more police protection.

One of the gimmicks was that zone cars must change crews in the street rather than go to the station. The theory was that there would be cars in the street at all times and presumably giving the good citizens more protection. The trouble with the idea was that many times the crew who was supposed to relieve you in the street didn't show up on time, consequently you had to take their radio assignments and work overtime. For a while I had a lieutenant relieve me in the morning and he'd arrive in his car, shirt open, pants unbuttoned, and shoes unlaced and have the zone car follow him to

CITY OF CLEVELAND

DEPARTMENT OF PUBLIC SAFETY

230 CITY HALL

ELIOT NESS
DIRECTOR

December 9, 1938.

Mr. Edward A. Stein,
15604 Greenway Road,
Cleveland, Ohio.

Dear Sir:

This is to advise that you have been
promoted to the position of Sergeant of Police,
Division of Police, Department of Public Safety,
effective December 16, 1938.

Very truly yours,

Eliot

Director of Public Safety.

EN:MM

Appointment by Elliot Ness

the station so he could get dressed properly. He must have jumped out of bed and into his clothes like a fire laddie. One did not complain, it wasn't done. Actually, changing crews in the street was good newspaper publicity, something new in Cleveland but from the standpoint of doing any good it was ridiculous. We went along doing our sworn duty the same as always.

Changing crews in the street meant that one had to drive one's car to the location and park it in the street. One time I had my car parked next to a church. It was the afternoon shift and during the evening we received a complaint of a car having been broken into at that location. When we arrived the complainant showed me the trunk of his car which had been forced open and his new spare tire stolen. My car was parked directly in back of his and I expected it to have been forced open also but a cursory examination showed it to be untouched. I noticed I had, unintentionally, left the door unlocked and after taking the report, I reached under the front seat of my car and found my tire iron missing which I always kept there for protection and easy access. I knew what had happened, my tire iron had been used to pry open the trunk of the car. Did I tell the man about it? Hell, no! He might have blamed me for the whole episode. I was out a tire iron but my car hadn't been worked over, perhaps in appreciation for the tool, so I had no complaints.

The city had bought more cars for this zone system and it did have good points. Instead of beat men now they were mobilized and we also had two-way radios which was a great improvement in answering complaints. All information was relayed to the Radio Unit, such as descriptions, requests for detectives, for assistance or emergency vehicle to take away prisoners. Police call boxes were seldom used now although they were still around.

Chapter 27

*I*n the mid 1930's, on Harvard Avenue in Newburg Heights, was the Harvard Club, a gambling establishment owned by James "Shimmy" Patton. I knew "Shimmy" from working in the 8th Precinct when he had a liquor "joint" at the corner of Jay Avenue and W. 25th. His clientele at the place was not of the best and not usually of the caliber one would take home to lunch. He was raised in the Old Angle and well-known in the area, having gone to St. Malachi's School. His upbringing, I suppose, was as good as anyone's there; however, he became a minor booze and gambling king on the west side. "Shimmy" lived on West Boulevard not far from our home on Bernard and it was said that he never drove his car into the garage or into the backyard at night for fear of being gunned down with a shotgun from behind his garage.

It was rumored that he left his car in front of the house or the front part of the driveway and ran to the front door which was opened by his wife. It could very well have been so since, one evening, a man by the name of Patton lived on Bernard east of W. 105th, who was reading in his living room when someone shot him dead through the front window. He was no more than, perhaps a distant relative of the Patton clan, if that. Mr. Patton was a good family man with no enemies, therefore, it can be assumed that a competitor of "Shimmy" must have picked the wrong Patton from the phone book. The murderer was never caught.

Quite a while ago a Brian Albrecht wrote an interesting account in what I believe was the Sunday story section of the Cleveland Plain Dealer headed, "Whatever happened to the Gambling Palaces of the Great Depression" which was very interesting and sums it up pretty

335

well since I recall the names of the places, the locations and their goings-on being frequently mentioned during my time in the department.

The flagship of the gambling resorts was the Mounds Club on Chardon Road across the Lake County border. Once it was nothing but a good-sized chicken farm but now it was a top watering hole for the wealthy and prominent Shaker Heights crowd. Shondor Birns, a shady character, whom I knew, was one of the big spenders and, about 1978, was blown up one night when someone wired his car with a pineapple in the vicinity of W. 25th and Detroit.

Geauga Lake Park was blessed with the Geauga and Portage County line which ran through the middle of the park. The slot machines were on wheels so that if one county invaded the park for a raid, the slot machines were pushed over the line into the other county. Then we had colored man Benny Mason who was in his heyday during my time. He was a numbers operator and operated the Cedar Country Club. Following a raid on one of his numbers establishments he complained, "I'm just trying to do something for my race and the white folks don't like it." And so it was in the 30's.

Frank Sinatra is a good singer and a good actor and at this writing must have almost 40 years in the show business. I never cared much for him. Admittedly I'm a bit biased, perhaps because of the hard time he unwittingly gave me on his visit to Cleveland or because of his supposed Mafia connection at one time. However, give credit to his good showmanship.

About the time I'm writing, in the late forties or so, teenagers went a bit nuts about "Frankie." Now they have Rock and Roll music about which they go crazy but at that time it was "FRANK-E-EEE." Still, I can understand that music tastes of an old-timer like myself wouldn't be the same as that of a teenager. Since everything changes and everyone to his own taste as the old lady said when she kissed the cow.

It was after the war, about 1949 or so, when Sinatra appeared at our Public Auditorium. I was detailed there with a young patrolman. It was a very cold January or February night with a stiff, icy wind blowing off of the lake, straight from Canada. Also, there were policemen from the traffic division who were working the afternoon shift and detailed to handle crowds on the outside or inside. The young officer and myself stayed near the stage at the front of the auditorium to give Sinatra protection while the traffic men were scattered here and there. The auditorium itself had their own guards who, I found out that evening, weren't worth a damn when it came to trouble. They were just there, drawing their pay and their breath.

The hall was packed with teenagers and, as the show progressed, kept calling, "Oh! Franke-e-e-eeee. Oh! Frank-e-e-eeee" in the meantime sliding up the aisle on their bottoms to get close to the stage. They were mostly girls. The longer the show lasted the more the girls screamed. Towards the end of the show I could see from their glassy-eyed look that they were in an emotional state; that it was getting the better of them and a mob spirit could take over. When some of the screaming "Frankie-e-e-e-e" enthusiasts tried to climb on the stage with Sinatra the show ended and he disappeared. He was smart. He knew what was coming so he left for his hotel by a rear exit. This left the nutty teenagers swarming towards the exit doors in the hopes they could get a final glimpse of him.

When the show was over our worthy traffic officers, their bosses too, scattered for home and their warm firesides. They were smart too. They didn't want trouble, weren't used to it and just wanted to get the hell away from there. I didn't know all this and couldn't have done anything about it anyway but it left me and the young patrolman to handle the crowd, plus the auditorium guards who were no damn good anyway in trouble, and kept out of sight. One can say we should have left also but no, it wouldn't set right with me. One just doesn't leave a ticklish situation like that. It was lousy planning by those responsible for setting up the police detail, who ever they were.

On the inside of the building, surrounding the auditorium itself, is a wide hall with exit doors to the outside. At one end of the hall, on the west side of the building and about in line with the stage, was a closed door, locked. Some in the group had the idea that it lead behind the stage and to dear Frankie. They hammered on the door and by the time we arrived in the hallway and realized what was happening the teenagers were swarming around, pushing on the locked door and screaming. The hall was jammed, the girls had gone cuckoo and some were being crushed against the wall and couldn't get away. It was a brainless mob for sure. I couldn't get to a phone because there was none there so I forced my way between the girls and the wall and, holding up my arms, yelled to them to clear away. It was useless! No one paid any attention and I couldn't be heard anyway.

I was being crushed against the wall and thinking I'd be no good dead, I squirmed my way to the side. I looked for help from the guards and saw them clustered around the door window, on the inside of the auditorium, looking out at me with white faces. They seemed scared as hell. I can't say I blame them since it was, perhaps, their first experience with a nutty crowd. In the meantime the young officer with me was working in the back pulling girls away from the mob so I started to help him but saw it was not much use. One or two girls fainted, one had been trampled but, luckily, not seriously hurt and one mother was trying to pull her daughter out of the mob but was unsuccessful since she paid no attention and kept screaming and pushing her way in. The mother was worried and frantic but there was nothing she could do. There was only one thing I could do since I couldn't control them and that was to call for help before some were crushed to death.

At this point, and I have been forever grateful, the young officer had the best idea of the evening. He opened the doors leading to the outside and the icy, zero wind blowing off the lake swept through the crowd and brought the teenagers to their senses and they dispersed. I complimented him many times and I'm positive his move saved lives that night. You see, I never thought of the doors, the action was so heavy at the time. It was a golden opportunity the reporters missed and I believe the bitter weather had much to do with keeping them hold'd up. There was never a thing about it in the papers. The ironic part of it is that the closed and locked door against which the teenagers were pushing was a broom and mop closet with cleaning equipment, leading nowhere.

Meanwhile we were enjoying our new 6-room brick home on Greenway Road where life was rich and full for may years. Little Martin was a joy and Leona kept things running in apple pie order at home. I seldom had time for anything else and after work headed for home by the quickest route. We had a mortgage of $2900 to pay off which took us 11 years. The price of our sturdy home was $6550, lot included. I recall when we were looking around before settling on the Greenway location, we could have bought a two-story, completely furnished, brick home with full attic in a nice neighborhood west of Warren Road for $9500. We didn't have the means.

What had helped was our saving Leona's salary for several years after our marriage and, also, the sale of Mom's two-family home on Bernard Avenue after her death, the proceeds being divided between us four children and my share being about $2500., part of which we invested in a Model V-8 Ford coupe. Our Model A Ford Coupe, having seen better days, was used as a trade-in. It was a bit thin going at times but Leona was frugal and I didn't waste my nickels in beer parlors or at the races. Leona did much of her own baking and in the fall, canned tomatoes, fruit, and kept our fruit cellar well stocked. We had plenty of good wholesome food and Leona set a good table. We weren't in the Rockefeller class but lived within our means and were happy. Good Pocahontas coal, lump or egg size, was $9.00 per ton and we used six ton per winter.

Marty was going to Our Lady of Angel's School and receiving excellent marks. On the evening of May 31st and morning of June 1, 1942 I spent anxious hours at St. John's Hospital until our son Ed was born. The nurses named him the Fuller Brush baby because he had a head of black hair which stood up like a brush. They also referred to him as Butch since his hair resembled the butch haircuts worn by men at the time. He was baptized Edward Anthony after me by the sisters and was later christened at Our Lady of Angel's Church and went to school there.

In the 30's Adolph Hitler was stomping around, showing his muscle in Germany. Daily headlines told of Adolph and his Nazi Brown Shirts and their doing. Benito Mussolini, fascist dictator in Italy, was not far behind. Benito and his Black Shirts came into power in Italy. He was a short, cocky rooster, about 4 foot 4 inches in elevated heels, and whenever he harangued a crowd he place his hands on his hips and jutted his meaty jaw at the horizon. He was a jackass.

340

Arthur Neville Chamberlain, Prime Minister of Britain, pursued a policy of appeasement towards Germany and Italy in an attempt to maintain peace. He was blamed for selling Czechoslovakia down the river at the Munich meeting with Hitler on September 30, 1938 when he agreed to Czechoslovakia's partition. I recall seeing Chamberlain, either in a movie or on T.V., proudly waving a copy of the "No More War" pact which he had signed with Hitler. Hitler figured he had things going his way and took over all of Czechoslovakia. Had he been satisfied with Czechoslovakia and stopped, I'm sure we would have had no Second World War, since nobody wanted war in the first place.

For me to go into the causes and details of these wars is a waste of time since accurate accounts can be found in any history book. I will, however, tell of my impressions at the time.

Ras Tafari had become Emperor Haile Selassie of Ethiopa and in October, 1935, Mussolini attacked this defenseless country and the next year annexed it as an Italian possession. Selassie never denied the story that he was a direct descendant of King Solomon, or some such. I remember the TV showing his tribesmen with spears and rifles, about their only weapons, declaring loyalty to their emperor. However, they never had a chance against the pasta and pizza eaters.

After a year of diplomatic maneuvering by Hitler and the signing of a non-aggression pact with Russia, Germany invaded Poland and that's when Britain and France declared war. They saw the handwriting on the wall--they would be next. World War II had started.

I recall Hitler on TV ranting and raving and the crowds eating it up-Ya Wohl, Meine Vok Genossen. Ein Volk, Ein Reich, Ein Fuehrer. Heil, Sieg Heil! The Nazis had bitten off quite a chunk. They

341

invaded Denmark and Norway while the Russians invaded Finland; they had the German Siegfried Line and there was the "phony" war of 1939-40 when there wasn't much doing on the western front. Hitler invaded the Netherlands, Belgium, and Luxembourge and the French Maginot Line was a farce. England was hanging on the ragged edge and, I believe, if Hitler and his generals would have, or would have been able to, follow up the British withdrawal at Dunkirk in 1940 he may have come out on top, for a while anyway. Britain called the withdrawal of 300,000 troops a victory. Calling it so was like turning a frog into a prince. Certainly, it was good for home consumption but was hogwash none the less since Hitler had driven them out of France and had them boxed in and pinned on the beach against the Straits of Dover at Dunkirk. The honor goes to the boys who were in the box and the seamen who rescued them with whatever watercraft was available while the Germans bombed the hell out of them.

The Germans under General Erwin Rommel, known as the Desert Fox, drove the English back to El Alamein, Egypt, where the Fox was eventually defeated and driven back across Libya, Tunisia, and the rest, by Britain's General Montgomery. You see, the line was too long and Hitler, because of the allies bombing the supply lines, could not get supplies or gasoline to Rommel. Rommel is said to have been of the opinion that Hitler abandoned his Africa Corps. Hitler recalled him to organize the defense along the coast of France but by this time, the German generals were waking up to the fact that Hitler was a bit hysterically nuts, that his plans wouldn't work and that the war was being lost. They plotted an attempt on Adolph's life which failed and the story is that Rommel was in on it too. Rommel died before the end of the war but the place, time, or cause of death was never clear. It was said that Hitler ordered him to commit suicide or be killed.

As for Benito Mussolini, near the end of the war in 1945, the Italian partisans hung him and his lady friend from a pole by their necks until dead, after which they reversed their positions and hung them by their heels. This was the little chore which finished the Fascist regime. It was a time--I tell you.

In 1940 Congress passed the Selective Service and Training Act which was peacetime conscription of men for the armed services and the first in our history, but call it what they liked it was a preparation for war. I registered for the draft too. The Allies suffered severe losses and England was hanging on the ropes with the rest of them and needed help again from the United States, so Roosevelt called for all-out aid to Britain and for the U. S. to convert itself into an "Arsenal of Democracy." The Lend Lease Act was passed with the expectation that all we furnished to the Allies in material and manpower would be paid back by them after the war. It was a lot of nonsense fed to the good citizens and pure fantasy since everyone knew they still owed us from the first World War, the only nation paying its debt having been little Finland. If they had wanted to pay back the billions owed us nobody had the cash anyway.

Japan wanted to expand in Asia and counted on the unpreparedness of the United States in the Pacific and, although we didn't like it, we continued to ship scrap iron and petroleum products to Japan since we feared placing an embargo on it would result in the Japs invading the Netherland East Indies. General Hideki Tojo, one of the big shot Japanese Army Generals, became Premier and was very hostile to the United States. He belonged to the Japanese military clique and at the end of the war attempted suicide by shooting himself, recovered, stood trial, and was executed. The Jap and United States ambassadors were playing ring-around-the-rosy with the Japs wanting us to agree to their expansionist policy and our government turning thumbs down.

On December 7, 1941, the Japanese Air Force assaulted our Pacific Fleet at Pearl Harbor, sunk most of our ships, wiped out our air fleet at Clark Field and were not long in attacking our forces on Guam, Wake and Midway Island. Roosevelt called December 7, the "Date that will live in infamy." On December 8, 1941, the U.S. declared war on Japan and about three days later Germany and Italy declared war on the United States. Now we were in World War II.

Compared to World War I with its bands playing and flags waving, this war was grim on the homefront. There seemed to be little horray and waving of banners about, rather it was a determined, serious business. We had a war on two fronts; had to supply men and arms in two directions and knew many of our boys would not come back.

General Douglas MacArthur came out of retirement and was assigned to the U.S. forces in the Far East. He defended the Bataan Peninsula, Phillipine Islands under attack by the Japs and was ordered to leave Corregidor by President Roosevelt to organize the defense of Australia. He was made full general again and appointed commander of forces in the Southwest Pacific. General Jonathan Wainwright was left in charge of besieged Corregidor when General MacArthur escaped with his wife and small son by motor boat and submarine. Corregidor fell and General Wainwright was captured with all his men. The Bataan Death March is history.

At home the men were being drafted and the police ranks were being thinned as were those of the fire department. There was a scarcity of many food items, such as butter and meat, most of it going to the Armed Forces; however, no one complained, it was part of the war. At the butcher shop one took what they had and was grateful. Leona shopped around and managed somehow, while I had a friend or two at the Sheriff Street Market who sold me a pound of butter or an occasional roast beef if it was available.

Prices then, of course, were high but we managed. Gasoline was rationed but we were allowed stamps for a certain number of gallons and with my being in Civil Defense and on the organization end, so to speak, like the rest of those officers in Civilian Defense I was allowed a few extra stamps in compensation for gasoline used in traveling about the Report Center 7 Area. You can be sure there was black marketing going on in both food and gasoline stamps. Driving was kept to a minimum and the streets were not crowded with autos. Leona and I saved our gasoline stamps wherever possible for a short vacation trip when my furlough time came.

I believe I was working in the Second District when one summer evening a police cruiser came to our house and Sergeant McManamon told me I had been transferred to Civil Defense and was to report to Report Center No. 7 the following day. The report center was located in the fire station at the east end of Carnegie Bridge where the Hay Market used to be when I was a boy. In charge of it was Lieutenant Frank Perrell whom I knew from the old 9th Precinct and who had asked that I be transferred to work with him. This was something entirely new now. Gone was the hurly-burly of outside work, although still in uniform I now worked mostly days with Saturday and Sunday off.

I worked with Lieutenant Frank Perrell keeping the Civilian Defense members organized with meetings, office work, letters, notices, and the rest. We had the section from the Cuyahoga River to E. 55th and from the south side of Euclid to Walworth Run, mostly colored. They were good patriotic people and worked hard to do their share. The purpose of Civilian Defense was to keep the public on the alert in case of air attack by the German Luftwaffe. We had practice sessions in case of an air attack when the whole city was darkened at the wail of sirens situated on buildings. It was good for the war effort and kept the people on their toes, dramatizing the seriousness of war, although I don't think Hitler ever planned or had the means, to fly across the ocean and attack our cities.

I was in my early 40's then and the draft included men up to the age of 45 yrs. Quite a few of the older policemen, some of whom had served in World War I, joined the Navy Shore Patrol since that was about all that was open in the service to men in our age bracket. The job was the same as the Military Police and experienced police were welcome since they were used to this type of work. I also wanted to enlist but had two children and broached the subject to my Leona and she turned thumbs down--naturally. She said I had a family to support and enough to do on the homefront. She was right and I didn't blame her, but I would have liked to have gone. Too young for the First World War and too old for the Second.

Winston Churchill became Prime Minister of the United Kingdom in 1940 and was the rock and strength the English people needed. He was the epitome of John Bull with his big cigar and two-finger victory sign. He had a liking for Americans since his mother was American-born. He had a way with words like no one else and when elected he said he didn't become prime minister to lose the war and that all he had to offer Britain was blood, sweat, and tears. On one of his visits to the United States, after the bombing of London by the German Luftwaffe, he appeared before our Congress and remarked, "Hitler said he would wring our neck like a chicken--SOME chicken." Churchill found out somewhere along the line that Hitler's name had been Shickelgraber and many times thereafter referred to him by that name in derision. He and Roosevelt hit it off fine.

346

Chapter 28

On the homefront all manufacturing was going full blast. The members of the department were now permitted to work an extra job for the war effort so a friend of mine, Detective James Benasek, who was working as foreman in the grinding department of the Arrow Aluminum Company on Berea Road, asked me to work with him. I did, one buck an hour, 6:00 to 10:00 p.m. five nights a week. It was a dirty job and I had to learn how to grind the seams off new aluminum castings with a large emery wheel. There's a trick to it but I soon got the hang of it. To this day I haven't forgotten how to dress an emery wheel to make it sharp. In a way, it was a bit dangerous since the wheel revolved at high speed, sometimes developed a crack, and if it broke and struck you in a vital spot you'd be dead.

Beside the furnace on one side of the building where the castings were poured there was a sand-molding department where molders were employed. Any good molder is in demand since it's quite an exacting trade and dexterity is required. Before a casting can be poured a sand mold is made and put into an oven and baked hard so the aluminum can be poured over it to make the casting. The foreman, I forgot his name, would stroll through our grinding department and watch us. One day he asked me if I would like to work for him and learn the molding trade. Of course I said yes, it was something new to learn. He put me to work at the lowest and dirtiest level cleaning sand out of the castings--he was starting me from the bottom up but I didn't mind. After a bit he put me at the molding bench, forming sand molds for small items. It was a bit tricky to make the damp sand stay in place since, if a corner or small lump of sand fell off, it had to be repaired or made over because the casting would show a fault.

The regular molders had the dexterity which I still had to learn but I was slowly making progress until one fine night I was put back in the grinding department. The molding department foreman was aggravated but there was nothing he could do but comply since a few of the young men in the department who were in the Molders Union objected to me not belonging to the Union and therefore was not an apprentice officially, blah, blah, blah, etc. etc. etc. Had they asked me to join I would have. To keep the necessary peace I was moved. I saw the point. Further, I'm convinced it was done because they knew I was a policeman and only working part time; these things get around. That was the end of my career as a molder. Anyway, I was a good grinder.

Pilots were being trained to fly the big bombers destined for the war front so every day we had fleets of them thundering over our house. They took off at Dayton, Air Force Base and flew to Canada and returned. It was a sight to make one think and brought the war closer. We had aluminum kitchen ware, tin can and tire collections. Mom and I contributed what we could in the line of aluminum pots and flattened our tin cans for pickup, besides driving our car as little as possible to conserve the tires. New tires could not be generally bought so good seconds were in demand.

There was a place in the E. 40th wholesale commission house neighborhood which advertised horse meat for dogs and cats. They didn't pull any punches with their advertising--it was sold as horse meat and that's what it was. Remember, beef was very hard to come

348

by and horses ate the same things cattle did. I don't know where the horses came from or what they had been doing before they met their demise, but there were the carcasses hanging from hooks.

I was at this meatery a few times and it was surprising how many people had suddenly become the owners of dogs and cats--people from Cleveland Heights and Shaker Heights, even. In big cars, yet.

Meat was rationed and one had to have food stamps to buy it. However, horse meat could be bought without ration stamps. There was a restaurant on E. 55th near St. Clair which served all the meat one wanted and was patronized by the shop workers in the area. It wasn't advertised but it was generally known that it was horse meat. A sergeant friend of mine ate there regularly and enjoyed it, especially the tenderloin section. Came the day I brought home a roast of horse meat, unbeknownst to Leona. Roasts had been scarce and one gets tired of eating odds and ends from the butcher shop. I had to lie a little because I knew that if Leona knew it was horse meat it would have been thrown out but she knew that, occasionally, I was able to buy a roast of beef at the Sheriff Street market, so in a day or two we had it for supper. Marty was at the table too. Outside of it being a bit dry, it wasn't bad at all and to the uninitiated was roast beef albeit a little strong of flavor. I told Leona in a day or two. Blame the horse meat on Hitler.

At the fire station where we had our report center, the fire laddies had a small commissary in the basement for their own use. They worked on 24-hour shifts so, many times, they cooked their own meals. In a large locker they stored their staples such as canned soup, coffee, and sugar. If a person wanted a bowl of soup or a cup of coffee, it was paid for, the money being used to restock the commissary.

UNITED STATES
OF AMERICA

War Ration Book One

WARNING

1 Punishments ranging as high as *Ten Years' Imprisonment or $10,000 Fine, or Both,* may be imposed under United States Statutes for violations thereof arising out of infractions of Rationing Orders and Regulations.

2 This book must not be transferred. It must be held and used only by or on behalf of the person to whom it has been issued, and anyone presenting it thereby represents to the Office of Price Administration, an agency of the United States Government, that it is being so held and so used. For any misuse of this book it may be taken from the holder by the Office of Price Administration.

3 In the event either of the departure from the United States of the person to whom this book is issued, or his or her death, the book must be surrendered in accordance with the Regulations.

4 Any person finding a lost book must deliver it promptly to the nearest Ration Board.

OFFICE OF PRICE ADMINISTRATION

N⁰ 415923 −312

RATION STAMP NO. 1   RATION STAMP NO. 5   RATION STAMP NO. 8   37 SUGAR

Food Ration Stamps
Courtesy of John and Anna Radkowski

One day I walked downstairs to buy a can of soup and found the cook of the day and the lieutenant of the shift counting ration stamps to see if they had enough to buy enough ground meat for chili con carne for the shift for their evening meal. When they remarked it was going to be a close squeeze I told them I could get them all the meat they wanted without ration stamps. They both said, "Horse meat." I said yes and that I would get them all the wanted. They conferred a moment or two and asked me to get six pounds but swore me to

350

secrecy. They didn't want the members of the shift to know about it since it perhaps, would not be eaten. I purchased the ground meat for them. In a few days I asked the cook of that day how it went and he said everything was fine; that no one suspected a thing and that one of the men had changed his allowed dinner hour to partake of the chili con carne which was his favorite.

Dwight Eisenhower was General of the U.S. forces in Europe. Winston Churchill wanted Hitler attacked through Italy, "the soft under belly of Europe" as he called it but Eisenhower preferred the attack through the west coast of France, which they did. General Montgomery of the British Army had chased Rommel out of Africa by this time and later fought through Europe.

Every country has a general who makes a mistake here and there. As I recall, somewhere along the line, General Clark of the U.S. Army, pulled a boo-boo during the invasion of Italy; however, those things happen. Our General George Patton was not exempt. He was quite a guy. He was rough and ready, had boundless energy, plenty of daring-do and took chances which kept pushing the Germans back.

He made a mistake one time which was witnessed by a reporter who publicized it and, I believe, it was blown all out of proportion to the actual happening. It seems he slapped a shell-shocked soldier at a rest area. What it was all about I do not know but the papers made quite a to-do about it with the result that General "Ike" Eisenhower ordered him to publicly apologize. I gather his public apology was more a statement than an apology, but it passed.

General Montgomery was a slow mover and was just the opposite of General Patton. He didn't move until he had everything bunched around him and ready to go, material, man-power, everything. It was said that Churchill was aggravated at this slowness and wished he'd get off his duff and move faster. I think it was Patton who said that Montgomery could never make up his mind whether to pee or poop.

Willie Barotta, a neighbor of ours, was in Patton's outfit and said that many of the other officers didn't like Patton because he was always ahead of them. Keep pushing, never let them rest, was his style. It was our loss when he was killed in a jeep accident while there. I saw the movie about him the title of which, I think, was "Patton" and he seemed to be quite arrogant. However, what officer, in the higher echelon, isn't? Willie Barotta told of Patton having a small dog as a pet which accompanied him everywhere. Barotta didn't know the dog's name until one morning the dog decided to go out on his own private inspection tour and Patton called it back with a "Willie, come here, you son-of-a-bitch." Willie Barotta at first thought Patton was calling him and that's when he found out the dog's name was Willie.

Chapter 29

I 'm a graduate of Purdue University. You bet! I have a certificate to prove it, somewhere. I matriculated and graduated in ten days and it happened like so.

The War Department assigned army officers in the higher echelon to teach the report center controllers, and other select persons, in fine points of Civilian Defense, what to expect, what to do, and so forth. Actually, I believe any of our boys could have taught them a thing or two since we were teaching it ourselves at our report centers back home. It was a series of lectures held at Purdue University, Lafayette, Indiana, and the government picked up the tab. The first group of police officers sent there were those in the upper bracket, like deputy inspectors, captains, and lieutenants. Then came the sergeants, a few patrolmen, and civilians. They were sent there from all over the state and beyond. Railroad trains were running to capacity and filled with servicemen going to or coming from camp. The train had an assignment of Navy Shore Patrol and Military Police on board to keep order if necessary among the men in the service. There were no reserved seats, it was first come, first served, and when the seats were taken there was standing room in the aisles.

We were to report at 7:00 a.m. one morning at the Terminal Tower, Public Square, to take a Nickel Plate train to our destination. The train was to be made up in Cleveland and I knew there would be a scramble when it came time to board. We had our orders a few days prior to that so I went to a friend of mine in the New York Central Railroad Police Office in the Terminal and arranged that we, as being engaged in the war effort, could board the car before the gates were opened for the public and the rush began.

Came the time, our group was all ready when the train caller in his New York Central Railroad uniform, shiny buttons and all, led us through the waiting crowd at the gate to take us downstairs to the waiting train. As he walked us forward he said to the crowd, "Step aside, please. Security. Security," and it was remarkable to see the people step aside willingly and make way for us. The word security had done the trick and, of course, we were all in civilian clothes so, in their minds, they perhaps thought we were from the F.B.I., the Secret Service, spies, cloak and dagger stuff, things like that. We never batted an eye, walked as though we expected the good citizens ogling us to make way and followed the caller downstairs like ducks going to a pond where we boarded, had our choice of seats and remained together.

The ride to Lafayette was tedious and we arrived in the afternoon where we were met, signed in, and taken to the student's building at the university and each given a room. Like at conventions we cleaned up before supper and met in the lobby to get acquainted with the other citizens and eyeballed each other. These civilians were from all walks of life, business people, bankers, and housewives. All good, solid, first-class citizens. Our group was on its good behavior and the usual joking, bantering, and raillery was absent. We were lounging around in the lobby, our clothes in order, shoes shined, looking as intelligent as possible and trying to make some sort of good impression when one of our group, an officer from a report center, began telling of his experience one night in the police department. He was quite a talker and not used to choosing words which would normally be used in church, just telling it as it was. He had their full, undivided attention. He told of one early morning hour while cruising around the Sheriff Street Market he saw a man acting

354

suspiciously. It was the morning after market day and the cleaning crew had not arrived to clean up the odds and ends lying about after market, such as old lettuce, discarded fruit, bananas, banana stalks, and the rest. He said "I got out of the car to check him out and turned away for a minute and he jumped me from behind so I grabbed the first thing I could lay my hands on and hit the son-of-a-bitch in the bazoo with a banana stalk." Goodbye good impression.

They had curfew and the place was under control of the military with guards here and there. I think we were supposed to be in our rooms about 9:00 p.m. but a few of us decided to see the downtown at night, maybe lift a few beers, so without telling anyone, we went downtown and wound up in a bar. The town was small, there wasn't any action, the sidewalks having been taken in about 7:00 p.m. so we had a few drinks and went back to our "hotel." We couldn't get in the grounds since the soldier on guard pointed a rifle at us and barred the way. We talked to him, told him what the score was with us but he had his orders and wouldn't budge until his lieutenant gave him the okay. He did some calling out loud and soon a young lieutenant came, questioned us, and reluctantly let us in. We didn't give a hoot and thought it was a big joke; however, we could see their point.

We listened to lectures, saw movies of the London Blitz, which all of our crowd had seen a number of times, and had three good meals a day. It was hard to keep awake at times since it was summer and, not having slept too well, we were all a bit drowsy. The upper army personnel, colonels, majors, and other officers hung together and, I could see, it was a piece of cake for them. Something like a vacation, so to speak. Actually, I believe they were in only for the duration and had been civilians like we 'uns shortly before donning uniforms.

355

They didn't impress us since they couldn't order us around and they knew it. However, we went along with it for the good of the war effort and gave them no trouble.

In about ten days, at the end of the seminar, we lined up on the front steps in a group, had our picture taken, were given our "diploma" certificates and headed back to Cleveland. The train was jammed, many standing all the way and I was glad to get home to my family. That's the only time I was in Lafayette.

California had a large Japanese population and after the attack on Pearl Harbor and during the war in the Pacific the feeling in this country ran high against them. The President ordered the establishment of internment camps and all Japanese were taken to the camp, losing their property and everything they owned. They were forced to stay there for at least two years under the guard of soldiers. It mattered not that many of them were citizens of the United States and had been born here. They were interned solely on the basis of race and nationality origin. I recall it well, the feeling in the country was bitter against them and, while now it seems to have been the wrong thing for the U.S. to do, at that time it was a protective measure and looked on with favor. I approved at the time and still do. I can see where it was a protective measure for the Japanese too, since riots could very well have occurred because of the hatred for them. I just heard on television that Japanese in California have formed an organization demanding 3 billion dollars restitution for property lost at that time.

During the war years and certainly not before, gas furnaces were not as prevalent as now so homes were heated with coal. The city was dotted with coal yards and it was a big trade. Two of the old standby coal companies were the Albrecht Coal and the Zettlemeyer Coal whose names I recall being on coal wagons since I was a child. All schools, hotels, and office buildings were heated with steam from their boilers which was generated by burning coal. The hotels and buildings downtown seemed to have a daily supply of coal delivered to their boiler rooms so, you see, there was quite a coal trade. Came the winter of about 1943 we had a coal shortage because the war and manufacturing came first. The shortage became so acute one winter that it was decided to let the police department, through its police civilian defense controllers such as me, handle it so a large room was set up in the upstairs north end of the public auditorium with rows of desks and phones where calls for coal could be received.

The idea was to sort out the most needy and to do this we relied on the Welfare Department a great deal since they had their needy people listed and, while some on the list were fakers, by and large the list was fairly accurate. Then the calls from homeowners who were low on coal came in too, and to be fair with everyone, we sent a policeman to their home and checked on the bareness of the coal bin. It had a restraining effect on the chiselers. Being a somewhat behind-the-scene quasi-coal dealer now you can be sure that I saw to it that our home on Greenway was warm that winter. My family wasn't about to be cold if I could help it. So, with a warm house in mind, I reviewed the coterie of acquaintances I had in civilian defense in my report area and came up with a coal yard on the east side where I was known. They had agreed to work with and deliver coal to those persons whose names we sent them, just like other coal yards during the emergency. The problem was one had to take whatever coal they had on stock, whether it was anthracite, pocahontes or cheap soft

357

smoky-burning coal. This friend told me to call in my order when I was low on coal so I was all set. There were no promises made nor was the coal paid for until delivered.

I had a couple of other irons in the fire in that respect in one or two more coal yards. Just in case. The coal dealer should have done okay since I phoned all requests for coal to him which were nearest his coal yard thus making short hauls. I'm sure he noticed. I kept our coal bin filled all winter. One load of coal was soft coal which I named Smokey Joe. It burned with a heavy black smoke and made plenty of soot; however, it burned and we were grateful. The following spring I had trouble with keeping the smoke out of the basement, open draft or not, so on a quiet day I opened the clean-out door of the chimney, put a mirror in it and saw the sky through a small hole. I knew the chimney was practically blocked up by soot from my friend Smokey Joe, so I had it cleaned out in a hurry.

I received a phone call from a woman who said a lady a few doors down her street had stolen her coal. It developed that her coal was to be delivered that morning and when the truck was driven down the street the neighbor lady stepped out, waved the driver into her driveway and had him unload the coal into her bin. The driver had assumed he had the right address but never checked it. She was a resourceful woman and, perhaps, did not know the actual destination of the black diamonds and all she saw was COAL. I appreciated the humor of it but I could see her heart wasn't exactly saturated with honesty so I sent a policeman to the lady's home and shortly thereafter she and her children were carrying coal out of her coal bin in buckets and delivering it in person to the rightful place.

The war was going on full blast; the allies invaded Sicily, the mainland of Italy, the west coast of France under Eisenhower while

Russia pushed back the Germans who had been stopped at Stalingrad and Leningrad, formerly St. Petersburg. The turning point for the U.S. in the Pacific came at the battle of Coral Sea when our fleet defeated the Japanese fleet. Not known until some time after the war was the fact that we had broken, or obtained, the Japanese code and, also, that of the Germans and knew what the moves of each were going to be so we could shift our forces accordingly. It is said to have been one of the best-kept secrets of the war. Only for this I believe we would have had a much harder time in both war theaters.

President Roosevelt was an ailing man when he attended a conference with Winston Churchill and Joe Stalin at Yalta, a city of the Soviet Union and a port on the Black Sea. Mother Russia had a tricky jerk in Joe Stalin who had a doctor pass as one of his waiters whose job was to observe Roosevelt and pass on to Stalin his opinion of Roosevelt's state of health. Pictures of Roosevelt show him to be thin and definitely in ill health. In fact, it was later stated that he should not have gone there in the first place. I read an account one time, true or not, of Stalin holding a meeting of the politburo after the war when there were straws in the wind of he being ousted by them. He wanted to find out who his friends were so he feigned illness, or a seizure of some kind, fell from his chair, gasped, struggled for air--a real good act. Some of the politburo figured he was a dead turkey anyway so they said what they thought of him, called him names, hoped he'd die, interesting things like that, all while he was on the floor. He rose to his feet, brushed himself off and continued the meeting. It wasn't long thereafter there were new faces in the politburo. It's a good story and may have happened.

359

military service. Another time we saved our stamps was when we took a trip to Toronto, Canada, on our way to Detroit and back home. It was on the way there that we learned from a gas station attendant that we did not need stamps since the war was about over. On arriving in Toronto we found that the war was indeed over and a great doings was going on downtown. After eating dinner we went downtown to see the action and found crowds, crowds, crowds, whooping and yelling and having a good time--the roof was the limit. We decided the best place for us was back at the motel.

Harry Truman was Vice President when Franklin Roosevelt died of a heart attack, or stroke, at Warm Springs, CA in April, 1945. To him was left the awesome decision of turning loose the atom bomb.

Very few knew that we were working on the bomb and Truman first learned of it after he became President. Japan was losing the war and knew it and may have been preparing to defend its shores from our invasion. Truman decided that bombing Hiroshima with the atom bomb as a warning to Japan of what would be done was better than the loss of thousands of our boys in an invasion. A great deal of Hiroshima was erased on August 6, 1945, as was Nagasaki on August 9, 1945, and shortly thereafter, Japan surrendered.

I have a great admiration for Harry Truman since he was honest, outspoken, and came up the hard way. At one time he had been part owner of a haberdashery store, went bankrupt and paid back all his debts. His mother-in-law apparently always thought her daughter Bess had married beneath her and gave Harry a hard time on occasion. Harry was born in Lamar, Missouri, in 1884 and before going into politics was a farmer. His ma-in-law was a staunch southern Democrat, had been raised in the southern atmosphere after the Civil War and had no use for Republicans. On her first visit to the White House, they installed her in Lincoln's bedroom and the next morning she demanded to be moved to another room because she wasn't about to sleep in Lincoln's bed.

Harry Truman, as senator, gained respect for his honesty and was named to head a committee to investigate contractors who were chiseling on government contracts. I believe it to have been called the Truman Committee, or some such. During the war there was plenty of chiseling going on among manufacturers with war contracts who hired more people than needed so they'd have plenty of help on hand, consequently the people didn't have enough to do and the government was picking up the tab. He tells of one concern they called on where everything seemed in order when he spotted a door and was told it lead to the basement and that there was nothing of importance there. He had the door opened and up came a slew of men who had been told to remain there until the door was opened, presumably when the investigating committee had left.

For interesting reading see the book "Harry Truman." He had been a captain in World War I, received a couple of promotions and I believe, his opinion of the upper echelon in the Army was not of the highest.

General MacArthur did a good job in the Pacific as did General Eisenhower in the European theater. Civilian Defense was disbanded and I was transferred to the 3rd District, Central Station, where I worked on zone cars, desk duty, and beat sergeant. I had good superior officers, one of whom was Captain James McArthur who had also been in Civilian Defense. For a while I was assigned to investigate liquor permit applications which meant that before the owner of a liquor permit could have the permit renewed I had to inquire of the neighbors as to how the place was run and if they had any objections to a renewal. This also meant a rechecking of the owner's record. I was smart enough not to make any recommendations for renewal or denials but laid out all the information I had obtained in a report which was forwarded to the Ohio Liquor Control Board, Columbus, who made the decision.

I recall one report I made, which drew amusing comment, of a woman I interviewed who lived in an apartment directly over a liquor parlor in the colored neighborhood. Bars in that area were usually noisy, especially on a Friday and Saturday night. This particular widow said she had no objection to the place "except the shootin'" thru the floor. One night I woke up when there was a "shootin'" and I heard a ping and the next day found a bullet in the bed springs.

When General Eisenhower came home from Europe he received the proper ticker-tape reception in New York and Cleveland did him honor too with a parade, dinner, and the rest. I was in the parade detail that time and stationed on Euclid across from the May Company when he came by in the car. The crowd was cheering and waving flags so he stopped in front of me, got out of the car, shook my hand, gave a shrill whistle and waved to the people on the side lines and those looking out of the office building windows, reentered the auto and was driven on. There was no particular reason for him to shake my hand other than I just happened to be in front of him. Naturally I was pleased. I met him again, with Nixon, at the airport when he was campaigning for President.

I was detailed at the Union Terminal one time when President Truman came to Cleveland. He walked through the lobby of the Terminal Tower at the entrance to Public Square, waving and smiling at spectators. His daughter Margaret and his wife Bess were with him. I believe their destination to have been the Cleveland Hotel. His dismissal of General Douglas MacArthur for not obeying orders is history. In his book he tells, in no uncertain terms, what he thought of MacArthur and Eisenhower.

I had served 25 years in the department and my thoughts were moving slowly towards retirement although I was feeling fit and not quite ready. Captain James McArthur became Inspector of Police, was put at the head of the detective bureau and one fine day his secretary Clarence Hawking, who had sounded me out several times before, told me that I was going to be transferred to the detective bureau. Apparently it was at the wish of Inspector McArthur. Things moved in mysterious ways.

When I was transferred to the detective bureau as detective sergeant I was assigned to the east side where the greatest percentage were colored. Beside my own crew, I supervised three others on my shift. There were other crews and detective sergeants assigned here and there throughout the city. Again it was a phase of police work different from what I had been doing. Gone was my uniform. I now worked in my regular citizen clothes. There were some things I had to learn and some things I had to become used to. A detective in civilian clothes is not in the public eye like a uniformed man; he is free to move about without observation by the public and, I noticed he received more respect. The shifts were split three ways, 8:30 to 8:30.

On the morning shift we attended lineup where those arrested for crimes or investigation of crimes in the preceding 24 hours were brought before us behind a screen on a raised platform. While the detectives were in darkness the arrested persons were under strong lights, made to face us, and turned until we had viewed them from each side. Each person's name was called, age, and why apprehended. There were usually a dozen in a lineup and the number of lineups depended on the number of persons arrested. I conducted many of them. As is generally known, the purpose of the lineups is to acquaint the detectives with arrested persons so if they were seen on the street under suspicious circumstances they'd be recognized. It was impossible to remember each one in a lineup since it was a daily affair and the arrested persons were not always the same, some never being involved with the law again. However, if a person was frequently in the lineup, as many hoodlums were, he'd soon become known to the detectives. Further, frequently a detective would spot a man in the lineup for whom the police were looking in connection with a crime.

Chapter 30

*A*fter 15 years of retirement I know that some laws have
changed; that arrest methods have changed along the line of
constitutional rights, which may all be to the good but, in
general, it seems to me that police have been hampered and their
hands tied by court rulings. Our judges would be wiser men if it
would be obligatory for each to have spent one or two years in a
police uniform, in a tough neighborhood, before being elected or
appointed to the bench. They'd have more compassion for the victim
and less for the criminal. Indeed, it wouldn't hurt members of the
media either. It will never happen.

In the meantime everything was going along fine at home. Marty
was going to St. Edward's High School. Ed was going to grade
school at Our Lady of Angel's and, several years after Mother's
death, Lucy lived with us, where she stayed until we sold our home
in 1977, a total of about 35 years.

I suppose the popularity of detective stories began with Sir Arthur
Conan Doyle, creator of Sherlock Holmes, but any good detective
will tell you that the tracing of a criminal through fingernail clippings
or a strand of hair is rarely, if ever, done; however, they can be an aid
in an investigation. Occasionally I enjoy a good mystery story but I
am not an avid reader of them since I know that the stories originate
in someone's head and the answers always dovetail to perfection.
We, too, had our Scientific Investigation Unit which was manned by
experienced and excellent men in the field of fingerprint
identification, ballistics, photography, polygraph, and the rest, who
were of tremendous help and the police department could not do
without. Their scientific help is a story in itself. Real detective work

consists of a lot of work gathering evidence, climbing stairs, knocking on doors, interviewing people and, mainly, persistence in following bits of information.

The idea that a detective sits at a desk in serious thought and solves some crimes through reasoning power is pure hogwash. Basically, someone must talk. Somewhere along the line someone must talk. Let me explain: If a person witnesses a crime, sees the culprit and gives a description to the police who apprehend him because of the description, we can say he was apprehended because the witness talked. Again, if a person commits a crime, there are no witnesses, and he is later picked up for another reason and he then tells of the crime he committed, HE has talked. So, you see, if there are no witnesses, no direct evidence and no one talks, it's doubtful whether a case can be made. There are endless examples.

I recall one time it was dusk when a man held up the lady clerk behind the counter of a dry cleaning establishment on Euclid while the owner was in the back room. The woman was thoroughly frightened and saw nothing but the gun and later could give very little description of the holdup man who made his escape. Certainly she would never be able to identify him. The owner heard the commotion, ran into the street and fired several shots at the rear of the car in which the holdup man was escaping but was not at all sure that he had hit the car.

It was the area of about the 7000 block and the next day an auto was found on a side street which had been reported stolen the evening before. It was a street of large old homes and apartments buildings and the owner of the auto was a young man who lived in one of the apartments in the vicinity. He lived alone and we didn't like the looks or actions of the young man and, knowing it was an old trick to report a car stolen after using it in a holdup, we brought him in for investigation. In checking his record we found he had been arrested for holdups before. We spent a lot of time and hard work on the case since we were quite sure he was the man we wanted. He denied everything and firmly maintained he was in his apartment at the time of the robbery. Maybe so.

There was one slim chance we had of making him confess and that was by having the store owner identify the auto as the one which he saw the holdup man escape in. Being dusk the owner of the laundry could not identify the man either. We were holding the car which, incidentally, had no bullet holes, in the police pound and I decided we would give it a try. I had the car moved in among a line of other autos of about the same color and make and covered all the license plates. In order to cover all angles possible and leave no loopholes for the defense in case it ever came to trail, I brought the store owner in the lot at dusk, about the time of the holdup and asked him if he could identify the car which he saw drive away. He looked at the line of cars from about the distance he had shot and picked out our man's car without hesitation. We still had no solid evidence that the man in the clink was the driver but hoped when confronted with this bit of evidence he would confess. He didn't. You see, he had been in jail before and, if he was the man, he had become wise. We had to turn him loose although we were sure he was our man. If he was the culprit, he had saved himself by not talking.

When I think of all the work a policeman does to make sure he has the right man and all the laws of evidence which must be met to protect the accused person, the claim that "I was framed by the police" doesn't hold water with me. To be sure, it has happened somewhere and, perhaps, will again, but I never found it to be so. A

367

policeman does not have to produce a certain number of arrests to hold his job since enough come his way just doing his duty.

There are cases where it is not necessary that the accused person stand in a police lineup; however, in line with the old saying "I was framed by the police" let me explain the procedure the police follow to make sure the accused person had been properly identified as the culprit. I should know, I have held many lineups. We'll take a theoretical case where a holdup has been committed in which there are the victim, several witnesses and the culprit who had escaped but later was picked up. During the questioning the arrested person denies all knowledge of the holdup, so the next step is to arrange a time for the witnesses to appear at headquarters as soon as possible after the occurrence.

The accused is brought out in a lineup of five or six men, the same color, approximately the same height and similar clothing as worn by the accused. The victim is advised that he will view several men behind a lighted screen and that he, himself, will be in darkness; that each man in the lineup will verbally be given a number and turned around in several positions so that the victim can view him from all sides. He is instructed to stay silent until he has studied the lineup and if he sees the culprit he should say his number out loud. After the identification, the accused is brought face to face with the victim who is instructed to make the identification again and, in front of him, tell what he has done. There are times when the victim then decides that he is not sure and, unless someone else identifies him or he admits the crime, he is turned loose. The same procedure is gone through if there are a number of witnesses and if some identify the accused and some do not. Statements are taken and presented to the prosecutor for evaluation. This is a good system and, I presume, is still followed without much variation.

An incident comes to mind when I was a teenager, had no thought of joining the police department when, while walking with three or four of my friends past the 9th Precinct Station one summer evening, an officer came down the front steps and stopped us. He asked us to come in to stand in a line with someone else to be viewed. This was something new to us, an adventure. We asked him what it was all about and he said there was nothing to it and we could go on our way afterward. In the station, where in a few years I would stand roll call, they formed us into a line and brought out two young men and stood them between us. Then a nice-looking young lady was brought out from a side room and she walked slowly down the line giving us a good looking over. She was pretty and I would not have minded dating her. She identified none of us and we went on our way. In retrospect I can see what would have happened. If she had picked me or one of my friends the "nothing to it" statement by the officer would quickly have been forgotten and replaced with "something to it." We would have been held and thoroughly investigated.

In every veteran officer's police experience there is life and death. Certainly, the job is not all fun and games and many times it's grim. Without going into the finer details I'll relate a few instances in my experience.

There was the time one summer forenoon when we picked up the body of a middle-aged woman who had jumped off of the Denison Avenue bridge. She had left a purse at the railing with a note to her son, "Now you can get the car you wanted." What drove this poor soul to suicide?

There was the time we were called to a room in an apartment building on Detroit near W. 25th where we cut down an elderly man who had hung himself from a steam pipe. There was no note and in his dresser drawer he had over $700 in paper money. He had no kin. He must have been in despair over something.

Then there is the time I saved a 4 year old boy's life by the resuscitation method after he had fallen through the ice in a creek in back of his home on a cold winter day. There is a newspaper article about it in my scrap book.

The despair of growing old without means of support and no money or food was brought home to me one forenoon during the Depression when we were directed to a home by a man who had seen his neighbor with a bloody face looking out of the door window and waving to him. We found the aged husband and wife lying side by side in a double bed with their wrists slashed. In a weak voice the woman managed to say that they had nothing, nothing. They had decided to end it all. The husband survived but the wife died.

There was the long, long night I was detailed at the Ellington Apartment fire at E. 9th and Superior and watched tenants jump to their deaths from upper-story windows. The screaming is still with me to this day. One old man refused to go down the fireman's ladder until he returned with his fiddle. It was arson.

Then there was the father and two small daughters we saved from a gas-filled home on Holmden Avenue. We carried them out and laid them on the lawn in the dusk of a summer evening. The gas burner had accidentally been extinguished. They recovered but in another half hour they may have been beyond help.

There was the neat man who lived alone in a room in a building on Euclid. He was dressed neatly, his shoes were shined and in a row under the bed and the apartment was spic and span. So he wouldn't soil the bed sheets he lay down with his head in his leather jacket and shot himself in the temple. No note--no reason given.

We were called to a home in the Polish neighborhood and told by a man that his next-door neighbor had planted the cut-off limb of a tree in his front yard the day before; that he had made some strange remarks and they hadn't seen him since. He suspected something had happened to him. We found him hanging from a rafter in the attic. His wife had died--he was alone.

I won't go into the grisly details of what I saw in the posting room at City Hospital--cadavers in various phases of dissection with whistling students sewing them up.

Then there was the cab driver who picked up a colored girl as a fare who wanted to see the lake one cold, zero, winter night. At the end of the E. 9th Street pier she got out and said, "So, this is Lake Erie" and jumped off the pier. She broke her leg on the ice. The water was frozen. Suicide miscarried.

Why do so many people die in bathrooms? And so it was--And many more.

I won't go into detail of my time spent in the detective bureau since the memoir of cases in which I have been involved, the arrests made and the work performed could very well be repetitious and become boring. I will tell you; however, of an incident which may interest you before I close the narrative of some of the occurrences in my life.

General Eisenhower was persuaded to run for President on the Republican ticket and during his campaign Cleveland, on Sept. 8, 1952, was one of his stops. A big affair was planned by the G.O.P. with speeches, dinners, and all the foofraw which goes with it. I was detailed with about four or five detectives to meet him at Hopkins Airport to give him protection from the mob which would surely be there and stay with him until evening when another crew would take over. We were bodyguards, you might say, and necessary with all the

371

kooks floating around on such occasions. When Ike got off the plane he was met by various politicians such as Congressman George Bender, Congresswoman Frances Bolton and others. Police in uniform were in the background controlling the crowd while our detail mingled with the politicians and managed to stay near and around Eisenhower without being conspicuous. The idea is to face the crowd and look for troublemakers. We had no trouble and everything went along fine. There were various political signs around such as "Clean House Washington--Eisenhower-Taft."

While Ike was shaking hands here and there and giving his rubber smile I notice a large plane cruising over the airport which soon landed. From the plane came Richard Milhous Nixon, Vice-Presidential running mate of Eisenhower and later President of the United States who resigned because of the Watergate scandal. There were greetings and smiles all around and I was beside Eisenhower with Nixon facing us, sort of a three-corner deal, with the crowd around when Nixon told Ike that he had been flying by on his way to Chicago, or some place, to make a speech when he saw the large crowd below and thought it was for him so he had the pilot land and was surprised to fine Eisenhower there. The laughter, ha-ha, hee-hee, was general. At this time a man with a camera asked them to face the camera and they did--me too, between Nixon and Eisenhower. At the time I thought it was a politician taking a snapshot but that evening on the front page of the Cleveland Press was the photograph of Ike, Tricky Dicky Nixon and my head between them, felt hat with snap brim and all. I have the picture. The oddity of the picture is that it shows Eisenhower with hair on the back of his bald head but it is the hair of a politician standing directly behind him.

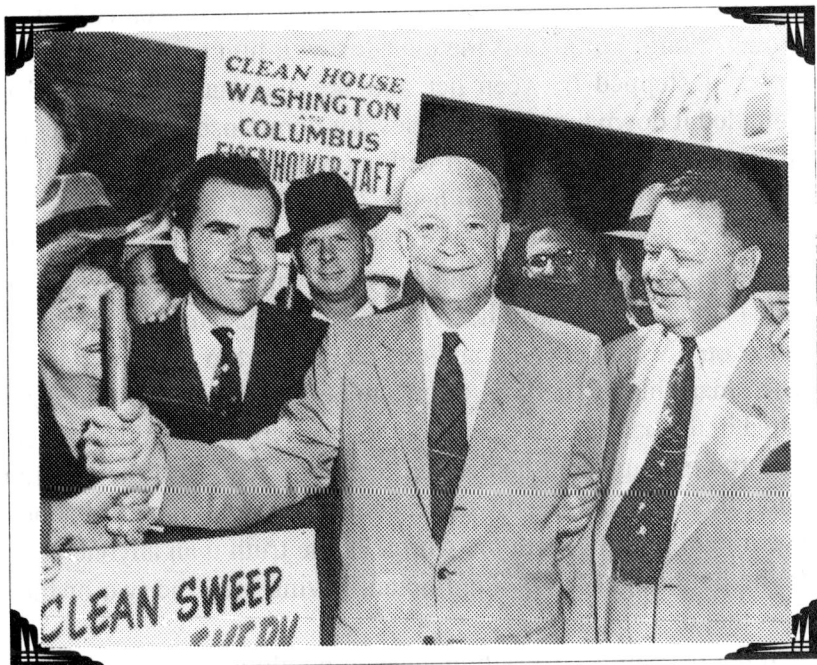

Richard Nixon, Edward Stein, Dwight Eisenhower

We drove in the Eisenhower cavalcade directly in back of his car to the Carter Hotel at E. 9th and Prospect. At the dinner he had his talk while we lingered in the area keeping our eye on the crowd in general. I followed him to the lobby where he was buttonholed at the elevator by a woman who insisted on talking to him and boarded the elevator with the rest of us. Ike listened closely to her and by this time I was alert to the fact that she did not belong in our party, that she was a bit nuts, did not have both oars in the water and was just one of those people who appear at a time like that. Ike was still

373

listening closely when the elevator stopped. I had decided that the woman should not get off the elevator with him so, when the door opened I stepped between her and Ike and our future President hightailed it down the hall. The elevator door closed and we went to the first floor where she got off without protest and walked out of the hotel. I was glad to get rid of her.

The newspapers and media in general had been on Nixon's tail about his income, how much property he owned, what money he had in the bank and how much he saved--nosy things like that. He was to appear on TV that evening and make his report to the public which was a smart thing to do if he wanted to be Vice President. Our detail waited in the hall until Ike came out to hear Nixon on TV in a special room the management had set up for him. We heard the program which Ike listened to and when leaving, he said to me, "I'd sooner have a man running with me who tells the truth than anyone else." Maybe he thought I was a politician, having seen me two or three times that day.

On the homefront everything was going along fine. We had two fine sons: Marty was going to high school and later to John Carroll University. Ed graduated from Our Lady of Angel's School and later from St. Edward's High School, while Leona went back to work to assist in paying expenses for medical school. Marty graduated from St. Louis University Medical School on May 9, 1959.

It was in the 50's that Chief Frank Story wanted someone to take over the supervision of the chief's office personnel. Inspector McArthur told me that the chief has asked him if he knew of anyone who could do the job and McArthur recommended me. He said he didn't like to lose me but it would be a good job for me if I wanted it. The chief had me report to his office for an interview and told me of the difficulties he had been having with office records and other things and thought it needed reorganization. He said the job was mine if I wanted it and I asked to let me try it for a month but that I didn't want to take a cut in my detective sergeant's pay. Chief Story said it would not be cut and to report to the office the next morning. After trying it and observing what changes should be made I told the chief I'd take the job and I was transferred, staying there for the next ten years.

Eventually Chief Story retired and was replaced by Chief Richard Wagner whom I knew since the day he entered the department. He was a fine, upstanding man, very knowledgeable and I liked him immensely.

My target year for retirement was 1963 and when November rolled around I handed in my resignation effective January 12, 1964, a total of 38 years, 7 months, and 23 days in the department. I was the oldest man in point of service in the department at that time. I would not have believed it in 1925. I left work in November since I had accumulated furlough and overtime days and the boys in the office gave me a farewell dinner with luggage, money, portable radio, and other gifts. To this day I appreciate all they did for me--their loyalty, hard work and dependability. I never worked with a finer group of men.

At first we had planned to retire to Florida but our friends Millie and Ed Jacobs, whom we had chummed around with in our youth, had settled in Prescott, Arizona and told us to try Arizona before we made up our mind. Their suggestion and that of Dr. Barr at home decided us to give it a try. In November, 1963, Leona and I took off for Tucson, and on the way there we stopped at a motel on the western end of St. Louis. The following morning it poured, so we western end of St. Louis. The following morning it poured, so we decided to stay over a day when, before lunch, it was announced over TV that President Kennedy had been assassinated. He had been shot while riding in a motorcade in Dallas, Texas. Leona and I had last seen him in Cleveland.

Marty and Jane had moved to Palo Alto, California, where our two grandchildren, Martin Edward and Juliet Marie, were born and Ed Jr. with his wife Rita moved to Euclid, Ohio, and have presented us with two fine grandsons, James Joseph and Anthony Edward. (Note to Reader: a granddaughter, Theresa Annlee, was born after this writing.)

This, then, gentle readers, is the end of the narrative of a few occurrences in my life which, I hope, has interested you. There has been good seasoning to my life and with Leona at my side, and our two fine sons Martin and Edward, our lives have been rich and full.

There are several things in this account which will be obvious:

    1) We are of German descent

    2) We were raised in the Catholic faith and

    3) The best swear word we have is Son-of-a-bitch.

GESUNDHEIT!

Edward A. Stein, Sr.
Tucson, Arizona

DECEMBER 31, 1980

EPILOGUE

*A*bout September of the year following their retirement, Dad and Mom drove to Arizona. There they rented and later purchased a condominium near Tucson, remaining there 21 years.

Mom suffered from at least one stroke in the early eighties. Following that her health deteriorated until Dad, whose heart had weakened, could no longer care for her.

Marty, who had made arrangements for Dad and Mom to live with him, took

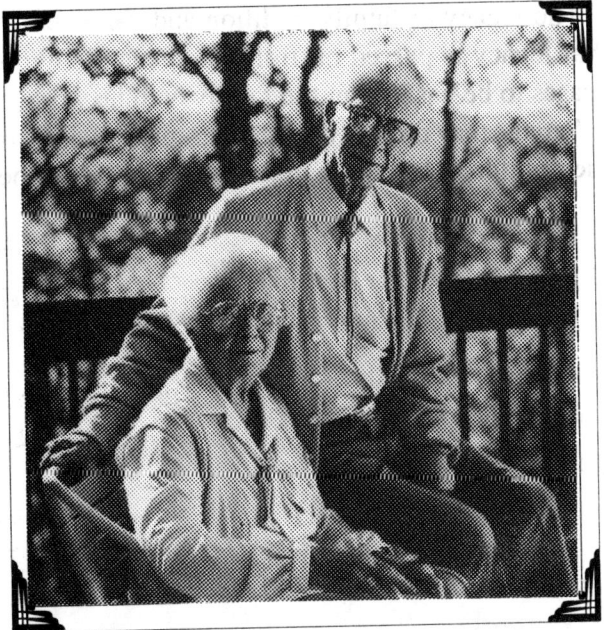

Leona and Edward Stein

Mom first. In the meantime, I went down to assist Dad break up housekeeping, do those chores he was no longer capable of doing, and to help him pack for his move to be with Mom.

After talking it over with Marty, Dad chose the risk of bypass surgery, but did not recover due to his already weak heart. Dad, was 85 at the time of his death in 1986. So far Mom has lived longer than anyone in her family; she passed away in 1994 at age 93.

A poet once said that we become adults only when the umbilical cord which ties us to our parents is severed through their death. Their death is our passport into adulthood while, at the same time, its their passport to freedom from all care and worry.

The legacy of family tradition and value remains only as long as that legacy is passed on from one generation to the next. When it ceases to be passed on, the family and the world are the less for it.

Parents may pass away, but their memory lives on not only through their children, but through those they have touched along the way.

Edward A. Stein, Jr.
August 9/22/97

REMINISCENCES ....

SON, MARTIN

As I think of Mom and Dad in those days, many wonderful things come to my mind. Mom and Dad were happy people, and home was a happy place. I remember that they laughed a lot about happenings in the neighborhood, and the comic events Dad encountered in his work. Sometimes they laughed so hard that they could barely finish their story. Dad and Mom didn't kiss or hug each other in our presence, but their love for each other was something we could sense, and took for granted. "How's my honey?" was often Dad's greeting to Mom when he got home. He never forgot Mom on special occasions, especially her birthday and mother's day. In reminding us that an important date was coming up. Dad would say, "Don't you ever forget about your mother. I don't care if you remember me."

I don't remember an argument or a voice raised in genuine anger between our parents or our relatives, although I had heard of a notable one between Dad and an uncle. I can't imagine that Mom and Dad and our relatives didn't have occasional arguments. They all certainly had their strong opinions about lots of things, including politics and religion.

Our parents didn't entertain the neighbors much, but they knew everyone well on our street, since people lived for decades or even lifetimes in their family homes. Mom and Dad especially enjoyed getting together with our aunts and uncles, or with a few close friends. Often these visits were dinners together, games of pinochle, or picnics in the valley or Fairview Park. Sometimes Mom's bridge club met at our house. For all these events Mom or Aunt Lucy prepared special delicacies, and we usually managed to sneak away with one or two. These were happy times, with laughter drifting into the evenings as we fell asleep in our beds.

I keenly remember Dad's story-telling abilities. After tucking us in at night he sometimes lay in bed with us and told us a story in serial format, a new chapter each night. He could entertain us and the neighborhood kids with his tales of Snerds and other whimsical creatures. He made up stories as he told them, and I noticed that when we asked him to tell the same story again the tale was never really the same. When we were older, and a younger crop of kids was growing up in the neighborhood, one or two of them sometimes came to the front door on a summer evening and shyly asked Dad to tell them a story. Dad loved children. He always spoke to the neighborhood youngsters with the same respect that he gave adults. If a child seemed interested, Dad always took the time to explain what he was doing.

Punishment of children seems to be out of fashion now (even against the law!), and I want to comment on it here. A certain amount of corporal punishment was considered acceptable when raising children in those days, and I am absolutely certain that I am a better person because of it. I think Dad and Mom set reasonable limits and expectations for us. I always knew where the line was drawn, and I got many more second chances than I got lickings. Those spankings were something to be feared, however, and had great deterrent value. I don't recall Dad administering a spanking in anger, probably because of the way Mom ran the household. When she had enough from me she rarely spanked me, but she would finally say those dreaded words, "Wait 'till your father gets home." If I couldn't talk her out of it, she would tell Dad. Then I got a good talking-to from Dad, who would tell me exactly how things had to be. If it was a repeat offense or something pretty egregious, punishment was prompt and predictable: "Upstairs, young man!" was followed by the climb upstairs to Mom and Dad's bedroom, where Dad administered two or three painful whacks with his belt squarely on my rump. The spanking stung like hell, but did little damage except to my ego.

I don't think that I was ever punished unfairly or that a spanking was excessive, but that isn't saying I enjoyed them. There were times when Mom never said anything to Dad despite her threat, and times when they realized I may not have understood the rules, and let me off. Sometimes I was given the choice of a "licking" or something else like staying in the house after school, or no radio for a week. (No radio? Gad!) I remember that I sometimes chose the painless punishment, but after a day or two decided to get it over and take the licking so I could go out to play. I once put padding in my pants before I told Dad I'd take the spanking. It worked, and although Mom knew, she didn't tell Dad.

In our parents' decision-making, money was often a limiting factor. Mom and Dad followed a tight budget which they codified in a series of envelopes kept in the dining room buffet. Sometimes after going to bed I would hear the rumble of their voices in the dining room; then I would steal down the stairs and sit in the dark, listening to their worried conversations about how to divide up too few dollars among the budget envelopes. As I look back on those times I'm struck by the fact that I never heard them argue about money; their approach was one of discussion and consensus.

I always had the feeling that worry about finances was never far in the background at home, and I'm sure it touched both my brother and me. He and I have always spent our money conservatively, and for myself I trace that attitude directly to Mom and Dad's need to be very frugal. Although I knew that we were not poor, I also knew very well that we had no spare change. Mom and Dad required me to earn an allowance and save my own money for things I wanted. When my "payday" came (usually Saturday), Dad would sometimes sit down with me at the dining room table and watch me divide up my twenty or thirty cents. Usually he urged me to put a little into my envelopes for church and for war-bond savings stamps.

Neither Mom nor Dad liked to buy anything "on time." They planned a significant purchase well ahead, and saved money every week in a special envelope for that purpose. Only twice in their long lives did Mom and Dad buy a new car; the first was a Ford Coupè in the 1930's, and the last was a 1940 Ford sedan. After that they got by with second and third-hand autos, which a friend or relative sold to them at a reasonable price. Dad made many friends among merchants in the course of his time as an honest beat cop. Now and then one of those merchants would offer Dad an item at a special price, making the unaffordable affordable.

Dad and Mom treated the disabled and the poor with kindness and respect. A young man who lived in our neighborhood was mentally handicapped, and he was the brunt of teasing and jokes by many of the other children. Mom and Dad were always kind to him, and went out of their way to say hello and talk to him whenever he came around. My brother and I knew that we should treat him the same way. I learned much later that his family remained in our neighborhood because of our kindness to him. When I was four or five years old I remember strangers occasionally coming to our back door to beg for food. Mom was always gracious and fed them a warm meal. At times when I was with Dad downtown, someone begging on the street would ask Dad for money for food. I think Dad could judge whether a person was really looking for money to buy liquor. On more than one occasion Dad answered that he would not give money, but he would gladly buy that person a meal. We then all walked to the nearest restaurant, where Dad paid for the man's meal. Thanks to Dad's example, I've sometimes taken this approach myself.

Dad and Mom were fervent Catholics. They attended mass faithfully, and contributed to the church whatever they could afford. Once or twice when we were traveling on one of our little trips I remember Dad being drawn by others into conversations about religion. He didn't agree with the idea then common in the Church that those outside the Catholic faith might not go to heaven. He felt that divorce was just a fact of life that had to be accepted when two people couldn't make a marriage work. Those ideas surprised me then, since they weren't the party line we were taught in our Catholic grade school.

The lot of a policeman and his wife wasn't easy. There were times when Mom was very worried because Dad was extremely late coming home from work. Once Dad came home with his uniform torn and eyeglasses broken from a scuffle with some scofflaw. All repairs, of course, were at Dad's expense. I felt personally insulted when I learned that trash collectors in Cleveland were paid more than many policemen. Policemen in those days never carried out a strike or "work action," as it's now euphemistically called, so they were last on the list for pay raises.

It was against Police Department policy to hold a second job. Although some of Dad's coworkers held extra jobs, he didn't take one. Dad certainly needed extra income, but he believed in living up to the spirit of the regulation. During the latter part of the War, second jobs were officially encouraged to aid the war effort, and Dad worked in an aluminum foundry. At that point he was working sixteen-hour days, not counting time for court appearances and commuting. I remember how tiring that period was for Dad.

Budget constraints were probably a reason Dad became a jack-of-all-trades. He seemed to be able to do just about any job that needed to be done around the house. He was carpenter, electrician, mason, painter, plasterer, tiler, and overall maintenance man. He replaced some of our house siding, laid a new sewer line, plumbed the down spouts, poured a new garage foundation, paneled the basement recreation room, and rebuilt the furnace, even adding a "modern" electric thermostat. He seemed to accomplish those many projects by himself, although I'm sure with lots of advice from others. Dad even took up watch repairing when he realized that he could save much-needed money by repairing his own watch. He bought the necessary tools and learned the techniques. He ended up repairing watches for others, as well as renovating old mechanical clocks. It beats me how he ever fit everything into his days. He built a workbench in our basement and installed racks for the tools he accumulated over the years. It was there he taught me how to use a plane, a saw, and his other hand tools. I still have many of Dad's old tools, and I use them with special fondness.

Although I managed to earn some of my tuition through part-time jobs and scholarship assistance, my education placed an enormous financial demand on Mom and Dad. They never made me feel that my needs overburdened them, however, and they always encouraged me to set my sights as high as I wanted. During our grammar-school years Mom and Dad bought an expensive set of encyclopedias for my brother and me. It became an important means of self-education for us. Mom and Dad never discouraged me from taking things apart that I couldn't put back together, or from spending all my earnings on things they didn't understand. They endured all sorts of stinks and commotion from my advanced chemistry lab in our basement; their only caution was, "Don't do that when the wash is up!" My great interest in the sciences is a direct result of our parents' very liberal and encouraging attitude. I'm sure it was difficult for them to put up with a kid who engaged in such impractical, sometimes odoriferous and unsettling activities.

Dad tried over and over again to pass the civil service exam for promotion to lieutenant, but he never got a score high enough to get one of the few appointments available each time. For months before each exam Dad would pour over heavy maroon tomes of criminal law and police regulations. In the end he remained a sergeant, but his fairness and integrity earned him the very highest respect of his peers. Police Chief Frank Storey knew Dad's reputation, and asked him to take over as supervisor in reorganizing the Chief's Office. Dad did a fine job, and until he retired he was the chief's "right-hand man." At last Dad had a regular day-shift schedule, and a small pay raise.

Dad retired at age sixty-two. He told me, to my surprise, that he never went back to visit the department afterwards. Dad and Mom had a comfortable pension, and they had saved wisely. They eventually settled in Tucson, but we remained a close-knit family. We talked and visited as often as we could, and Mom and Dad got to know and enjoy their five grandchildren. In Tucson they made many, many new friends, and there I think they enjoyed the happiest and most carefree years of their long life together.

REMINISCENCES.............

SON, EDWARD, JR.

I recall the day in my parents home in Arizona when I was working in Dad's den removing framed pictures from the wall for wrapping and packing. As I continued, I came across a framed letter I had written for the occasion of his 80th birthday. In that letter, I thanked him for all he had done for me throughout my life. On the opposite wall, was a framed letter from my brother, Marty, expressing the same sentiments. I often think of those letters, what they must of meant to him, and how they must have validated Dad's fatherhood.

Dad and Mom were private homebodies who never partied, had many acquaintances, but only a few close friends, and who felt that familial closeness was what mattered most.

We lived in a neighborhood where married couples raised families and remained until the day they passed on to a far better life than we have in this vale of tears. Dad and Mom knew their neighbors and their neighbors knew them. When tragedy struck a family they, and the rest of the neighbors, pitched in and helped the family through the crisis. Neighbors trusted each other. We often left our back door open when we went to the store and gave a neighbor a key when we went on a vacation--we did the same for them. The amount of crime, violence, greed and lack of trust we now have, just didn't exist then.

When Dad and Mom finally sold their home, the name Stein had been part of our neighborhood and of our Lady of Angels parish for over 41 years. Today few know their neighbors, let alone trust them.

My brother and I are products of time when respect for the elderly was taught both by instruction and example. We were taught to have respect for the property of others and to take responsibility for our actions. We also learned never to talk back to our parents and elders, and never to poke fun at those who were mentally or physically challenged, or less fortunate than we.

Dad, who was a first generation American of East Prussian ancestry, ran a tight ship at home. He was a fair though a strict disciplinarian, who believed that there was a definite connection between the tail bone and the head bone, and that pain, administered judiciously, was an effective teacher.

To Marty and me, the phrase "up to the wood shed" meant a licking with a strap or paddle. This was before physical punishment through their use became looked on as child endangering or detrimental to a child's emotional well being--Marty and I got our fair share of lickings and no doubt deserved every single one. I am still of the opinion that a little pain in the right place is an effective teacher, reminding a child of what is acceptable and what is not.

Mom, who was of Alsatian/German descent and born within 8 days of Dad in the same month, could also lower the boom on occasion. She however, preferred to leave the punishment for the larger childhood "crimes" to Dad. Her comment at those times, and there were few, was, "wait till your father gets home". Even though Mom didn't always carry out the threat, we never knew when she wouldn't. This always left us on pins and needles--the threat of telling Dad our transgressions was often punishment enough.

Dad and Mom were the product of an age when outward signs of affection such as hugging and kissing each other in front of their children were frowned upon--this they did in private.

That Dad loved Mom deeply could be seen by the things Dad did for her--unasked. He remembered her through greeting cards, a box of candy, a bouquet of flowers, or a plant on days which had no special significance, and by helping her around the house through cleaning house, washing clothes and even making dinner--on occasion.

Mom, in turn, showed her love for Dad by making him the special dishes he liked, making pies or other pastries and desserts he enjoyed--unasked--and, in general, making life easier for him.

That my parents marriage was a close one, could be seen from their concern about each other and their solicitude for each other's well being. This solicitude showed me the two had become as one flesh. Dad's only worry was that we make sure that Mom was taken care of if he passed away before her. This my brother, Marty, willingly and lovingly did at a time I was unable to contribute anything due to conditions beyond my control.

During the summer, Dad and Mom always took me with them on vacations. I was fortunate that Dad had a sense of American history and always made sure that we stopped not only where they had planned, but at places of historical importance in the development of America. Later, as my interests turned to Civil War history, Dad and I would take vacations to various Civil War battlefields. My dad and I deeply appreciated these vacations together because we got to know each other better.

When I was about 15, Dad started an unusual hobby that would keep his interest even after he moved to Arizona--he began to collect insect and butterflies. It was at this time that I began to get even closer to Dad. I used to accompany him on his collection forays. After Dad began his hobby, there were usually three nets in the trunk of the car. Two were light ones for butterflies and the other a larger "sweeping" net for insects. It must have looked funny for others to see an adult and a teen chasing butterflies. I enjoyed it and became quite adept at catching them.

Since Mom had been a bookkeeper, she did the bookkeeping in the family. She saw to the weekly distribution of allowances, and work-related spending money. Dad had absolutely no problem with this arrangement and, as far as I can recall, I never heard them squabble about money. This, I admit, may have been because there just wasn't enough worth squabbling about after utility bills, the mortgage, and other absolute necessities were budgeted.

Our parents attitude toward education was a strong one. Marty and I were both told, in no uncertain terms, that we were in school to learn, and that if he found out we'd been "horsing around" to use another of Dad's expressions, our butts were grass and that he would be the lawn mower--Marty and I didn't dare get in trouble. Knowing that Dad trimmed "might close" with the belt he used as a lawn mower, was enough to keep us on the right path.

Dad, because of his upbringing in a German ethnic neighborhood, could read, write and speak German fluently. He offered to teach me conversational German when I was growing up, but I wasn't interested--I now regret my unwillingness.

Dad and Mom lived in an era when it was still possible for the average middle-class white and blue collar working person to purchase a home, pay the mortgage off, and pass it on their children. Today, of course, all that can be done is to pass the mortgage on to children who, if they can't afford the payments, either rent it out or sell it--sometimes, at a loss.

As a police officer, Dad worked shifts. Shift work, of course, meant that my brother and I had to be quiet when Dad was sleeping during the day. Noisy play indoors meant a reminder with a shoe pounding the floor. When the weather was nice, Mom usually put us outside or we went to a friends house to play.

The years passed, and the time came when Dad had gained enough seniority to work days. His last assignment was as sergeant in charge of the clerical work in the Chief's office.